THREE ENGLISH EPICS

It was the eighteenth century which really fixed most of the static allegorical labels on Spenser's characters and led his readers to believe in them. It is time now to return his allegory to its own century, to the Protean changefulness, that volatile subtlety conjunct with syncretic naiveté I have already mentioned.

Thomas Greene, *The Descent from Heaven*

The gods were not expecting to see [man] in more shapes when, behold, he was remade into one of their own race, surpassing the nature of man and relying entirely upon a very wise mind. O great Jupiter, what a spectacle for them! At first they were astonished that they, too, should be brought to the stage and impersonated by such a convincing mime, whom they said to be that multiform Proteus, the son of the Ocean.

Juan Luis Vives, *A Fable about Man*,
trans. Nancy Lenfeith

Art is more than art, literature more than literature. The arts are forms of expression for human life and experience, and as such they register changes in the condition of man over the ages. But they are also more than forms of expression, and they do more than merely register. By giving expression to latent reality, and thus bringing it to consciousness, they make wholly real what has been only potential. They create the cultural atmosphere of each given age. And by virtue of this function they play as active a part in man's development as other, seemingly more practical human activities such as science, technology, and politics. The evolution of artistic forms of expression is one of the most important evidences we have for the changes in man's consciousness and the changes in the structure of his world. Only when viewed in terms of this dualistic aspect—the development of consciousness and the development of the reality corresponding to it—do the arts gain their full human significance.

Erich Kahler, *The Inward Turn of Narrative*

Thomas E. Maresca:

THREE
ENGLISH EPICS

STUDIES OF *TROILUS AND CRISEYDE,*
THE FAERIE QUEENE, AND *PARADISE LOST*

UNIVERSITY OF NEBRASKA PRESS
LINCOLN AND LONDON

Portions of chapter 2 have been adapted from *Epic to Novel*, by Thomas E. Maresca, published in 1974 by the Ohio State University Press.

Library of Congress Cataloging in Publication Data

Maresca, Thomas E
  Three English epics.

  Includes bibliographical references and index.
  1. Epic poetry, English—History and criticism. 2. Chaucer, Geoffrey, d. 1400. Troilus and Criseyde. 3. Spenser, Edmund, 1552?–1599. The faerie queene. 4. Milton, John, 1608–1674. Paradise lost. I. Title.
PR509.E7M3   821'.03   79–1080
ISBN 0–8032–3059–1

Manufactured in the United States of America

For the Shades of 408–B

CONTENTS

PROLOGUE

The motif of the descent to Hell forms the spine of English epic tradition. The studies of Chaucer, Spenser, and Milton in this volume flow from that statement and its corollaries; it is both the premise and the argument of this book. Most of my presentation works explicitly to demonstrate not merely the presence of the motif of the *descensus ad inferos* in the work at hand but also to show its richness and variety and the multiplex uses to which master poets can put it. The analogy of a spine conveys exactly what its function is within the epic tradition: a core, a structural principle, a channel through which flow the ideas and themes and actions which each individual poet will flesh out and embody in his own unique way. To put it another way, the descent to the underworld in its various senses provides the basic grammar of epic, over which any number of rhetorics can be and have been laid.

I have chosen in the essays that follow to devote attention to the three most masterly of those rhetorics that the English language possesses. In so doing, I imply what I here wish to make overt: that the generic motifs, demands, conventions—what you will—of epic mold the practice of individual poets approaching the genre just as much as the genre itself is in turn reformed and redirected by the peculiar concerns and talents of its individual practitioners. Modern scholarship has generally tended to view

Troilus and Criseyde, The Faerie Queene, and *Paradise Lost* first as self-contained entities (the heritage of no-longer-New Criticism), second within the context of their authors' other works (the corpus theory), and third within selected contexts of their respective ages (more or less historical criticism). A few important works—Rosemond Tuve's *Allegorical Imagery,* Thomas Greene's *The Descent from Heaven,* A. Bartlett Giamatti's *The Earthly Paradise and the Renaissance Epic,* Peter Hägin's *The Epic Hero and the Decline of Heroic Poetry*—have substantially broadened the area within which English epic poetry must be located and examined, and to these and studies like them I am heavily indebted. I have tried in this book to push beyond their examination of strands of epic poetry to look closely at epic itself; following their lead, I have attempted a fusion of historical and generic criticism in order to see epic whole. That I have not wholly succeeded I am only too well aware, but the attempt has been in itself worthwhile. The descent to hell, however limited as a focal point (no grammar is the totality of a language), does illuminate the mutual affiliations, modifications, and rearrangements effected by Chaucer's, Spenser's, and Milton's poems. The structure that grows from it does clarify the articulation of those epics; its insistent concern with corporeality and spirituality, with the acquisition of knowledge, does provide an enlightening frame within which to grasp the appearance of those themes in an individual epic.

More important even than that, however, is the basic realization that the demands of epic as genre can and do frequently outweigh the private concerns of the poet, whether they be the philosophic/theological bias he displays in his other writings or the manner in which he normally employs imagery. To give a specific example: in *Paradise Lost,* one makes much more sense of the role of the Son if one minimizes the tenets of the *Doctrina Christiana* and emphasizes instead the functions of the epic hero as defined by the *descensus ad inferos.* In the same way, Spenser's Neoplatonism in *The Faerie Queene* derives far more directly from the Neoplatonism of the Virgilian commentators than from that of the

Florentine Academy. In fact, even when a commentator on Virgil happens to be a member of that group, as is the case with Cristoforo Landino, his remarks and attitudes still reflect far more of the ethical Platonizing of his predecessors Fulgentius and Bernardus than they do the more intricate and more metaphysical speculation of his friend Ficino. The Neoplatonism inherent in epic tradition almost coerces would-be writers of epic to conform their poems to it, to somehow come to terms with it. Dryden reveals this when, in the course of discussing the prerequisites for writing a great epic poem, he requires that his ideal poet be "conversant in the philosophy of Plato, as it is now accommodated to Christian use" and adds the following telling parenthesis: "for, as Virgil gives us to understand by his example, that is the only proper [philosophy], of all others, for an epic poem."[1] This is only one way of saying that developments in literary history are more often literary responses to literary problems than our old-fashioned reliance on political dates or our new-fashioned reliance on sociological data would seem to concede. Poems work poetically; epics work epically. That is hardly a profound truth, but it is one that needs stating, and I hope I have made a good case for its utility in these essays.

A few words about method. I am not a professional student of Chaucer, Spenser, or Milton; my normal areas of teaching and research are late seventeenth- and early eighteenth-century English literature. I was, in fact, betrayed into this study of medieval and Renaissance epic by research I began on the relations between mock epics and Fielding's comic epic in prose; that resulted in my *Epic to Novel*, to which this present study of epic stands in a rather horse-behind-the-cart relation. To the nonspecialist, the bibliographies accrued around *Troilus and Criseyde*, *The Faerie Queene*, and *Paradise Lost* appear awesome in their sheer bulk, and frequently insular and inbred in their concerns, particularly in their general ignoring of an ongoing epic tradition. I have made a determined effort to work through these bibliographies, starting with book-length studies and monographs and pushing on through periodical publications as far as my eyesight and sense of relevance permitted me, but it early became clear that to attempt to annotate my studies for complete correlation with the existing scholarly literature would produce a text very like a Renaissance edition of Virgil, in which a poor postage stamp of argument would founder in a vast sea of enveloping footnote. Rather than bring forth such an unreadable monster, I have chosen in each essay to provide a note listing the works that helped me most and to cite further only what seem to me the most crucial correspondences or divergences between my argument and the relevant body of scholarship. Needless to say, neither of these devices exhausts either the available scholarly material or that portion of it from which I personally profited, and I wish to make an inadequate but sincere acknowledgment here of all the unnamed Chaucerians, Spenserians, and Miltonists whose fields I have gleaned. In many cases in the following essays I am no doubt telling them what they already know about specific passages, sections, images, actions, etc. of their poems: I only hope that the overarching perspectives of epic and the descent to hell offer them the kind of illumination their works so often provided me.

A last word on method. I have placed the essay on *Troilus and Criseyde* last because that poem seems the least familiar in the context of epic. I hope by establishing the terms of this discourse first for poems where they appear more immediately relevant that their appropriateness to the *Troilus* will be made more apparent; that, in effect, *The Faerie Queene* and *Paradise Lost* will retroactively illuminate *Troilus*. This is purely a tactical decision on my part and in no way implies judgment about the merits or success of Chaucer's poem, or even about my degree of interest in it. It is in fact in some ways the most provocative and complex of the three in its attachment to the descent to the underworld tradition.

I am grateful to the SUNY Research Foundation for a summer grant in 1974 that enabled me to begin writing these essays and to the State University of New York at Stony Brook for a sabbatical leave in 1974–75 that enabled me to complete them. I also wish to thank Ohio State University Press for permission to use some material that originally appeared, in slightly different form, in my *Epic to Novel*. I am grateful as well to the Reverend Thomas H. Stahel, S.J., for permission to quote extensively from his as-yet unpublished translation of Cristoforo Landino's commentary on Virgil. My greatest debt, as always, is to the peace, patience, benignity, mildness, fortitude, and intelligence of my wife Diane: she endured.

THREE ENGLISH EPICS

1

Spenser:

THE FAERIE QUEENE

Let us start with a truism: the epic poem is always the product of its cultural matrix. In the case of an English Renaissance epic poem, like *The Faerie Queene*, that matrix is a rich broth of national aspirations, Tudor propaganda, Neoplatonic philosophizing, Petrarchan and Ovidian imagery, and the history, development, and generic demands of epic itself, plus whatever else may have struck the poet as interesting or useful. The epic poem was a learned poem, encyclopedic and inclusive; it had to present, to paraphrase Tasso, a complete and coherent world of its own which stood in clear relationship both to the actual world in which men lived and to the ideal world to which they aspired and which they thought to animate, underlie, and prefigure that brazen one. With all that, it had to be single, one, integral in the way that that ultimate reality, that golden truth beyond the quotidian and phenomenal, resolved itself into unity.

Those are the goals of Renaissance epic. In the case of *The*

Faerie Queene, the reality is an incomplete poem, a torso of epic, six books and some odd cantos of a projected twelve (perhaps twenty-four), studded with inconclusive actions, unresolved events, characters named and interesting (Sir Sophy, Sir Palladin, Sir Brunel) whose stories are never told. As readers we have no choice but to work with what we've got, to examine the torso to see how closely it fits the prescription and to what extent, if any, the proportions of the epic body reveal the configuration of its uncreated limbs.[1] Two factors help this kind of inquiry. One is the internal development of epic itself, the directions and expectations set up within the genre by its series of exemplary practitioners from Homer up to Spenser and by the scholars, dilettantes, synopsizers, and commentators whose works symbiotically derive from epic, nourish it, and to some extent alter it. The second is Spenser's own peculiar practice, the very tightly closed and limited imagistic system he has chosen to employ.

❧

BACKGROUND

Putting aside for the moment the question of Renaissance allegoresis of classical epics will help us to see more clearly a few facts about those poems which are obscured both by the habit of allegorizing and by our historical remove from the poems (as well as by our embarrassing cultural illiteracy). First, the protagonists of Homer's and Virgil's epics are "heroes" only in the most qualified sense. They are by no means paragons, are not wholly admirable, and are only selectively useful as positive exemplary figures, and they are, with the qualified exception of Aeneas, not remotely national or racial heroes (very few heroes of successful epic poems ever fit that description or prescription; it seems to be a *canard* introduced by French and English neoclassical criticism). Second, the "heroic ideal," "epic conduct," "heroic code" or whatever it questionable may be called has never existed *as an ideal or norm of behavior*. There is no such thing in the *Iliad*, and whenever one character

2

Homer

speaks as if there were, he is flatly contradicted either by another character or, through subsequent narrative, by Homer. Achilles' realization that the brave man dies exactly as the coward constitutes the total subversion of anything a "heroic code" could have encompassed, a point Homer drives home in the *Odyssey* when he once again uses Achilles (his wraith, at least) to inform Odysseus that the meanest corporal existence is infinitely preferable to sovereignty over the whole kingdom of the dead. Indeed, we underrate Achilles' intellect—and Homer's—terribly if we see him only Style as a dumb strong-arm man who spends most of the poem in a snit because the big bad king took away his bowling trophies. What angers Achilles—justifiably—is not just his loss of glory or renown, but Agamemnon's undoing of the social fabric and his destruction of the consonance between public honor and personal valor. Achilles' later realization of the futility of all fame in the face of death is the logical extension of a situation and a perception created at the very start of the poem by the character who most should be the protector and preserver of whatever heroic code existed. The remainder of the poem is devoted to more and more detailed questioning of whatever tattered shreds of that heroic glory are left. Certainly Hector's ignominious death, in defense of a cause he knows to be bad and at the hands of a berserker whose wrath and grief have drowned his reason, and the genuine pathos of his funeral, which is for all practical purposes Achilles' funeral as well—certainly these are the Homeric goodby to all that. In a similar manner, both Odysseus and Aeneas in their respective poems are brought to shed their old warrior identities for new self-conceptions which are much more strongly rooted in notions of the "immortality" of an ongoing society than they are in an eternal afterlife of fame. Third, unity of action exists in classical epic only in a very broad sense. The *Odyssey* of course is the easiest proof of that, but the *Iliad* and the *Aeneid* as well corroborate the statement: think only of Aeneas's after-dinner speech in Carthage, or the heroic games in Book 5, or the multiple skirmishes, challenges, and divine or human councils of the *Iliad*.

All three poems use as their protagonist and are most definitely *about* a flawed human being who is struggling to shed one calcified and obsolete definition of himself in order to grow a new one suitable for his changed world. The gods forbid Aeneas to be an old-fashioned vengeful strong-arm hero: he may not fall with Troy, just as he may not stay with Dido. Like it or not, he must learn to metamorphose himself from Trojan to Roman, to shift his allegiance and his sense of himself from the old dead world to one he may just possibly be able to bring into existence. In the same way, Odysseus has to be weaned from his identity as "sacker of cities"; he must become Nobody and learn, from Achilles, among others, in just what ways he is in fact nobody before he can assert a whole identity predicated on entirely different terms—son of Laertes, father of Telemachus, husband of Penelope, preserver of his family and home, justicer, and king of Ithaca. Odysseus masters chaos with a lie, flux by immersing in it; he counters force with guile, opposition with what moralistic critics would call treachery in anyone else. He uses all the weapons of the conventional villains (of epic as of pulp fiction); it's no wonder that we and the Renaissance love him—he's an artist (Spenser thought him the "model of a vertuous man").

The Odyssean creative use of truth is a luxury that Virgil does not allow his hero but reserves for himself. The cliché that the *Aeneid* marks the beginning of the tradition of major "artistic" epic is false insofar as it implies that Homer is inartistic or unconscious of his craft, but true insofar as Virgil's practice for the first time (in a major poem) intrudes that artistic self-consciousness about the poem's means upon the reader's awareness. Virgil's poem insists that you notice its style, its language, its structure, and its manipulations. The Homeric poems are evidently artificial—formulaic language could never have been the colloquial speech of their audience—but they do not demand our constant consciousness of their artifice. The *Aeneid* does. Artifice in the *Aeneid* is the means of control, whether it be Virgil's control of his poem, Aeneas's control of himself, or the Roman *ars pacis*

4

that controls the world. The shade of Anchises makes Virgil's analogies explicit:[2]

> "Others, I doubt not, shall beat out the breathing bronze with softer lines; shall from marble draw forth the features of life; shall plead their causes better; with the rod shall trace the paths of heaven and tell the rising of the stars; remember thou, O Roman, to rule the nations with thy sway—these shall be thine arts [*hae tibi erunt artes*]—to crown Peace with Law, to spare the humbled, and to tame in war the proud." [6.847–53]

Aeneas—and Rome—must learn from all, take from all, use all to govern all, just as Virgil as Roman poet must appropriate Homer and all the learning and art of his own contemporaries and predecessors in order to celebrate both those Roman *artes*.

These aspects of Virgil's poem were of course quickly appreciated, as the commentary of Servius and Macrobius's *Saturnalia* bear ample witness. But they left a larger and more important mark in the Middle Ages through the work of Servius and Macrobius, through the commentaries on the *Aeneid* and the ideas of poetry (and particularly of epic) they generated, than they did in and of themselves. Virgil's poem passed through the alembic of the hermeneutics it sponsored to emerge a transformed thing, more confirmed in its artifice, more ranging in its erudition, and redirected in its aim. In such commentaries Virgil appears as magician and scholar, a polymath whose learning is inexhaustible. Indeed, in Fulgentius's commentary the poor author abases himself in awe before the shade of Virgil, who *de haut en bas* addresses him as "little man" (*homuncule*) and provides him with a relentlessly ethical understanding of the *Aeneid* (extraordinary how much information wraiths provide, in the precincts of epic). Fulgentius in a crude enough manner turns his attention to the Virgilian *ars*, at least to the extent of using etymology (which he regards as providing the root and therefore true meaning of names) as his major means of opening up the poem; unfortunately he does that frequently at the expense of grammar, syntax, and logic.

5

Nevertheless, patterns of meaning and interpretation that Fulgentius discerns in the poem become some of the mainstays of the Virgilian tradition. Ignoring the chronology of the poem, Fulgentius reads the *Aeneid* as a history of the stages of human growth: Aeneas—man—being born in the first book, acquiring speech in the second, passing through childhood and adolescence in the third and fourth, and so on. This ages-of-man theory of epic appears to have been quite widely held throughout the Middle Ages, and its basic pattern is preserved by Bernardus Silvestris's later commentary on the *Aeneid*, even though his remarks terminate in Book 6. Fulgentius himself in fact quietly drops the ages-of-man motif after Book 6, which receives a disproportionate share of his comments (this too becomes a recurrent pattern in Virgilian exegesis). In Book 6, Aeneas/Everyman acquires maturity, defined as learning, wisdom, or understanding, and subsequently takes to wife Lavinia, the road of labors (*labor via*), and takes up the struggle against rage (Turnus) and impiety (Mezentius) and destruction (Juturna). In all later commentaries on the *Aeneid*, Book 6 continues to hold its place as the educational center and the fulcrum of the poem. The implicit pattern that Fulgentius establishes—action (Books 1–4)-contemplation (Book 6)-action (Books 7–12)—and the explicit one that he puts in Virgil's mouth—man's nature, what he learns, his attaining to prosperity; to possess, to control, to ornament; corporeal substance, intellectual substance, judgment—these threefold patterns remain important in themselves and give rise to yet other triple rhythms and structures in both later appraisals of Virgil's poem and in new poems that directly or indirectly grow from such appraisals.[3]

Bernardus Silvestris's most obvious continuation of Fulgentius's endeavors lies in his adaptation of the etymological mode of proceeding. However, he subtly and sensitively extends its range by a very flexible system of analogies which enable him to anchor his exegetical points fairly firmly in Virgil's text. He reads the *Aeneid* as the journey of a flawed and fallen Everyman through a process of purgation and maturation to the attainment of wisdom—scarely a shocking distortion of the text of the first six books at least, and only a slight realignment of the ages-of-man perspective on the poem. He lavishes most of his attention on the sixth book, making of Aeneas's descent to the underworld the climax of his interpretation of the poem and the pivot of its narrative.

Bernardus understands the *descensus ad inferos* quite complexly. There are, he tells us, four ways to accomplish this descent. One is by necromancy, and the mode of this Virgil as magician—or at least mage—describes in the funeral of Misenus, which Bernardus understands as a magical and sacrificial rite to invoke demons. Another is by simple vice; in that way anyone can descend to Hell, at any time, but in this mode of descent the way back is hard indeed. The third is according to the Platonic opinion—his argument here draws heavily on Macrobius's commentary on the *Dream of Scipio*—by birth, when the soul descends into the underworld (*inferos*) of the material body, which will be its prison and its grave in this life, which is itself a death of the spirit and an underworld; in this manner all men descend. The fourth way is the way of the mind; the intellect descends to the contemplation of created and corporeal things in order that in and through them it may come to know the Creator and thus return to him. This indeed is the way in which Aeneas, as man in the process of perfecting himself, is to be understood as descending in the company of the Sybil. Interestingly, Bernardus's reading of the *Aeneid* really has Aeneas accomplishing his *descensus* in all four modes: by magic and by contemplation, as I remarked above; by birth, which is the common lot, eminently so that of an Everyman figure, and prescribed, in effect, by the ages-of-man theory; and by vice, which has been his fate in his wanderings up until his arrival in Italy and the beginnings there of his intellectual discipline. The modes of contemplation and of birth, Neoplatonically understood, alter substantially the nature and direction of the descent, since both provide for—indeed, demand—a corresponding return and ascent. In the light of this reversal, the last six books of the *Aeneid* should then be implicitly understood as the return of the now prepared, disciplined, and informed mind or soul to the world to confront once again and to overcome those pitfalls of *temporalia* and material temptation that had earlier overwhelmed it and formed its *descensus* of vice. Alternatively and Platonically, they present the gradual reascension of the soul to its purely spiritual, noncorporeal state and its freedom from the underworld of the body (Mapheus Vegius many years later seems to have read the *Aeneid* in this manner; his *Thirteenth Book of The Aeneid* provides Aeneas with the merited apotheosis he felt lacking in Virgil's poem).[4] That is, Bernardus's lengthy treatment of Book 6 offers us more elaborate and more potentially fruitful versions of Fulgentius's triple progressions of action-contemplation-action and corporeal substance-intellectual substance-judgment.

In either of these modes, the *descensus ad inferos* becomes an oxymoron; it becomes simultaneously and paradoxically an ascent to knowledge or the *summum bonum* or the One or God. This is not an idiosyncratic, bizarre, or restrictedly medieval understanding of either the descent or the poem, and Mapheus Vegius does not offer the only testimony to that effect. The *Aeneid* itself bears witness to it in the very sequence of episodes in the sixth book: Aeneas in his first encounters in Hell meets allegorical and abstract figures (Grief, Care, Age, Disease, etc.) who are clearly intelligible as the defects incumbent upon the simple fact of corporeal existence; Landino's commentary on the *Aeneid* also stresses this obvious fact.[5] The first group of shades he meets constitutes a concise review of his past life with all its errors and misdirections and offers him the sort of rudimentary self-knowledge he must possess before he can receive the full revelation of his destiny from Anchises. As Landino puts it,

> There must be for him a mental repetition of the entire course of human life so that he may clearly understand not only how enslaved to crime are those who, having put aside their nobler part, place all their hope in a body and its pleasures, but how oppressed they are with misery. [242]

The Sybil has already warned Aeneas that his life, after this revelation, will be a redoing of his past; there will be another Grecian camp, he will have to face another Achilles, again for the sake of a foreign bride—but this time, rightly instructed and freed from his former vices, he will win through these obstacles. Bernardus's use of Macrobius's Platonic explanation of the descent of the soul into the body offers another corroboration of the validity of his reading of the *Aeneid*: the *Dream of Scipio* shares with the *Aeneid* crucial aspects of the same journey of education, the same review of vices and virtues, the same preparation for ideal Roman citizenship. Indeed, many early and late medieval ascents share a root in Aeneas's descent. Winthrop Wetherbee has argued this more ⟨ learnedly and more concisely than I can, so I will merely quote a passage of his case:

> One final instance of syncretism, equally characteristic and much more important for literary purposes, is worth mentioning: the relationship which Bernardus intuits between the *De nuptiis* and the soul-journeys of Virgil and Boethius. In his prologue, commenting on Martianus' purpose in the *De nuptiis*, he asserts:
>
>> The author's purpose is imitation, for he takes Virgil as his model. For just as in that poet's work Aeneas is led through the underworld attended by the Sybil to meet Anchises, so Mercury here traverses the universe attended by Virtue, to reach the court of Jove. So also in the book *De consolatione* Boethius ascends through false gods to the *summum bonum* guided by Philosophy. Thus these three *figurae* express virtually the same thing. Martianus, then, imitates Virgil, and Boethius Martianus.
>
> In this comparison historical, intellectual and moral themes are reduced to images for the same spiritual experience. The three works, do, to an extent, illuminate one another: Vergil's purpose is in some respects clarified by the translation of his poem into the terms of late-classical Neoplatonism, and the implications of Martianus'

Odd assumpt° [margin note]

9

mythology are sharpened and become more profound when applied to the moral and philosophical concerns of the *De consolatione*. But in Bernardus' hands they become, as it were, the "types" of a kind of allegory which, though many of its characteristics are perceptible in Martianus and Boethius, is fully realized only in the twelfth century. In his *De mundi universitate* Bernardus takes these authors—lovers, and, as it seemed to him, imitators of Plato—as his models. His poem is a genuine response to the challenges presented by theirs, and so extends a chain of influence and reaction which links together the work of these *auctores* and, in a real sense, brings the twelfth-century Chartrians into a living relationship with the *Timaeus*. This was the classical tradition for Bernardus and his contemporaries; so Alain de Lille will imitate Boethius, Virgil, and Martianus in his *De planctu naturae* and *Anticlaudianus*, and will declare that the philosophical allegory of the latter work, dealing with the regeneration of man, is more truly an epic subject than the conventional themes, Troy and Alexander, treated by his contemporaries. We will see twelfth-century authors of vernacular romance coming to terms in various ways with Bernardus' definition of the heroic theme, and in succeeding centuries the *Roman de la Rose*, the *Vita nuova*, and the *Comedia* will reveal in countless points of theme and structure the enduring vitality of this tradition for the later middle ages.[6]

And not just for the Middle Ages. Through the transmission belt of Cristoforo Landino's commentaries on the *Commedia* and on the *Aeneid* (which two poems he compares structurally and explicitly in the precise terms Wetherbee indicates and we have been discussing), through the Florentine Neoplatonists who were Landino's friends and intellectual associates, through Tasso who in theory and practice endorsed and promulgated Landino's views,[7] through Spenser (as I hope to show in this work), such notions came down intact to John Milton who also thought, like Alain of Lille, that the regeneration of man offered a subject "Not less but more Heroic than the wrath/Of stern *Achilles* . . ." and who preferred to celebrate "the better fortitude/Of Patience and Heroic Martyrdom" rather than "to dissect/With long and tedious havoc fabl'd Knights/in Battles feign'd."⁸ Moreover, he chose to do this in a poem whose structure and subject are descents resolving themselves into ascents, whose metaphors consistently work out the interchangeability of up and down, rise and fall. *Paradise Lost* is a poem so rooted in the epic tradition (at least in that aspect of it that concerns me here) that the poet can play with it, can joke with it, to the extent of letting his villains travesty and distort it: Satan so addresses his legions:

> Powers and Dominions, Deities of Heav'n,
> For since no deep within her gulf can hold
> Immortal vigor, though opprest and fall'n,
> I give not Heav'n for lost. From this descent
> Celestial virtues rising, will appear
> More glorious and more dread than from no fall.
>
> [2.11–16]

That remark can only take on its full significance when played back, by the aware reader, against the right kind of descent to the underworld by which man can in fact perfect himself and rise to celestial virtue.

I do not mean to imply that these notions about epic remain unchanged and monolithic up until Milton's climactic handling of them. Far from it. What Bernardus does to Virgil's poem in his commentary, more so in his own poetry, is already a major reorientation of epic, and Landino, for all his fidelity to the basic values and directions of Fulgentius's and Bernardus's interpretations, alters it even further—probably in a disastrous way—when he shifts so much of his emphasis in interpretation onto the journey itself that that portion of epic comes to seem the whole of it; and again, perhaps just as dangerously, when he construes Aeneas not as Bernardus's flawed Everyman but as the exceptional man who is destined for glory—glory being somewhat ambiguously allied to Christian beatitude.

Milton too radically rearranges epic's components when he

11

abandons a traditional form of the epic narrative (in its most skeletal form, the pilgrimage/journey, which the no less Christian and philosophic Dante preserved intact) for the overt retelling of the archetypal form (in terms of Christianity) of what Bernardus and the others recognized as the substance of epic; that is, Milton discards the poetic fiction of the integument to replace it with the allegory. But even within those crucial changes, the broad outlines of the tradition have been preserved. The epic poem consistently dramatizes a descent which is paradoxically an ascent. It consistently presents the human mind, spirit, or soul—Man himself— descending into corporeal matter and coming to terms with it and, illuminated about his dual nature, at last freeing himself from the grave clothes of the flesh. The epic poem understands the underworld in richly multivalent ways—as the abode of souls in the afterlife, a place of rewards and punishments, as this time-bound world below the fixed stars, as bodies or souls in bodies or the principles, effects, and affects of corporeality, or the psychology of minds dealing with or dealt with by matter—and surrounds these ways with images and metaphors that further extend them: grave and prison, earth and sea, cave and forest, drunkenness and carnality, wandering, dreaming, recovering one's father, one's home, one's identity. These are basal images for basal acts; they are among the primary images and archetypal locations of myth. Epic is in this sense, in its most fundamental reality, the vehicle of the central myth of the West, the myth of consciousness, of the acquisition of new knowledge. The process depicted in the epic poem and the process enacted by the narrative itself is centroversion: the raising to consciousness of what had previously been latent, unknown, unappreciated.[9] In John Barth's phrase, the key to the treasure is the treasure.

What I mean by that is simply that epic took up the slack after the primal myths of discovery had lost their efficacy, and that what epics always overtly described was the process of discovery itself, of the necessity of plunging within for knowledge which can then be carried without, of exploring the unconscious to return

12

with its riches to a heightened and intensified consciousness. Think of Odysseus passing through the portals not of death but of Circe, that female, chthonic guardian of the powers of annihilation, of submission to the animal and nonself (she will not only metamorphose him; she is also capable of un*man*ning him) to interview the reconciliatory, androgynous figure of Teiresias before passing through Circe's isle once again, equipped now with all the knowledge he needs to return home to himself. Dante the pilgrim performs exactly that same journey; the only difference lies in the scope and kind of knowledge each hero brings back—and that expansion of scope, that increase in depth and breadth of knowledge, is only possible because of the successful journey of each preceding pilgrim hero to the depths of his world and himself. In epic you can't go home again, at least not to the identical home and self you left, but neither can you go anywhere else. Milton, again, words this most succinctly and acutely—if most ironically—when, at the point of Satan's ascent into this lower world of ours, the demon realizes that "myself am Hell" (4.75).

We all are, of course, and that too is one of epic's main points.

❧

The pattern of the descent to the underworld—descent, illumination, ascent—resembles many other such threefold movements, from the Stoic process of purgation through to Joseph Campbell's monomyth, stopping by the way for such old standbys as the Christian meditative pattern of memory, understanding, and will, or the psychological trio of wit, understanding, and memory, or the two Fulgentian trios mentioned earlier (action-contemplation-action, corporeal substance-intellectual substance-judgment). These resemblances are, to my mind at least, neither coincidental nor necessarily superficial, since all those patterns simply present slightly different versions (in most cases, different largely in terminology alone) of a basic rhythm of mind, an almost archetypal pattern of the exploration and expansion of consciousness and control. Epic, because of its primacy among the genres and its early association with education, offered itself as a natural vehicle for both the form and its contents, and continued to serve that function up until the historical point at which the observation of nature began to be construed as the recording of outer nature rather than the interpretation of inner nature. *Paradise Lost* roughly marks the chronological watershed; for all Milton's emphasis on the paradise within, after that poem the world that lies before epic is a far different one from the world that lies behind it.

The Faerie Queene, like the commentaries on the *Aeneid*, belongs to that earlier world and shares many of its and their assumptions. For that reason, it makes sense to me to understand the pattern of the *descensus* as Spenser utilizes it and as it occurred in the commentators as allied to, loosely at least, a continuing Platonic or Neoplatonic tradition and related or analogous to the particular category that Edgar Wind has called a Platonic emanating triad. Even if there were no common roots in the generally Platonizing habit of mind of the Virgilian commentators (explicit in Fulgentius, taken for granted in Bernardus, explicit again in Landino, who argues quite simply that Virgil followed Plato in composing his poem, a sentiment later echoed by Dryden and many others), the descent-illumination-ascent of the epic would constitute a clear parallel to the emanation-conversion-return of Neoplatonic thinking—more particularly so since both processes ultimately express the relation of idea/mind/soul to matter and the steps by which those entities return from matter to their proper spiritual-intellectual sphere.[10] Spenser uses the pattern to show the gradual entanglement of the human soul in the complications of its temporal, corporeal existence; the time and space of Faeryland provide the psychological geography within which the soul explores and masters its abilities and limitations and from which it begins its return journey to its home with God. Landino's comments clarify precisely the aspect of the tradition that Spenser

14

exploits. Our souls, while they dwelt in "the celestial realms," participated "in that harmony which resides in the eternal mind of God;" now, "weighed down by the desire for mortal things and therefore already fallen to the inferior," "impeded by earthly limbs and moribund members," locked in "this irksome prison of the body," they "strive to imitate that divine music with this music of ours" (42).

> For while our souls are immersed in corporeal shadows, they do not recognize divine things except by certain shadows and images which present themselves to our senses. [65]
> For all perspective is taken away from [Aeneas] by cloudy shadows. . . . All evils come to us from corporeal matter, which the philosophers call a forest, for it hinders, dulls, and disturbs our minds and darkens them with shadows. [68]

Thus the underworld and its major properties are defined—corporeal existence, entered through the forest of matter and perceived as the flickering shadows on the wall of Plato's cave—and thus *The Faerie Queene*, had Spenser completed it, would have been bounded (as he tells us in the letter to Raleigh) by Cleopolis and Gloriana, from which the Red Crosse Knight's departure initiates the action of the poem and to which city of glory all the poem's heroes would have returned. Into the *inferos* of the poem as we have it each knight and lady carries the spark of the virtue he must master; each is an aspect of Gloriana, as all are related to each other and all are facets of Arthur. They are the many reflections in finite time and space of the infinite unity of the One.

This is true, I think, of everything in Faeryland, and is the simplest explanation of why there are so many repetitions and near-repetitions of character and event in *The Faerie Queene*. The metamorphosed nymph-fountain which debilitates the Red Crosse Knight, the metamorphosed nymph-fountain which kills Mordant, the literal nymph-fountain which tempts Guyon—all are aspects of one fountain, and bear relation to the Well of Life for

15

which Fradubio waits and into which the Red Crosse Knight falls. They unfold, in time and space, the idea and metaphor of fountain, presenting under varying guises to various human minds their central content, transformation. Each individual transformation manifests itself in Faeryland under the particular form that time, space, and the peculiar psyche of the protagonist impose on it, but all point past time, space, and idiosyncracy to the final change beyond all change, to the new heavens and earth of the Mutability Cantos' final Sabbath. Nature's remarks in these cantos also offer us another clue to the understanding of Spenserian transformation or change:

> I well consider all that ye haue sayd,
> And find that all things stedfastnes doe hate
> And changed be: yet being rightly wayd
> They are not changed from their first estate;
> But by their change their being doe dilate:
> And turning to themselues at length againe,
> Doe worke their owne perfection so by fate;
> Then ouer them Change doth not rule and raigne;
> But they raigne ouer change, and doe their states maintaine.[11]

This does not argue that change is illusory, but rather that change offers creatures a means to expand their beings, to improve or increase their existences, literally to have more being or to perfect what they have, and by and through change to return perfected to their original condition. Nature is here describing "in speeches few" a pattern of emanation, conversion, and return, and postulating that it governs all of the permutations of—at least—the sublunary world where, the poet agrees, Mutabilitie "beares the greatest sway" (7.8.1). So Spenser employs, in *The Faerie Queene*, a very limited vocabulary of images, each internally referable to each other, as the finite explication of the complication of infinite unity. Just as Agape "dilates her being" in Priamond, Diamond, and Triamond, just as Love, Hate, and Concord are folded up in the hermaphroditic Venus of Book 4, so all the other aspects of Faeryland stand in relationships of expansion or contraction to each

16

other, relationships of explication or complication. Their place and time constitute the order of their apprehension, and their existences are fundamentally dialectical and psychological. For example, Red Crosse Knight encounters Despaire not when he is languishing in Orgoglio's dungeon, which would seem emotionally the most appropriate moment, but after his rescue thence, when he is reunited to Una; *then*, seeing all the things Una is and does, then his faith is shaken.

This example will also serve to make my last preliminary point, to wit, that the allegory of *The Faerie Queene* resides (with one notable exception) not in the characters but in the action. If the point of the encounter between Red Crosse Knight and Despaire were merely the clash of faith, or the will to faith, with despair, or the fear of damnation, that is, if Spenser's goal were only a juxtaposition of concepts, it could occur almost anywhere in Book 1; indeed, in that case it probably should occur during Red Crosse Knight's imprisonment. But occurring where it does, and in the manner it does, the episode manages to present a very precise psychodrama about the workings of awareness of truth and wrongdoing, about the presumption of power in ignorance of one's own weakness, while at the same time presenting a tableau vivant displaying the workings of grace and sin, election and guilt: all in a textual matrix which makes it impossible to distinguish which is the "level of narrative" and which the "level of allegory." The meaning of the episode is carried in the action of the episode, in what Despaire says to Red Crosse Knight, in the reactions those statements provoke in him, in Una's intervention. Rarely, very rarely does Spenser's allegory ever lapse to simple personification; in every important case even the pat identifications are heavily qualified by their attendant circumstances. That is in my view the characteristic Spenserian mode of procedure.

The Faerie Queene begins, however, uncharacteristically

with that one notable exception I alluded to above. The first six stanzas of the first book present us with a flat tableau, almost an emblem, of nameless knight and lady who are clearly meant to be known and interpreted, in the manner of static personifications, by their attributes. The youthful knight with old and dented arms blazoned with "a bloudie Crosse" embodies the archetypal Christian soldier or Christian soul, generalized and abstracted, armed for the equally generalized and abstract moral warfare of this life. The lovely lady bears along with her most of the traditional symbols of purity, innocence, and truth, and by her pedigree must be understood either as the soul languishing for faith and Christ (the *sponsus-sponsa* relationship of the Song of Songs) since the Fall (the wasting of her parents' land by the "infernall feend") or as true religion, whose kingdom has been usurped, or both; they are not incompatible, and the characterization—it can hardly be called such at this point—is so abstract as to allow of either. Amid this welter of static props, we find only two dynamic attributes: the knight and lady are in motion, and they are going toward the land dominated by "that infernall feend." For us as readers, in fact, motion was the first thing we knew about these characters; the poem began for us *ex nihilo* with movement—"A Gentle Knight was pricking on the plaine. . . ." I suggest that these first six stanzas must be read as a *gestalt*, a configuration which reveals its meaning not in terms of the poem—that for us is a not-yet—but in terms of the background of epic as we have so far discussed it; those are the *res* of which *The Faerie Queene* begins *in medias*. The simple fact of motion locates us loosely below the fixed stars, outside of the Macrobian realm of intellect or the Christian or Dantean realm of changeless spirit, where everything exists in God. The generalized attributes identify the two characters as souls or minds or ideas, depending on your theological or philosophical preference, and the goal of their movement (the fact of movement alone is enough to show their separation from God or One, who is unmoved) indicates that they are proceeding toward the corporeal *inferos* of this world. These stanzas are imagistically depicting the beginnings of a de-

18

scent to the underworld, the emanation of ideas which are going to be more and more clothed in flesh, made progressively more specific and concrete as they enter more deeply into the material world. When the storm drives them into the woods, they enter the same woods in which Dante wandered; the forest—*silva*, matter—"that heauens light did hide,/Not perceable with power of any starre" (1.1.7) delights them with its diversity (though each stanza of enumeration ends forbodingly with "the Cypresse funerall" and "the Maple seeldom inward sound"), but it also obscures their return, leading them labyrinthan ways until "it brought them to a hollow caue." Any reader of epic would at this point surely recall the storm that drove Dido and Aeneas to another cave; any Renaissance reader would be delighted to find, a few stanzas later, that this was not that predictable one, but Plato's, the cave of Error, where the Red Crosse Knight encounters the first of the monsters who breed in darkness—

> For light she hated as the deadly bale,
> Ay wont in desert darknesse to remaine,
> Where plaine none might her see, nor she see any plaine.
> [1.1.16]

It is wrong, I think to read this ethically; at least it is certainly wrong to read it exclusively as moral allegory. The two travellers commit no sin in entering the forest, though they do make a mistake in not keeping track of their path, in letting the variety of the forest distract them from their business. And if the Red Crosse Knight is somewhat rash and foolhardy in his encounter with Error, he still has not fallen into sin (Error, with large or small *e*, is not sin), since Spenser explicitly tells us, after his battle, that they leave the forest "with God to frend." What the episode is depicting, in quite orthodox Platonic fashion, is the soul's confusion (drunkenness is the conventional term) upon its immersion in the body. Material existence—matter in the abstract—is the principle of multiplicity and the attractions of that multiplicity both obscure the soul's heavenly origin (thus the

19

forest hides the light and the stars) and enmesh the soul more deeply in its corporeal state (thus the forest paths are all "With footing worne, and leading inward farre"). The natural culmination of that is the cave of Error, which constitutes an almost direct reference to Plato's explanation of the relation of this corporeal world and its uncertain knowledge to the disembodied and certain knowledge of the world of ideas. Spenser's wood does not act as a moral trap for Red Crosse Knight and Una, but as a necessary stage in their journey to the world. After the wood, neither the travellers nor the readers return to a world of static allegorical correspondences or abstract ideas but to a world of confusion where there is no longer any necessary consonance between appearance and reality—as the pat arrival of Archimago in the guise of a pious hermit demonstrates. After the wood, we have left the realm that properly—of its very nature—pertains to Una, and entered the world of Duessa, the world not merely of moral duplicity but of physical multiplicity. Here all things which are one in the spirit world are fragmented and reveal themselves only partially, by fits and starts, in the multitudinous objects and persons of sublunary nature. In the world of *The Faerie Queene*, the deepening darkness of night gradually obscures the clear sunlight of "the plaine."

Spenser announces this almost literally early in canto 2, after the success of Archimago's scheme:

> But subtill *Archimago*, when his guests
> He saw diuided into double parts
> And *Vna* wandring in woods and forrests,
> Th'end of his drift, he praisd his diuelish arts.
>
> [1.2.9]

What has preceded this and immediately caused it was the parodic *descensus ad inferos* of one of the spirits that Archimago invoked, summoning up false dreams to tempt and weaken the Red Crosse Knight (the whole elaborate descent forms a succinct mock epic, its main action being accomplished by the demon in the form of a fly) and Archimago's subsequent embodying of the two demons under the appearance of Una and a young squire (I would suggest that this is another parodic *descensus ad inferos*). That is, the two apparently separate first actions of *The Faerie Queene* also form between them a *gestalt*, whose central action is the descent of the mind or spirit to matter; the first of these is the legitimate, normal, and morally neutral emergence of the human mind and soul from God or One into the material world which it must inhabit for a time (also, of course, from the purely literary point of view, it delineates the generation of symbol and the basis of Spenser's allegory); [12] the second is the ethically conceived descent—literally by magic, allegorically by vice—of the embodied mind or souls into the toils of concupiscence and wrath: when the Red Crosse Knight sees the coupling of the Una-demon and squire-demon, "he burnt with gealous fire,/The eye of reason was with rage yblent . . ." (1.2.5). The spirit is blameless in entering the body, but blameworthy in surrendering to it, even though the fallen body carries with it the danger of further fall in the consequences of original sin (succinctly displayed here in the ready power of concupiscence and irascibility). [13] This fallen world, dominated by the body and defined by its limitations and its encroachments on the spirit, forms the stage on which *The Faerie Queene* is enacted, and it will remain so for the six whole books we possess. Calidore, in Book 6, initiates a metaphoric ascent which, symbolically at least, rounds and closes the action of the descent with its corresponding return. The pointed parallels between the opening actions of *The Faerie Queene* and the closing ones of Book 6 are numerous and important. Red Crosse Knight, in the false dream vision conjured up for him by Archimago, sees Una presented to him carnally in a setting that is fully counterpointed by Calidore's vision on Mount Acidale:

> And she her selfe of beautie soueraigne Queene,
> Faire *Venus* seemde vnto his bed to bring
> Her, whom he waking euermore did weene
> To be the chastest flowre, that ay did spring
> On earthly braunch, the daughter of a king

21

Now a loose Leman to vile seruice bound:
And eke the *Graces* seemed all to sing
Hymen io Hymen, dauncing all around,
Whilst freshest *Flora* her with Yuie girlond crownd.

[1.1.48]

If the Red Crosse Knight's false vision shows the spiritual Una, model of chastity, reduced to the simplest carnality, Calidore's and Colin Clout's vision in the tenth canto of the sixth book shows the reverse process, Colin Clout's beloved, an earthly maid—"a countrey lasse"—raised by her "Diuine resemblaunce, beauty soueraigne rare,/Firme Chastity, that spight ne blemish dare" (6.10.27) to be another Grace and to assume Venus's place in the center of the dance of the Graces. So too Calidore's rather easy victory over the Blatant Beast recapitulates in many points the Red Crosse Knight's more ambiguous struggle with Error—first in the common nature of the beasts, both of whose weapons are language used to distort the truth; second in the initial flight of the quarry and its being brought to stand by the protagonist; third in the inutility of weapons in each fight; and fourth in the oral serpents of the Blatant Beast, whose spitting of "poyson and gore bloudy gere ... licentious words, and hateful things" (6.12.28) is the exact equivalent of Error's vomit of "bookes and papers.../With loathly frogs and toades" and "Her fruitfull cursed spawne of serpents small" (1.1.20,22). Moreover, both Calidore's subduing of the Blatant Beast and his rescue of Pastorella from the robber's cave (a "hollow" cave, like Error's, and like it shielded from and shunning the light, its darkness, like Error's, producing "A doubtfull sense of things, not so well seene, as felt" [6.10.42]) Spenser describes as ascents from the underworld, one in Christian terms and one in terms of classical myth. Pastorella "thought her self in hell,/Where with such damned fiends she should in darknesse dwell" (6.10.43: the next stanza [1.044] implicitly describes her as Persephone); Calidore accomplishes her rescue by bursting the doors of the cave and leading her back "to the ioyous light" over the slain bodies of the fiendish brigands:

So her vneath at least he did reuiue,
That long had lyen dead, and made againe aliue.

[6.11.50]

Spenser's images strikingly remind me of the many paintings of Christ bursting the bonds of the tomb, leading the souls of the righteous with him (over prostrate fiends) back from the underworld where they have awaited him; the effect is heightened in Spenser's text by the fact that Calidore does all this attired as and playing the role of a shepherd. In fact, Spenser so lards his text with conventional images and language that, baldly extrapolated like this, the effect is almost ludicrous; happily, it is far otherwise when these images arise in their rightful place in the narrative flow. The fight with the Blatant Beast presents the classical version of the same images: "this hellish Beast" is compared to "the hell-borne *Hydra*, which they faine/That great *Alcides* whilome ouerthrew" (6.12.32); his huge jaws appear "like the mouth of *Orcus* griesly grim" (6.12.26). Calidore, after binding him, leads him in a triumphal procession:

Like as whylome that strong *Tirynthian* swaine,
   Brought forth with him the dreadfull dog of hell,
   Against his will fast bound in yron chaine,
   And roring horribly, did him compell
   To see the hatefull sunne, that he might tell
   To griesly *Pluto*, what on earth was donne,
   And to other damned ghosts, which dwell
   For aye in darkenesse, which day light doth shonne.
So led this Knight his captyue with like conquest wonne.

[6.12.35]

This conflation of classical and Christian motifs works once again to establish out of the apparently divergent episodes a single configuration, the triumph of civilized and illuminated (by art and the Graces) virtue over the limitations and constraints of the flesh (Plato's cave, Error's cave, the brigands' cave, the body itself) and the distortions of misused intellect (error, Error, Blatant Beastli-

23

ness). As such, the two episodes are cognate steps in the ascent from the *inferos* and respond with neat symmetry to those first steps of the descent discussed before.[14]

Between these clearly marked *termini a quo* and *ad quem* lies the darkening landscape of the *inferos* and the Shandean path of the descent and gradual reascent. Book 2 explores the abilities and limitations of the corporeal body (most blatantly in the physical set piece of Alma's Castle) just as Book 5 delineates the workings of the body politic.[15] In the center of the poem as we have it, Books 3 and 4 depict the deepest penetration of the *descensus*, the overt encounter with matter and the principle of generation (physical generation of course) and their domination by spirit. The darkness of corporeal existence throws its lengthening shadow over these books, even literally: most of the major events of Books 3 and 4 take place either at night or in its equivalent, the sea (the sea is, according to the epic commentators, the trackless gulf of humors which constitutes bodily existence; Bernardus reads the storm at sea which opens the *Aeneid* as birth itself, the stormy entrance of the soul into the body). The action of both books is bounded by the flight of Florimell (who exists for us, in a manner similar to the Red Crosse Knight's mode of existence at the beginning of the poem, primarily as motion) toward the sea and union with the sea-born (Marinell). During the course of the two books' major actions, her motion is arrested, her flight stopped, and an ironic stability forced upon her by her imprisonment in the sea cave dungeon of Proteus, the principle of change himself, pure plastic matter unformed but capable of all forms. Motion may originate in the unmoved mover, particularly motion understood as love seeking its object, but it must rest, at least temporarily, in matter, before returning to its origin. So Florimell's flight from Cleopolis to Marinell and the sea is a recapitulation of the process of emanation with which the poem began, but also an extension and elaboration of that process into its next inevitable steps of conversion and return.

That conversion and return, in Florimell's case, take place

when Marinell frees her from Proteus's power and subsequently weds her. The background of this whole action is marriage—the marriage of the Thames and the Medway—which is one of the traditional metaphors for the union or coincidence of opposites. That notion and that image are crucial to understanding *The Faerie Queene*, since they constitute the obverse of the process of emanation-conversion-return or descent-illumination-ascent; the latter is the unfolding, the explication of unity into multiplicity; the former is enfolding, the complication of multiplicity into unity. Spenser presents another version of this, in slightly different terms, early in Book 4, where Agape (Love) brings forth the multiplex world (Priamond, Diamond, and Triamond)—that is, she unfolds her unity in that triad—which is later enfolded again into the triunity of Triamond "by traduction" (the technical term describing the entrance of the already created soul into the newly formed human body), which new unity is once again compounded by the multiple bonds of friendship and marriage among himself, Canacee, Cambell, and Cambina. Given the roles the characters have played in the preceding actions, their weddings must be seen as unions of opposites: the women, Canacee and Cambina, have respectively provided the source of strife and the source of concord, while the men, Cambell and Priamond-Diamond-Triamond, have respectively enacted the inviolable spiritual force of chastity and the unstoppable spiritual force of love. Such too is the case of Florimell and Marinell, whose names suggest a kind of elemental opposition and whose temperaments—she all fear, he all aggression—are clearly contradictory. And in both sets of marriages, a clear transformation of opposites occurs—Marinell from his scornful aggressive state on hearing Florimell's prison plaint, and Cambell and Triamond from their mutual strife on drinking Cambina's cup (much the same thing happens to the angry Artegal when he finally sees Britomart's face).

Such transformation and marriage of opposites mark the beginning of the ascending action of *The Faerie Queene*, and should be understood in at least a general sense as forming a part of the process of the poem by which Spenser's creatures "dilate their being." The Garden of Adonis offers another view of such a process, elaborating the particular kind of permanence within change or "eterne in mutabilitie" (parodically achieved by Florimell in Proteus's dungeon) that Spenser envisions:

> All things from thence doe their first being fetch,
>   And borrow matter, whereof they are made
> Which when as forme and feature it does ketch,
>   Becomes a bodie, and doth then inuade
>   The state of life, out of the griesly shade.
>   That substance is eterne, and bideth so,
>   Ne when the life decayes, and forme does fade,
>   Doth it consume, and into nothing go,
> But chaunged is, and often altred to and fro.
>
> The substance is not chaunged, nor altered
>   But th' only forme and outward fashion;
>   For euery substance is conditioned
>   To change her hew, and sundry formes to don,
>   Meet for her temper and complexion:
>   For formes are variable and decay,
>   By course of kind, and by occasion;
>   And that faire flowre of beautie fades away
> As doth the lilly fresh before the sunny ray.
>
> [3.6.37–38]

The Garden itself displays several similar transmutations of substances into different forms, most notably in the case of Adonis himself, who is converted there from the dying erotic figure he was in the tapestry in Malecasta's castle to the ever-living "Father of all formes," and in the case of Cupid, who there "laying his sad darts/Aside" plays the faithful husband to Psyche. What the entire garden presents is the relation of spiritual substance (soul, whether conceived as vegetative, animal, or rational) to matter, and matter itself as the principle of change in opposition/complement to the constancy of spirit—an extended and detailed version of what I have suggested is concisely offered to us by the embracing frame device of the imprisonment of Florimell by Proteus. The basis for Spenser's use of Adonis in this way is an early but accurate piece of cultural anthropology which linked Adonis with the eastern Adonai and with Thammuz, and interpreted him as the sun and therefore as the source of life (this links intelligibly with, and is foreshadowed in Spenser's text by, Chrysogonee's impregnation by the sun, which produces Belphoebe and Amoret, the latter then a quite appropriate resident of Adonis's garden).[16] The boar who legendarily slew Adonis is in this reading understood as winter, an element of the fable which, in Spenser's poem, forges an important subliminal link with the Persephone aspects of Florimell's and Amoret's imprisonments. Less learnedly, of course, the boar is frequently read as simple lust, which makes his confinement "In a strong rocky Caue, which is they say,/Hewen vnderneath that Mount" (3.6.48) a delightful final twist on the various caves of descent that dot the landscape of *The Faerie Queene*—particularly so, given modern scholarship's readiness to see that Mount as a none too subtle pre-Freudian enlargement of the mons Veneris: that is a *descensus ad inferos* with a vengeance, and must stand as the direct antithesis, allegorically, of Florimell's confinement.

∾❧∾

As Fulgentius, Bernardus, and Landino explain the action of the *Aeneid*, they implicitly and explicitly discern broad relations of synecdoche and metonymy between parts and the whole of Virgil's narrative. Aeneas begins in Book 1 a typical descent to Hell by birth, initiates another—by sin and vice—in Book 4 (or earlier, depending on the meanings found in Troy and his wanderings), and performs yet others—by magic and meditation—in Book 6. Indeed, Book 6, with its completed action of descent-illumination-ascent, stands as a miniature, a paradigm, of the whole twelve books, a synecdoche contained within a metonymy. Such ideas about Virgil's architectonics involve the rhythm of complication and explication into the very structure of the poem and posit an almost total continuity of form and content: the poem itself embodies the structures and patterns it contains. The relations of parts to wholes, in this vision of epic, repeat the patterns of complication and explication that epic is seen to be about. Whether because he was following such Neoplatonic beliefs about the containment of the whole within the part, or because he had resolved to confine the number of images around which to articulate his poem, or simply to indulge a personal taste for symmetry, Spenser has reproduced within the individual books of *The Faerie Queene* many smaller versions of its basic *descensus*. He varies them almost in the manner of a musical theme, here playing on the notion of the descent in its moral aspect as a degeneration into sin, there on its philosophical aspect as an intellectual exploration of creation, in another place exploiting its narrative possibilities in connection with magical rites and the invocation of demons, and yet again elsewhere using its imagistic props through the visual constellation of cave-night-darkness. Not surprisingly, the greatest concentration of these small descents occurs in the first half of the poem, since that consitutes, in the overall pattern, the downward leg of the descent's threefold movement; their antiphons in the latter half of the poem tend to be much more honorific—to be understood *in bono*, in effect—and to pertain more or less directly to the rising action of the *descensus's* final movement.

The first book is appropriately rich in such small versions of the main theme; Spenser even hints briefly that all the events of the book (and perhaps of the poem) are to be viewed *sub specie descensus* (which indeed would be a logical conclusion from the poem's opening) by beginning the third canto as follows:

> Nought is there vnder heau'ns wide hollownesse,
> That moues more deare compassion of mind,
> Then beautie brought t'vnworthy wretchednesse,
> Through enuies snares or fortunes freakes vnkind.
> [1.3.1]

"Hollownesse" is a concept which has already been closely as-

28

sociated with Error's cave, and such subterranean associations will be strongly reinforced throughout the remainder of the poem; indeed, "hollow" will become almost a fixed epithet of all caves in *The Faerie Queene*—thus this particular use of the word tends to conceptualize the whole created world as an enlargement of Error's cave (an appropriate and sound application of Plato's allegory) and all of human life as a prolonged *descensus ad inferos* (an absolutely literal and accurate application of the opinion of the Virgilian allegorists). If this is so, then the Red Crosse Knight's quest—and by implication that of every other Spenserian hero—will itself recreate the entire pattern of the descent, that is, descent, illumination, and ascent. Certainly that pattern can be discerned, at least in its broadest terms, quite easily in Red Crosse Knight's progressive degeneration into sin, culminating in his imprisonment in Orgoglio's dungeon, his purgation and illumination (begun ironically by Despaire and concluded by Contemplation), and his triumph over the Dragon and subsequent betrothal to Una, which has all of the properties of Christ's marriage to the soul or to *ecclesia*, even including a momentary manifestation to this fallen world of the heavenly harmony:

> During the which there was an heauenly noise
>   Heard sound through all the Pallace pleasantly,
>   Like as it had bene many an Angels voice
>   Singing before th'eternal maiesty,
>   In their trinall triplicities on hye;
>   Yet wist no creature, whence that heauenly sweet
>   Proceeded, yet eachone felt secretly
>   Himselfe thereby reft of his sences meet,
> And rauished with rare impression in his sprite.
>   [1.12.39]

As much can be said for the course of most of the quests of *The Faerie Queene* (the exceptions, as to so many other things, are Books 3 and 4), and for pretty much the same reasons. Every endangered hero in *The Faerie Queene* is threatened by one or another of the children of the Cave of Error, in one or another of their manifestations (the evil always takes the form appropriate to the protagonist, just as Archimago and Duessa shift their targets and their means after Book 1), and every successful quest reproduces—temporarily and fragilely—an earthly paradise or golden age which is an aspect of the unseen Cleopolis and the dim reflection of what lies hidden in brightness outside the cave of this life. Time and human imperfection mar the achievement of each hero in turn: Archimago escapes, Gryll repines at his return to human shape, Britomart never quite unites Amoret and Scudamor, the Blatant Beast reviles Artegal and in its turn escapes again to spoil the world.

Those similarities firmly locate the action of each book "vnder heau'ns wide hollownesse" and link it analogously to the overarching design of the poem, but it is the variations on the theme within each book which account for their differences and which define their peculiar topography. The opening episodes of Book 1 of course establish the theme for the whole of the subsequent poem, but they also introduce some of the specialized terms and images by which Red Crosse Knight's quest will be governed. The "litle glooming light, much like a shade" which Red Crosse Knight's "glistring armor" made (1.1.14) sets up an imagery and dialectic of light and dark which will eventually incorporate Red Crosse captive in the total darkness of Orgoglio's dungeon, Orgoglio dazzled by the light of Arthur's shield, and Red Crosse dazzled by the brightness of the heavenly Jerusalem, shown to him by the blind hermit Contemplation. The form that Spenser gives Error—the body of a dragon—prefigures the seven-headed dragon Duessa will ride and the final great dragon that Red Crosse will conquer, just as his rashness and unpreparedness in that initial fight foreshadow his later entanglements with Duessa and Despaire as well as his defeat at Orgoglio's hands. In the same way, Archimago's substitution of a demon for Una prepares the way for Red Crosse's deception by Duessa and his acceptance of her as Fidessa, while the magician's invocation of demons and the

30

demon-fly's message to Morpheus comically anticipate Duessa's far more somber and elaborate journey to Night and Hell.

Each one of these events is thus linked with the notion of the descent in some tangential way, though many of them are more significantly and more clearly so connected. The Red Crosse Knight's stay at Lucifera's castle, during which he pays homage to her, clearly constitutes a moral descent, the implications of which the Dwarf reveals to Red Crosse after he has spied the contents of the castle's dungeons. Duessa's excursion, in the company of Night, to visit Aesculapius in Hell is a more narrative and less figurative version of the same, complete with all of the props of the classical damned: Cerberus guarding the gate, the punishments of Ixion, Sisyphus, Tityus, and others. For Duessa, of course, this is going home, and the episode functions in the poem as the basal revelation of just what and who she is and what sort of threat she constitutes for the Red Crosse Knight—what her real identity as Duessa means, as opposed to her assumed guise as Fidessa. Beyond this, Spenser plays with heavy irony with the idea that Duessa goes to Hell to seek a resurrection, to have the damned Aesculapius restore Sansioy to life. The irony rests in part on the fact that the principles that characters like Sansioy and Duessa embody are in fact deathless and can no more die than can Despaire—

> He chose an halter from among the rest,
> And with it hung himselfe, vnbid vnblest.
> But death he could not worke himselfe thereby;
> For thousand times he so himselfe had drest,
> Yet nathelesse it could not doe him die,
> Till he should die his last, that is eternally.
>
> [1.9.ult.]

Partially also it resides in the fact that the *inferos* is indeed an appropriate place to seek for the care of the body, and Aesculapius, who rejoined the members of Hippolytus, an appropriate physician; similarly, Cymodoce will seek help, beneath the sea, for Marinell from Tryphon. More largely, however, the irony rests on

31

the implicitly Christian content of the pagan *locus* and the fact of seeking resurrection in the house of death. Just as Archimago's earlier embassy to Morpheus was a burlesque of the conventional and serious epic *descensus*, Duessa's pilgrimage here is a parody of the archetypal Christian *descensus*, Christ's harrowing of Hell and subsequent resurrection. As such, it stands in a clear prefigurative relation to the final episodes of Book 6, where Calidore will successfully accomplish a metaphoric but perfectly valid harrowing of Hell and a figurative resurrection.

The opening episodes of Book 1, in addition to forming the configuration that I discussed earlier, also establish a narrative/thematic pattern which Spenser employs frequently throughout the whole poem, the simple pattern of overt test followed by covert temptation to the same or similar sin, vice, or error. The sequence of events from Lucifera's castle to Orgoglio's dungeon follows this pattern: overtly exposed to pride in Lucifera's realm, the Red Crosse Knight partially succumbs but finally escapes, just as he did with Error; and as the subsequent events there, by Archimago's wiles, involved him in "Errors endlesse traine," so here the subsequent events involve him finally in a captivity to Pride. Having ostensibly escaped the coils of pride, darkness, and the *inferos* of the body, the Red Crosse Knight proceeds to fall victim to the *inferos* of his own body ("Pourd out in loosnesse on the grassy grownd,/Both carelesse of his health, and of his fame" [1.7.7]) and encounters purely carnal pride, the child of the cave:

> The greatest Earth his vncouth mother was,
>   And blustring *Aeolus* his boasted sire,
>   Who with his breath, which through the world doth pas,
>   Her hollow womb did secretly inspire,
>   And fild her hidden caues with stormie yre,
>   That she conceiu'd; and trebling the dew time,
>   In which the wombes of women do expire,
>   Brought forth this monstrous masse of earthly slime,
> Puft vp with emptie wind, and fild with sinfull crime.
>
> [1.7.9]

Orgoglio's origin parodies and debases the Genesis account of God's creation of man out of the slime of the earth; he is the purely material son of earth and air (interestingly, the mythographers associate Aesculapius with *aera*: see for example any edition of Charles Etienne's *Dictionarium poeticum*), and fittingly conquers Red Crosse by air: the wind of his blow knocks him over. Orgoglio is, of course, though Red Crosse doesn't know it, his *doppelgänger* and shadow self, a child of Heaven encountering a child of earth, soul meeting body, spirit meeting its purely material counterpart in the element of air. Thus Red Crosse Knight's imprisonment in Orgoglio's dungeon becomes, in Spenser's matrix, richly multivalent—a narrative event in and of itself, carrying all the complexity of Red Crosse Knight's psychological development to this point and, insofar as he is a representative figure, a typical pattern of Everyman's soul or mind in quest of truth in this world. It becomes also an allegory of the history of religion, indicting Roman worship of a Babylonian captivity to worldliness; a moral descent into sin; and either another step in the process of philosophic descent of the mind to creatures, indicating the greater and greater power of matter in and of itself to limit and confine spirit, or in the precise Ciceronian-Macrobian sense, the definitive moment of the absolute and irrevocable entrance of the soul into the body—in effect, the moment of birth—the beginning of the incarceration of spirit by matter. Such descents all bear back-reference to the initial entrance of Red Crosse Knight and Una into the *silva* of this world, but all these latter—whatever interpretation or interpretations one chooses—should be clearly distinguished from that former by the fact that these are sinful. The entrance into the wood and the fight with Error was morally neutral; conquest by Orgoglio is conquest by sin, or at least pollution by original sin. Spenser's vision at this point is on one level at least almost Manichean: Orgoglio is "fild with sinfull crime" for no other reason than that he is nothing more than a "masse of earthly slime." (This may, incidentally, shed some light on that thorny problem of Ruddymane's hands. Needless to say, Spenser is a poet

33

and amateur philosopher, not a professional theologian, so no defense of his orthodox standing seems to be necessary. In any event, the Neoplatonism of the Renaissance frequently, even in its most carefully orthodox formulators, flirts close to the edge of Manicheanism. Landino again makes this nicely explicit: "all evils come to us from corporeal matter, which the philosophers call a forest," he tells us, "and if, as Plato thinks, ignorance is from bodily darkness, then all vices will be from the body" [68]).

In whatever light one chooses to regard these episodes, they are evidently Red Crosse Knight's nadir, and the reader can reasonably expect some sort of turnabout. In keeping with the pattern of the *descensus*, this takes the form here not of a simple reversal of fortunes (though that is obviously included) but of an illumination, or the beginning thereof, about Red Crosse Knight as a self and what he has become thus far. This recreates literally and narratively an important part of the classical *descensus*, as it is exemplified in the *Aeneid*, where Aeneas in encountering the shades of Dido and of various Trojan heroes conducts what amounts to a mental review of his past life from which he learns about his mistakes and sins, as well as later learning what his future course should be. For the Red Crosse Knight this encounter with himself (the true self, not the shadow self as in the Orgoglio episode) begins with Despaire, who rehearses to him all of his derelictions only to lead him to a greater one; once again, as in the struggle with Error (of which this is yet another aspect), he is saved from himself only by Una's interruption and reminder of his role and putative virtues. (It is worth remarking that it is only after being rejoined to Una—whatever she may signify—that Red Crosse Knight is able to see the truth about himself; apart from her, he despairs of life, but rejoined to her he momentarily despairs of salvation, and then is saved from that despair by her greater knowledge of him. Clearly, he is a function of her and she of him: she offers him knowledge, he offers her power.) His illumination is overtly continued in the narrative by the instruction and discipline he receives in the House of Holiness, and it culminates in the

34

vision of the heavenly Jerusalem and Contemplation's revelation to him of his identity and destiny (that he is English born, and will become St. George). This narrative climax demands immediate relation to two similar occasions: one shortly before this, when Despaire gave him an accurate account of himself but drew the wrong conclusion from it, which Red Crosse leaped at, just as here he leaps at Contemplation's predicted sanctity—

> O let me not (quoth he) then turne againe
> Backe to the world, whose ioyes so fruitlesse are;
> But let me here for aye in peace remaine,
> Or streight way on that last long voyage fare,
> That nothing may my present hope empare.
> [1.10.63]—

a counterpoint that completes symmetrically the process of his self-knowledge. The second is, despite Spenser's comparison, neither of the biblical *loci* he suggests nor Mount Acidale (1.10.53–54; but the episode does bear comparison with Calidore's vision of the graces on Mount Acidale in 6.10.5ff.), but rather that point in the *Aeneid* when Anchises—the shade of Anchises—leads Aeneas to the top of a little hill from which they survey the future of Rome and where Aeneas at least learns the fullness of his own destiny and identity. This is the point at which the epic descent converts itself into an ascent; from here the way is clear, however many obstacles may yet remain, to the foundation of Rome or the liberation of Eden. That both acts are really restorations, of Troy and of earthly paradise, is the final point of their symmetry and a sure proof of their acclimatization in epic.

The *descensus* of the second book are, fittingly, both fewer in number and oriented toward the particular concerns of that book, the exploration of temperance. The primary concern of Book 1 had been, loosely, spirit—spirit encountering matter, learning to deal with it and to accommodate itself to it, and even attaining a brief vision of its ultimate freedom from it. The concern of Book 2, on the other hand, is body, its powers and limitations, and that concern in itself indicates a deeper penetration in the overall pattern of descent. The two *descensus* of the book, Guyon's visit to the cave of Mammon and the subsequent visit of Guyon and Arthur at the House of Alma, clearly conform to that presiding focus. In the course of both, the knights learn at least one aspect of what it means to be the "man of earth" that Contemplation called Red Crosse Knight.

Spenser links the cave of Mammon with the classical Tartarus by putting its entrance on the same road that "streight did lead to *Plutoes* griesly raine" (2.7.21), by locating a fairly orthodox battery of personified abstractions before its gates (see *Aeneid* 6.268–81), and by locating Tantalus within it; in these respects it resembles Duessa's and Night's visit to *"Plutoes* house," though there almost all similarity between the episodes ends. Guyon, without his Palmer to restrain him (that seems to be the Palmer's primary function), follows Mammon out of simple curiosity; after having prolonged their conversation by a catechism of questions and answers far beyond the point at which he knows all he needs to know to shun the "God of the world and worldlings," he asks about the place all his wealth is stored, and is lured into his kingdom by a simple "come thou . . . and see." What follows such a beginning clearly distorts the orthodox notion of the descent of the mind to the contemplation of creatures. The purpose of that descent is through knowledge of created things to arrive at knowledge of their creator. No purpose is served by Guyon's descent, except Mammon's, and that is not to inform but to tempt. Once in the cave, Guyon sees essentially not creatures, but creature: wealth in its myriad forms, including Mammon's daughter Philotime, who embodies a perverse version of the love of honor that Guyon so insistently asserts motivates him (she and her father, though unscathed here in Book 2, get their proper comeuppance in Book 5 under the guises of Pollente and Munera). This particular descent climaxes in the Garden of Proserpina, where Guyon sees the eternal punishments of Tantalus and—crucially—Pontius Pilate. Pilate's sin can in no ordinary way be related to the concept of

So, are we dealing with the right / most relevant model

temperance; his description of himself makes this clear:

> I *Pilate* am the falsest Iudge, alas
> And most vniust, that by vnrighteous
> And wicked doome, to Iewes despiteous
> Delivered vp the Lord of life to die,
> And did acquite a murdrer felonous;
> The whiles my hands I washt in puritie,
> The whiles my soule was soyld with foule iniquitie.
>
> [2.7.62]

All of the language of that passage, and Pilate's and Spenser's own emphases, point to the concept of judgment rather than temperance as being the standard of his damnation; as such, he seems more properly to belong to Book 5 (with which Book 2 is intimately related) than to Book 2. Even if one argues that what he sought to accomplish by his judgment was a sort of false tempering of the commonweal, that still, by its public nature, seems more fitting to the fifth book than to this. His presence here enlarges the conventional notion of temperance—the notion by which Guyon has to this point been governed and which was encapsulated in the Castle of Medina—to include judgment and at least that aspect of justice which will be displayed in the fifth book as personal justice, the government of oneself. (Conversely, in Book 5 Guyon will regain *Style* his horse—will? passion?—without which he remains, in Book 2, dependent literally upon the motive power of others—Phaedria, the boatman.) It serves as well to show the dangerous flaw in Guyon's subterranean grand tour, which results from intellectual error—from a false judgment—rather than from appetite. Guyon's immediately subsequent collapse demonstrates graphically the danger of lingering too long in the contemplation of material things; the weight of matter, as the Red Crosse Knight discovered, can oppress the spirit. Aeneas, at the very outset of his descent, is warned of this danger; so the allegorists understood his not lingering over the friezes of the Temple of Apollo. "Therefore on the doors through which there was access into the temple were depicted the killing of Androgeos, the foul deed of Pasiphae, and the pride of Icarus. And so in the beginning Aeneas contemplates these things; but there can be no long delay over the recognition of vices, for they should be recognized immediately and left behind immediately once they are recognized."[17] In addition, the sybil throughout his descent frequently reminds him of the need for haste; it is easy to go to Hell, but hard to return—as Guyon finds out.

Guyon's three days beneath the earth bear one more relation to Duessa's descent than I have yet mentioned: both parody, pervert, or distort the harrowing of Hell. In the case of Duessa's journey, this aspect is quite overt, as I discussed above; in the case of Guyon's, it is overlaid, at the end of his sojourn, so as to transpose the whole descent from the context in which we have so far investigated it to a wholly new area of reference. The sharp-eyed reader might pick up a hint of a Christic or Christian dimension to Guyon's descent from Mammon's succinct words of invitation ("Come thou . . . and see"), which echo Christ's invitation to his first disciples in response to a similar question about where he dwelt;[18] I confess I did not ,except by virtue of hindsight. Be that as it may, the introduction of Pilate, his self-indictment, and the closely following mention of the fact that Guyon has spent "three dayes of men" below the earth definitively yank the episode in the direction of Christ's three days in the tomb and subsequent resurrection. Here, however, Spenser reverses the aftermath of the *descensus*: death (symbolic, of course, but Spenser's language nevertheless resolutely insists we see it as such) occurs after the tomb:

> The God, though loth, yet was constraind t'obay,
>   For lenger time, then that, no liuing wight
>   Below the earth, might suffred be to stay:
>   So backe againe, him brought to liuing light.
>   But all so soone as his enfeebled spright
>   Gan sucke this vitall aire into his brest,
>   As ouercome with too exceeding might,

38

> The life did flit away out of her nest,
> And all his senses were with deadly fit opprest.
>
> [2.7.ult.]

So for Guyon, whose trip to Mammon's cave was needless and essentially unproductive of new knowledge, the real descent to the body takes place after his return, when what we call Guyon is reduced to a senseless body, to mere matter. At precisely that point the spiritual world asserts its hegemony over inert matter by the providential appearance of the angel (a descent in itself, I might point out) and the subsequent exertions of Prince Arthur. At the exact moment that the agent of Providence slays the paynim exponents of wrath and concupiscence, Guyon revives: "By this Sir *Guyon* from his traunce awakt, / Life hauing maistered her sence-lesse foe" (2.8.53). It is worth remarking that that second line refers equally and ambiguously to the resurrection of Guyon's spirit, its victory over dead matter, and to Arthur's conquest of his enraged opponents. They are simultaneous and indeed cognate acts. For this reason Arthur fights with Guyon's sword; similarly, because the opponent is the self—at least the bodily self conceived of as the house of sin and death—the two pagan knights can use Guyon's shield and Arthur's sword against them. For all practical purposes, Arthur and Guyon from this point on in Book 2 are one individual bifurcated into two aspects or explicated under two forms, and their final adventures should be seen also as simultaneous prosecutions of the same end. Arthur there, as here, pursues and vanquishes the foes endemic to and resident in the body—and it is his hardest fight in *The Faerie Queene*—while Guyon encounters and masters the distempered intellect (the Bower of Bliss is for this reason portrayed as a palace of artifice).

   The lessons about the limitations of the body or nature and about the interdependence of body and spirit that these episodes enforce are confirmed by the Castle of Alma, where the workings of the body, the mind, and the indwelling *Alma* are elaborately unfolded. The stay of the two knights there relates in two ways to the epic *descensus*: first, it is a literalization of the notion of the *descensus* as the entrance of the spirit into body, and so serves to put right the disordered and threatening *descensus* that have preceded it; and second, it functions once again, in the tradition of the narrative (as opposed to the allegory) of the *Aeneid*, and like the House of Holiness in Book 1, to provide the heroes with information about their identity, here by means of memory and history rather than foresight and prophecy. Both these functions work to simplify a situation that had threatened to grow far too complex (not at all successfully, if one can judge anything from the volume of scholarly argument about what consitutes the order of nature and what the order of grace in Book 2). What Guyon's swoon, Arthur's battle with Pyrochles and Cymocles, and Alma's castle all teach is the simple interrelatedness of body and soul, that the two apparent opposites must coincide. In this way it is a radical departure from the implicit philosophy of the castle of Medina: there is and can be no mean between soul and body, just as in the Christian system there is no mean between sin and grace. Medina is not even able to keep peace in her own house, while the castle of Alma is completely harmonious:

> The frame thereof seemd partly circulare,
> And part triangulare, O worke diuine;
> Those two the first and last proportions are,
> The one imperfect, mortall, foeminine;
> Th'other immortall, perfect, masculine,
> And twixt them both a quadrate was the base,
> Proportioned equally by seuen and nine;
> Nine was the circle set in heauens place,
> All which compacted made a goodly diapase.
>
> [2.9.22]

Criticized from the viewpoint of this coincidence of opposites, Guyon's notion of temperance has consistently gone wrong by simply trying to repress one half of the equation, by trying to deny any validity to the body's impulses. The cave of Mammon exposed the fallacy of that not by what Guyon saw there but by what he did there:

And now he has so long remained there,
  That vitall powres gan wexe both weake and wan,
  For want of food, and sleepe, which two vpbeare,
  Like mightie pillours, this fraile life of man,
  That none without the same enduren can.

[2.7.65]

Guyon's spirit is immediately thereafter overcome not by the strength of the body but by its weakness, and it requires a step outside the order of nature to return him to his "natural" condition. Alma's castle, built as it is out of "that *Aegyptian* slime," yet inhabited by that "virgin bright," displays the full dimensions of the divine creation of which Orgoglio was a sorry travesty.

⚵

Books 1 and 2 of *The Faerie Queene* provide a basic working manual of allegorical technique. The Book of Holiness, beginning as it does with the generation of its own allegorical matrix, offers after that an elaborate but perfectly normal allegorical narrative: the Red Crosse Knight fights spiritual foes with physical weapons, the symbolically understood armory of the spirit, as conventional allegorical thinking demands. In normal allegory, the physical portrays the spiritual: Red Crosse's shield images faith. The Book of Temperance in large part reverses that relationship and proceeds—with heavy internal irony and parody—to portray the physical in its allegory. For a large part of Book 2, Guyon and Arthur must fight essentially physical foes with spiritual weapons; that is the reason for the striking ineffectiveness, in this book, of those normally reliable tools—witness Arthur's struggle with Maleger as a case in point. But once the conventional allegorical relation is upset, paradoxes abound. Scylla and Charybdis, for example, are already present in the narrative as concepts, not as creatures. Acrasia and Maleger, ostensibly the most carnal of *The Faerie Queene*'s villains, are its most insubstantial: Maleger and his crew in fact offer the finest paradox in the whole poem, insofar

41

as Spenser insists that we see them as incorporeal bodies. Because of this basic displacement of the normal allegorical tenor and vehicle, Spenser is able to carry out his apparent intention of exploring the realm of body and the claims and limitations of body. By the same token, this displacement enables him also to return to some of the narrative elements he used in Book 1 from a totally different point of view. For example, the Ruddymane episode. That virgin spring, noumenally the same spring that revived Red Crosse and promises life to Fradubio, the pure spring as opposed to the polluted one that weakened him, here slays Mordant: in Book 2, the life of the spirit is the death of the body except in the most tempered souls (thus Guyon "dies" when he returns from the underworld, and the angel guards his "lifeless" body). The life of the body is the death of the spirit, the life of the spirit the death of the body: the principle of spiritual life is death to the death giver (Mordant). Ruddymane's hands are red because his hands are red; they bear a scar, blood, the sign of physical life and of physical limitation, of death itself, of physical antipathy to spirit, and of physical dependence upon spirit, and they tell right from the start what Guyon's difficulties will be: the shield of faith will not keep him from either hurting or dying. Man cannot live by faith alone any more than by bread alone: Book 2 is designed to present an immediate and heavy qualification of the apparent optimism of Book 1.

Books 3 and 4 continue Spenser's realistic assessment of the human situation, now exploring the mutual interaction of mind and body, of individual minds housed in individual bodies; he offers us here multiple examples rather than general representatives, since, at this deepest point of the *descensus*, the poem is most immersed in the principle of multiplicity itself; Archimago and Duessa almost disappear from these two books, to be replaced by Busirane and Proteus, by the monsters of the mind and pure plastic matter. Book 3 begins with body suffering because of mind—Florimell's panic fear, Britomart's love torment, Arthur's, Red Crosse Knight's; no archetypal incident presents itself, no chief villain presides over either book. Rather in both the initial strife is among the Knights of Maidenhead themselves and within themselves. Even the heroes of the previous two books are caught up in the discord, and the monsters of the mind they create are the enemies they must conquer by chastity and friendship, by love, constancy, and concord. The accomplishment of that and the beginning of the final, ascending movement of the Platonic triad will be signalled by Florimell's final freedom from fear and woe and her achievement of true rest in union with Marinell, a union already celebrated in the poem by the ritual marriage of their surrogates, the Thames and the Medway.

Books 3 and 4 constitute the central transforming unit of the triad—in its various senses, the life of the soul in the body, the mind learning from and about created things, the life of sin and potential damnation, magic and the invocation of demons. Book 3 consequently is the book of enchanters and enchantments: Merlin's world of glass, Merlin himself, Busirane and the masque of Cupid, Britomart's enchanted spear, Amoret's wound. Book 4 is the book of transformation and merging: Priamond, Diamond, and Triamond, the indissoluble bonds of Cambell and Canacee, Triamond and Cambina, the marriage of the Thames and the Medway, the joining of Florimell and Marinell, the meeting of Britomart and Artegal. They share common locales: the forest, the *silva* of this world, and night and the sea which are the forest's ideological equivalents; this is the world of the spirit in the body, the world of multiplicity, and what we witness here are the *motions* of spirit itself in and through time. This is why Spenser has here adopted a romance structure and utilized its principle of *entrelacement*; at this deepest point of the descent, at the farthest remove from unity, the apparently episodic format and the multiplicity of protagonists and narratives reflect with accuracy the diversity of the created world, its apparently infinite particularity, and its underlying unity in the ideal pattern of "beauties chace"—at once the pursuit of beauty and beauty's own pursuit of its proper object. For this reason too the whole two books are framed by Florimell's quest, from her passage through *silva* to her immersion in *humor*, through the ironic stasis imposed on her by the principle of change itself to her true stability and true union with Marinell. Again, for this same reason, Books 3 and 4 of *The Faerie Queene* imitate Books 6 and 7 of the *Aeneid;* Merlin's prophecy of the fate of Britain and the garden of Adonis recapitulating Anchises' prediction of the future of Rome and Aeneas's vision of the souls awaiting birth; and the meeting of Florimell and Marinell and the strife stirred up by Ate and the False Florimell recapitulating the first approaches of Aeneas to his destined bride Lavinia and the strife stirred up by Allecto and Juno upon her account (one can also see in Spenser's catalog of rivers, in the marriage of the Thames and Medway, a transformed counterpart to Virgil's catalog of the gathering opponents of Aeneas's marriage).

Because these books are located in the world, and concern themselves with the actions of souls in bodies and of spirits in time—because, that is, of their exact locus in the process of the *descensus*—they are even more susceptible than the others of *The Faerie Queene* to the kind of reading we can only call psychological. From the very beginning of Britomart's love, Glauce protests against her making "such Monster of your mind" (3.2.40), and it is against monsters bred of their own minds that all the protagonists of Books 3 and 4 must struggle until they achieve such constancy in the face of mutability as Florimell personifies, or such knowledge about the nature of corporeality and its relation to spirit as the Garden of Adonis exemplifies, or such confidence in the face of death and futurity and time as Merlin's predictions offer (and Britomart only fully achieves in the Temple of Isis in Book 5). Their life is beauty's chase, and the object they pursue defines the nature of the transformation they will undergo and the end they will achieve. The good they seek will conform them to itself; of this fact False Florimell's choice of Braggadocchio as her knight is emblem, as is—in an entirely different direction—the hermaphroditic union of Scudamore and Amoret in the deleted (in the 1596 edition)

44

concluding stanzas of Book 3. Malbecco is Spenser's most elaborate and, to my mind, funny treatment of this process. Torn between two creatures, his wealth and an entirely carnal love for his wife Hellenore, he loses both because he loved neither even for itself (which, in orthodox Christianity, would have been bad enough) but only for possession's sake. Committed to the most fragile of relations to created things, the attempt to hold, stop, freeze, possess forever what are by their very nature mutable and elusive, he suffers in kind: he is transformed into the insubstantial spirit of the fear of loss, himself frozen forever in an impotent desire and rage for and against what he can never have:

> But through long anguish, and selfe-murdring thought
>   He was so wasted and forpined quight,
>   That all his substance was consum'd to nought,
>   And nothing left, but like an aery Spright,
>   That on the rockes he fell so flit and light,
>   That he thereby receiu'd no hurt at all,
>   But chaunced on a craggy cliff to light;
>   Whence he with crooked clawes so long did crall,
> That at the last he found a caue with entrance small.
>
> Yet can he neuer dye, but dying liues,
>   And doth himselfe with sorrow new sustaine,
>   That death and life attonce vnto him giues,
>   And painefull pleasure turnes to pleasing paine.
>   There dwels he euer, miserable swaine,
>   Hatefull both to himselfe, and euery wight;
>   Where he through priuy griefe, and horrour vaine,
>   Is woxen so deform'd, that he has quight
> Forgot he was a man, and *Gealosie* is hight.
>
> [3.10.57, 60]

His sorry refinement from flesh grotesquely parodies the illuminated mind's return to the timeless realm of spirit at the same time that it ironically comments upon the materiality he sought. Within the *descensus*, he descends still further, discovering a mode of existence that we can only label a Platonic world of bad ideas, a region not of forms capable of informing substance but of forms deformed by it. Like Satan's darkness visible in *Paradise Lost*, Malbecco's rarefaction is both a travesty of the Good and a succinct mock epic.

Malbecco is not the only character in these books who wastes away till he is "like an aery Spright." In addition to Amoret and Marinell, who get very near to literally becoming ghosts and who undergo corresponding resurrection (as does Florimell, whom every other character at this point in the narrative believes dead), Britomart, Florimell, and Timias, all pine away through love and/or fear:

> [Britomart] still did waste, and still did wayle,
> That through long languour, and hart-burning brame
> She shortly like a pyned ghost became,
> Which long hath waited by the Stygian strond.
>
> [3.2.52]

> [Florimell], as one nigh of her wits depriued,
> With nought but ghastly lookes him answered,
> Like to a ghost, that lately is reuiued
> From *Stygian* shores, where late it wandered.
>
> [3.7.14]

> There he [Timias] continued in this carefull plight,
> Wretchedly wearing out his youthly yeares,
> Through wilfull penury consumed quight,
> That like a pined ghost he soone appeares.
>
> [4.7.41]

> Whom [Timias] when she saw in wretched weedes disguiz'd,
> With heary glib deform'd, and meiger face,
> Like ghost late risen from his graue agryz'd,
> She knew him not, but pittied much his case,
> And wisht it were in her to doe him any grace.
>
> [4.8.12]

As the last quotation clearly implies, each of these symbolic deaths has its symbolic resurrection, and each is effected by the power of love. Love mediates between gods and men, according to Plato; love is the impelling force of beauty's chase, according to Spenser. Love in the form of Venus is unfolded in the dialectic of the three

Graces (the *Carites*, i.e., the Loves), whose triple action of giving, receiving, and returning illustrates one mode of the Platonic dialectic of emanation, conversion, and return.[19] The knot of the Graces is the knot of love, and love in *The Faerie Queene* is the central (both narratively and ideologically) converting power that starts its protagonists on their upward journey to the One and initiates their liberation from the grave of the body and the *inferos*. This too is its function in Virgil, according to Landino's argument: divine love "attempts nothing else . . . except this: that, aroused by the sight of corporeal beauty, it might carry us to divine beauty" (65). Spenser shows this clearly in the second fight between Artegal and Britomart where, up until the point at which he sees her face, Artegal is described as "full of despiteous ire" and activated by "felonous intent" (4.6.11): "Certes some hellish furie, or some feend/This mischiefe framd, for their first loues defeature" (4.6.17). As soon as he sees her face, he:

> At last fell humbly downe vpon his knee,
> And of his wonder made religion,
> Weening some heauenly goddesse he did see.
>
> [4.6.22]

Even Scudamor sees in her:

> That peerelesse paterne of Dame natures pride,
> And heauenly image of perfection,
> [and] blest himselfe, as one sore terrifide,
> And turning his feare to faint deuotion,
> Did worship her as some celestiall vision.
>
> [4.6.24]

An exactly parallel instance occurs when Florimell is freed from Proteus's dungeon and brought before the pining Marinell:

> Who soone as he beheld that angels face,
> Adorn'd with all diuine perfection,
> His cheared heart eftsoones away gan chace
> Sad death, reuiued with her swete inspection,

47

And feeble spirit inly felt refection;
As withered weed through cruell winters tine,
That feeles the warmth of sunny beames reflection,
Liftes up his head, that did before decline
And gins to spread his leafe before the faire sunshine.
[4.12.34]

To make religion of one's wonder and one's love is obviously the proper sort of response in *The Faerie Queene*, and Spenser clearly intends the cultivation of that love to lead the various protagonists of the books of chastity and friendship (proper love of oneself and proper love of others) out of the forest of the world and into the unity of the noumenal. Of that unity, marriage is symbol and metaphor and is fittingly represented here by the only marriage actually celebrated in *The Faerie Queene*, that of the Thames and the Medway (the total physical merging of rivers analogizes a human spiritual union of ideal proportions), and that marriage appropriately serves as the ritual surrogate for the triumph of the only completely successful quest in the poem, that of Florimell for Marinell (although they are in fact married in the course of the poem, Spenser declines to describe their nuptials [5.3.3]). The marriage of Florimell and Marinell, as I said earlier, accomplishes a joining of opposites, an infolding of diversity into unity, which definitively marks the start of the rising action of the poem and the return portion of the *descensus*. Love and fertility unite with wrath and matter (Marinell is master of the heaped-up wealth of the Rich Strond). Their marriage antithesizes the false harmony of the coupling of Verdant and Acrasia: here, Venus truly tempers Mars, and their conjunction should bring forth Harmonia.

Within that ideal frame, the other characters emulate in their more limited and human fashion that constancy of Florimell, the devotion of her love, and seek for, never quite to find in the poem as we have it, her ideal conclusion. Love and the religion of love remain profoundly ambiguous in *The Faerie Queene*; the ambiguity is summed up in Scudamor's shield, which bears the image of the winged god. But which one? The cruel conqueror of

48

the Masque of Cupid, the power that holds and tortures Amoret? The bowless, docile Cupid of the Garden of Adonis, the faithful husband of Psyche? Clearly, Scudamor should owe allegiance to the latter: Amoret, after all, dwelt with Psyche in the Garden of Adonis, and Scudamor won her from the temple of the Hermaphroditic Venus, Venus Concordia. But precisely the ambiguity of his own allegiance prevents him—but not Britomart—from passing through the fires of lust and consequently enthralls Amoret to the religion of cupidity.[20] Spenser captures the exact nature of that ambiguity in the simple presence of the Masque of Cupid at Scudamor's and Amoret's wedding feast: the wrong Cupid has come to dominate their love. That is the monster their minds have made to torment them, and they can only be rescued from it by Britomart, who shares their love but not their lust, who can both see that it is a divinity she assaults ("We a god inuade" [3.11.22]) and yet know the limitations of that deity, who can be defeated by watchfulness and boldness. Busirane is merely the priest and magician of that god, cruelly serving him with sacrifice as his namesake Busiris served Neptune (his cruel and misplaced piety was undone by Hercules; Britomart is destined to wed a man who will redo the labors of Hercules).

The religion of love receives far greater distortions than this in the course of Books 3 and 4. The homage paid to the False Florimell leads inexorably to the discord and confusion of the misnamed Tournament of Beauty, of which she turns out to be the prize and Braggadocchio the fitting winner. The true Florimell's girdle becomes an object of idolatry:

> The first of all forth came Sir *Satyrane,*
> Bearing that precious relicke in an arke
> Of gold, that bad eyes might it not prophane.
> [4.4.15]

After the tournament, of course, it is thoroughly "prophaned" by the inability of all save Amoret to wear that ornament of chastity

49

and by its finally being awarded to False Florimell. Paridell and
Hellenore provide the climactic moment of all of the poem's ironic
uses of the language of the religion of love in their sacrilegious
communion at Malbecco's table:

> Now *Bacchus* fruit out of the siluer plate
> He on the table dasht, as ouerthrowne,
> Or of the fruitfull liquor ouerflowne,
> And by the dauncing bubbles did diuine,
> Or therein write to let his loue be showne;
> Which well she red out of the learned line,
> A sacrament prophane in mistery of wine.
>
> [3.9.30]

After that, her reduction to the level of the satyrs (whose attitude
toward her markedly differs from their attitude toward Una) concludes her "beauties chace," rewarding her with a drolly comic and
carnal refuge:

> At night, when they all went to sleepe, he [Malbecco] vewd,
> Whereas his louely wife emongst them lay,
> Embraced of a *Satyre* rough and rude,
> Who all the night did minde his ioyous play:
> Nine times he heard him come aloft ere day,
> That all his hart with gealosie did swell;
> But yet that nights ensample did bewray,
> That not for nought his wife them loued so well,
> When one so oft a night did ring his matins bell.
>
> [3.10.48]

The declension of the religion of love to this particular form
of matins marks exactly where we are in the large declension we
have been witnessing from Red Crosse Knight's shield of faith to
Scudamor's shield of love. To lesser degrees, all of the characters of
these books share this pervasive carnality; all are, with Florimell,
trapped by the sea, by *humor*, by Proteus who represents both
matter and man. Arthur is largely in abeyance here, himself wandering in beauty's chase and bewildered in the night which he
correctly links with death and "Herebus blacke hous" (3.4.55).

50

Timias is separated from him, lost in the forest and in Belphoebe's disfavor. Even Britomart, who is sufficiently chaste to rescue Amoret from Busirane, promptly loses her again to lust when she falls off to sleep and Amoret wanders into the wood. While Florimell is trapped beneath the sea—that is, while the spiritual force of love is held in stasis by material mutability and denied its proper object—events on land reflect that disharmony. Concupiscence and wrath have been with us from the beginning of the poem, of course, but nowhere do they wield such power, nowhere are they so ubiquitous as in Books 3 and 4. That is not because Books 3 and 4 are about friendship, love, and chastity; rather, that is the reason why those topics are the subjects of the central books of *The Faerie Queene*.

The forest, the sea, and the night of Books 3 and 4 are the underworld of the poem as a whole, through which most of the poem's heroes (all except Calidore, in fact) must pass. Matter and spirit reach their greatest depravity in False Florimell and in Malbecco: she, dead elements animated by a malignant sprite, he, dead spirit sustained by thirst for matter. The House of Busirane synopsizes all this: the house of bondage stands at the very center of Spenser's poem.[21] In its outer room, Britomart sees the "fowle Idolatree" (3.11.49) of the worship of Cupid; in the middle, wrought in gold, the decay of material prosperity in the "thousand monstrous formes" (3.11.51) of love and its spoils; in the inmost, the destruction of the spirit by its own powers in the Masque of Cupid:

> There were full many moe like maladies,
>   Whose names and natures I note readen well;
>   So many moe, as there be phantasies
>   In wauering wemens wit, that none can tell,
>   Or paines in loue, or punishments in hell;
>   All which disguized marcht in masking wise,
>   About the chamber with that Damozell,
>   And then returned, hauing marched thrise,
> Into the inner room, from when they first did rise.
>
>   [3.12.26]

Britomart's chastity sees her safely through the fires that surround the House of Busirane, and her "huge heroicke magnanimity" (3.11.19) forces Busirane to undo his spells and release Amoret. With that disenchantment with the illusions of impure love (*cupiditas* rather than *caritas*) ends the thralldom of the mind to lures of the flesh: Cupid has literally been seen through. This does not mean that all is perfect. Far from it. The characters and the poem are still very much in the underworld, and will remain there. Amoret will again fall victim to lust (external lust this time), and Britomart will have her own problems with Artegal—but the journey has reversed its direction, and the poem and characters are slowly ascending from the underworld of matter. Spenser is now free to show us the exemplary loves and friendships of Cambell and Cambina, Triamond and Canacee, even though they will be involved in the degrading Tournament of Beauty; he can allow Arthur to free Amoret from Lust and Timias to reestablish his virtuous companionship with Belphoebe. More strikingly, Scudamor, the source and partaker of so much of the disorder of Book 3, can now recount his winning of Amoret from the Temple of Venus, and Spenser can use that psychologically symbolic account of the progress of virtuous love to set the scene for the marriage of the Thames and the Medway and the coming together of Florimell and Marinell. Scudamor and Amoret themselves are never quite united again, and their unconsummated marriage must stand as emblem of the tentativeness of all victories, in *The Faerie Queene* as in the world; in the no-time and every-time of the poem, Amoret is simultaneously sitting in the lap of Womanhood in the Temple of Venus and bleeding at the pillar in the House of Busirane, where the dagger of the underworld's cupidity pierces every human heart.

Books 5 and 6 of *The Faerie Queene* form the return leg of the *descensus*, that portion of the process which returns the liberated mind or soul to its proper spiritual sphere of action. Even narratively Spenser preserves this thrust by concluding so many otherwise unfinished actions: Florimell and Marinell return to the world to marry; Britomart and Artegal finally straighten out their relationship to each other; Timias rejoins Prince Arthur; and Duessa is brought to justice and unequivocally punished. A literal understanding of Artegal's quest in Book 5—to establish the kingdom of peace—complements and expands the establishment of a purely personal, albeit symbolic, harmony by Florimell and Marinell at the end of Book 4. Indeed, Book 5 can reasonably be viewed, in at least one light, as the extension to the body politic and society at large of the concord established between individuals in Book 4: Irena's kingdom is the political version of a phenomenon we have already seen under differing species in the respective knots of Priamond, Diamond, and Triamond or Triamond, Cambell, Canacee, and Cambina or Thames and Medway. So too Calidore's quest in Book 6 completes and expands Artegal's. Artegal conquers the Blatant Beast for himself by his unquestioned achievement of inner peace, but Calidore vanquishes him for the world and by so doing establishes, at least momentarily, a golden world. The pastoralism of the Book of Courtesy prepares us for that, as does Calidore's vision of the Graces on Mount Acidale—a vision that directly counterpoints and translates into the idiom of the pastoral Red Crosse Knight's vision of the Heavenly Jerusalem in the first book. In exactly the same way, the restoration of Pastorella to her parents answers the reunion of Una and her parents, the giant Disdayne is "sib to great *Orgoglio*" and Defetto, Despetto, and Decetto correspond to Sansioi, Sansfoi, and Sansloi. All of this locates us at approximately the same depth in the *inferos*: that is, the characters and protagonists of Book 6 are about to emerge from the world of Archimago and Duessa in just the same manner that the protagonists of Book 1 entered it. The passage in either case is through error: the way down is to fall into Error; the way up is to conquer the Blatant Beast, who disseminates error. Calidore's victory frees the soul or mind from the last—and first—monster of its own creation and restores it to the state of equanimity it possessed before its immersion in the confusions of Error's wood. That Spenser conveys this all by parallel uses of a Christian and a pagan harrowing of Hell (discussed above, pp. 23–25) seems to me sure indication of the mind's and the poem's at least temporary liberation from the *inferos*: "vertues seat," he assures us in the proem to Book 6, "is deepe within the mynd,/And not in outward shows, but inward thoughts defynd" (5), and the pattern for it Spenser finds in Elizabeth's "pure minde," where "as in a mirrour sheene,/It showes" (6). The last stanza of his proem makes explicit the pattern we have been watching all through the poem and tells us exactly where, at the end of the book, we will be in relation to it:

> Then pardon me, most dreaded Soueraine,
>   That from your selfe I doe this vertue bring,
>   And to your selfe doe it returne againe:
>   So from the Ocean all riuers spring,
>   And tribute backe repay as to their King.
>   Right so from you all goodly vertues well
>   Into the rest, which round about you ring,
>   Faire Lords and Ladies, which about you dwell,
> And doe adorne your Court, where courtesies excell.
>
> [7]

The path of the ascent, once clear of the tangles of Books 3 and 4, is a relatively simple one. It starts with the honorific appearance of a cave—Astrea's—as a place of illumination about the nature of justice and passes through the dispelling of illusion in the evaporation of the False Florimell by simple juxtaposition with the true and the subsequent exposure and disgrace of the false knight Braggadocchio. That clarification leads in turn to the foiling of Dolon's plot—significantly, at night—and the first transformation of night and dreams into the vehicle of true vision in Britomart's dream in Isis's church. In the same way, Artegal and Arthur lure Malengin from his cave, frustrate his attempt to convey Samient therein, and thereby destroy him and nullify its efficacy; this leads in turn to the formal arraignment and punishment of the duplicitous Duessa and her removal from Faeryland. The parallel resurrections of Belge and Irena are fittingly capped by Artegal's achievement of personal peace in his ability to withstand Envy, Detraction, and the Blatant Beast, which then becomes the last enemy at large in *The Faerie Queene*. Spenser very firmly describes that quest as a mental one from the proem onward. For that reason he emphasizes throughout the book the necessity of mental discipline, as can be seen in the lessons he has Calidore teach Crudor and Briana and the Hermit impart to Timias and Serena. Such an emphasis also informs Calidore's sojourn in the pastoral life: Spenser presents it as a thoroughgoing excursion into the retired life as opposed to the active, with all of its attendant implications of the superiority of contemplation to action and with its built-in Boethian lesson about the necessity of the disciplined and informed mind's superiority and indifference to the vicissitudes of fortune (we should recall at this point Red Crosse Knight's premature desire to remain with Holy Contemplation). It is only by obtaining the tranquillity that retirement and contemplation can give, the contemplative life and knowledge which was the goal of Aeneas and of epic and which, according to Landino, provided the norms for action, that Calidore can conquer the Blatant Beast: Calidore must muzzle the beast in himself before he can subdue him in the world. Fortune is the presiding power of the sublunary world, the *inferos*, and the mind can only rise above that mutability by coming to know through contemplation—through the knowledge of creatures which is the very process of the *descensus* itself—the "eterne" which informs it and governs it. This Calidore accomplishes by his social declension from knight to shepherd, which mirrors in miniature the whole of *The Faerie Queene*'s passage from Una through Duessa, Proteus, Malengin, and the Blatant Beast, through "forgerie,/Fashion'd to please the eies of them, that pas" (Proem 5) to return to "So faire a patterne . . . of Princely curtesie" (Proem 6).

The initiation of motion out of stasis ("A Gentle Knight was pricking on the plaine") differentiates man from God, who is stable and unmoved—but only motion will bring man back to God and stability. Epically, Aeneas cannot fall with Troy, but must move through Crete and Carthage and Sicily to Italy and rest; Achilles must pass from inaction to action to his final rest. The perfect is stable and cannot duplicate itself; the imperfect is unstable and can only approximate stability through circular motion: thus the structure of *The Faerie Queene*, thus the progression in the poem from saint through exemplar to recognizable human being in realistic/symbolic situations, and thus too the inevitable escapes of Archimago and the Blatant Beast. *The Faerie Queene* ends in pastoral for many reasons: because of its associations with retirement and contemplation, because of its especially "literary" nature and its implications about the range of artistic vision—but most of all because pastoral is, as in Virgil's fourth eclogue, the genre par excellence of the reestablishment of the Golden Age, the achievement of rest after motion, the return of the triad to its proper infolding in God.

<hr />

However important Calidore's harrowing of Hell may be in knitting up the strands of the *descensus*, his vision on Mount Acidale seems to serve a greater purpose in the purgation of Faeryland and in the release of the human spirit from the bonds of infernal mutability. A.C. Hamilton has rightly stressed the importance of images to our understanding of Spenser's poem, and we must extend that emphasis to a comprehension of the centrality of *seeing* to the characters of the poem.[22] It is not merely that *The Faerie Queene* primarily offers itself to us, the readers, as an image, but also that it is almost exclusively under this form that it is apprehended by the personae of the poem themselves. This is crucial to epic generally: the example of Dante (as Hamilton remarks) springs immediately to mind, of course—but the pattern was established before he remade it. Aeneas must free himself from his accustomed helmsman Palinurus—"wandering vision," according to the commentators—must descend to the underworld to *see* Anchises, so that his father can show him the future of Rome. In the commentators' treatments of the *Aeneid*, the hero sees different things—the punishments of sin, the rewards of virtue, the limitations of creatures—but the act of his seeing and the importance of his vision remain central to the poem and crucial to his achievement: in the contemplative descent, the hero learns for the first time to see clearly. Vision is knowledge, and in *The Faerie Queene* Spenser attempts to clear for us the glass through which we now see so darkly so that, in Sidney's words, "our erected wit" can make us "know what perfection is," even if "our infected wil keepeth us from reaching unto it."

Calidore's vision of Acidale is not a vision of perfection face to face, but an apprehension of perfectibility under the triple modes of poetry, *descensus*, and *The Faerie Queene*. What he sees are the Graces, and especially the three principal Graces, Euphrosyne, Aglaia, and Thalia, and Colin Clout's beloved, "for more honor brought . . . to this place,/And graced . . . so much to be another Grace" (6.10.26). She has earned her place by her virtues:

> Another Grace she well deserues to be,
> In whom so many Graces gathered are,
> Excelling much the meane of her degree;
> Diuine resemblaunce, beauty soueraine rare,
> Firme Chastity, that spight ne blemish dare;
> All which she with such courtesie doth grace,
> That all her peres cannot with her compare.
> [6.10.27]

That list enumerates most of the virtues available to women in the poem, including an immunity to the bites of the Blatant Beast ("that spight ne blemish dare"), and at least in that respect she foreshadows the good state of the world, the restoration of the graces to earth, that Calidore will bring about by capturing the

Beast. Her placement in the center of the ring of Graces, her replacement of Venus, indicates that too:

> And in the middest of these same three, was placed
> Another Damzell, as a precious gemme.

[6.10.12]

The importance of this placement lies in the relative positions and functions of the Graces vis-à-vis Venus and vis-à-vis humanity:

> Those three to men all gifts of grace do graunt,
> And all, that *Venus* in her selfe doth vaunt,
> Is borrowed of them.

[6.10.15]

> They all are Graces, which on her [Venus] depend,
> Besides a thousand more, which ready bee
> Her to adorne, when so she forth doth wend:
> But those three in the midst, doe chiefe on her attend.

[6.10.21]

> These three on men all gracious gifts bestow,
> Which decke the body or adorne the mynde.

[6.10.23]

The Graces explicate, they unfold, Venus; Colin Clout's "countrey lasse" complicates, enfolds, the Graces.

That image encapsulates the threefold dialectic of the poem: giving, receiving, returning; emanation, conversion, return; descent, illumination, return. Through the medium of the Graces humanity and divinity are united and equated: what flows from the gods as unity is divided in them and through them is united again in man. Spenser's elevation of a "countrey lasse" to the status of Venus by means of the Graces' threefold channel of courtesy returns to its ideological source Calidore's descent from knighthood to shepherdry, from action to retirement, through the agency of his courtesy. Calidore is permitted to see the Graces because he embodies them just as much as Colin's beloved does, and he cannot retain the vision for the same reasons that humanity cannot keep bound the Blatant Beast. The Fall is a continuing process as much as is the Redemption.

This is signalled in the poem by the antithetical relation Spenser sets up between Calidore's vision as truth, the purgation of sight—it is crucial to remember that he actually *sees* the Graces with his physical eyes; he does not dream them, as Britomart dreams her vision of Isis and Osiris—and the false vision of the Red Crosse Knight which allowed sin to enter Faeryland and began the series of illusions and delusions which subsequently bedevil the Knights of Maidenhead:

> And she her selfe of beautie soueraigne Queene,
> Faire *Venus* seemde unto his bed to bring
> Her, whom he waking euermore did weene
> To be the chastest flowre, that ay did spring
> On earthly braunch, the daughter of a king,
> Now a loose Leman to vile seruice bound:
> And eke the *Graces* seemed all to sing,
> *Hymen io Hymen*, dauncing all around,
> Whilst freshest *Flora* her with Yuie girlond crownd.
> [1.1.48; compare 6.10.27, quoted above]

This false dream, the product of a parodic and ironic *descensus ad inferos*, a descent by vice and magic, directly antithesizes Calidore's vision of Colin's lass chastely encircled by the Graces. It provides the means by which Red Crosse Knight's mind, already confused by the multiplicity of the world (Error's numberless spawn) and the deceitfulness of appearances (Archimago as a reverend hermit), begins to succumb to the concupiscence and irascibility which the body carries with it as the result of original sin. Spenser confirms this when he has Red Crosse Knight *see* the copulation of the two demons Archimago has invoked and embodied as Una and a squire, "Which when he *saw*, he burnt with gealous fire,/The *eye* of reason was with rage *yblent* . . . " (1.2.5). From that blinding to Calidore's sight ("There he did *see*, that pleased much his *sight*,/That euen he him selfe his *eyes enuyde* . . . " 6.10.11; italics mine), through all the errors and disgressions of false vision and delusion, lies the path of *The Faerie Queene*. The map of its psychological space begins with the carnal Venus and

59

the Graces, falsely perceived, leading the Heaven-born Una in their dance and it ends by rounding upon itself, returning to the same psychological/symbolic spot, and showing us an earth-born "countrey lasse" enshrined in Venus's place, leading the Graces, now rightly known, in their proper rhythm of reciprocity:

> Therefore they alwaies smoothly seeme to smile,
> That we likewise should mylde and gentle be,
> And also naked are, that without guile
> Or false dissemblaunce all them plaine may see,
> Simple and true from couert malice free:
> And eeke them selues so in their daunce they bore,
> That two of them still froward seem'd to bee,
> But one still towards shew'd her selfe afore;
> That good should from vs goe, then come in greater store.
>
> [6.10.24]

The Graces' freedom from "couert malice" very pointedly distinguishes this vision from that conjured by Archimago, just as their nakedness, that "all them plaine may see," establishes the truth of their appearance by reversing Error, who "light . . . hated as the deadly bale,/Ay wont in desert darknesse to remain,/Where plaine none might her see, nor she see any plaine" (1.1.16). Calidore's later conquest of the Blatant Beast in a fight that recapitulates Red Crosse's struggle with Error confirms in action what he has here witnessed in contemplation (i.e. under the mode of the descent to the underworld) and returns the poem as a whole to its beginning in the noumenal world which precedes the phenomenal.

For this reason, Spenser's proem to Book 6 insists on the ideal nature of its subject and its essential interiority: "vertues seat is deepe within the mynd,/And not in outward shows, but inward thoughts defynd" (5). This proem exploits Sidneyan language and Sidneyan conceptions to distinguish between true and false mirrors of art, true and false courtesy, golden worlds and brazen, in order to identify and establish the "idea or foreconceit" of the work, which "faire . . . patterne" Spenser locates in his "soueraine Lady Queene,/In whose pure minde, as in a mirrour sheene,/It showes" (6). This pattern he is at some pains to restore to her again in a stanza that implicitly depicts Elizabeth and her court as Venus and the Graces:

> Then pardon me, most dreaded Soueraine,
>   That from your selfe I doe this vertue bring,
>   And to your selfe doe it returne againe:
>   So from the Ocean all riuers spring,
>   And tribute backe repay as to their King.
>   Right so from you all goodly vertues well
>   Into the rest, which round about you ring,
>   Faire Lords and Ladies, which about you dwell,
> And doe adorne your Court, where courtesies excell.
>
> [7]

That circularity of virtue, like the ring of the Graces, epitomizes the motion of the poem while it explicates the relation of the phenomenal world of physical reality to the poem's world of noumenal truth. Not accidentally, given the basic symmetries of the structure Spenser is employing, this whole cluster of images recalls the similar language and conceptions of the proem to Book 1. There he invoked Venus and Mars and the benificent Cupid:

> And with them eke, O Goddesse heauenly bright,
>   Mirrour of grace and Maiestie diuine,
>   Great Lady of the greatest Isle, whose light
>   Like *Phoebus* lampe throughout the world doth shine,
>   Shed thy faire beames into my feeble eyne,
>   And raise my thoughts too humble and too vile,
>   To thinke of that true glorious type of thine,
>   The argument of mine afflicted stile:
> The which to heare, vouchsafe, O dearest dred a-while.
>
> [4]

Elizabeth's role here is one she explicitly possesses in several other of the invocations: she is one of Spenser's muses as well as being occasionally the "real-world" pattern or exemplar of the virtue he is about to describe. As in several other proems, she is identified as a mirror of virtue or grace, and here particularly named as an antitype of Gloriana, "The argument of mine afflicted stile." But to think of Elizabeth or Gloriana as Spenser's "argument" and to see the one as a "type" of the other casts the imagery into another dimension; it is to see in these lines an implicit claim for *The Faerie Queene* not unlike the one that Dante makes for his poem in the letter to Can Grande della Scala, that the allegory of the poem shares something of the nature of the allegory of Scripture. Surely, Elizabeth as a "Goddesse heauenly bright" is being called upon to serve as Spenser's muse in a manner normally reserved for the celestial Venus or for Urania; to be precise, she is being asked to serve Spenser not only as an antitype of Gloriana but also as an antitype of that heavenly Wisdom who is in herself "the brightnesse of the everlasting light, and the undefiled mirrour of the majestie of God" (Wisdom 7.26; compare line 2 above). Sapience, "The soueraine dearling of the *Diety*,/Clad like a Queene in royall robes" (*An Hymne to Heavenly Beavty*, 184–85), stands in the same relation to God and to men that the Graces hold in respect to Venus and to mortals; she explicates God to men:

> Both heauen and earth obey unto her will,
> And all the creatures which they both containe:
> For of her fulnesse which the world doth fill,
> They all partake, and do in state remaine,
> As their great Maker did at first ordaine,
> Through obseruation of her high beheast,
> By which they first were made, and still increast.
> [*An Hymne of Heavenly Beavty*, 197–203]

More than that: like the Graces, she is man's road back to God, his passport from the prison of the flesh to the immutable world of spirit:

> Wherof such wondrous pleasures they conceaue,
> And sweete contentment, that it doth bereaue
> Their soule of sense, through infinite delight,
> And them transport from flesh into the spright.
>
> In which they see such admirable things,

As carries them into an extasy,
And heare such heauenly notes, and carolings. . . .
[*Heavenly Beavty*, 256–62]

As he has done so many times in the course of the poem proper, Spenser is, in his proems, linking a classical and a Christian image and merging them into a single vision of mediation between the Platonic ideal or Christian truth and the worldly and temporal fragmentary manifestations of that truth. Sapience and the Graces, Elizabeth and Gloriana, are the media through which the invisible light of the One must pass, taking on the colors perceptible to mortal vision, in order to be seen through and beyond to the "true glorious type" behind them. They are the only possible muses for a poem whose very "argument" is the process of that vision.

The Red Crosse Knight's encounter with Error initiates a gradual descent into darkness and an increasing obscurity of vision that leads inevitably to the primacy of delusion and equally inevitably to the dispelling of that delusion and the restoration of the sight of truth. Each book and each hero of *The Faerie Queene* pass through similar valleys of darkness to emerge on the mountains of light, just as the six books of the poem, as a unit, enact the same fall and purgation. The Red Crosse Knight's declension is easy to trace. From his fight with Error where,

> his glistring armor made
> A little glooming light, much like a shade,
> By which he saw the vgly monster plaine
>
> [1.1.14]

to his entrapment by Archimago and subsequently by Duessa and the passionate blinding of his "eye of reason" therein, he moves steadily toward the physical darkness of Orgoglio's dungeon, which he earns, appropriately enough, by laying his light-giving armor aside (1.7.2 et seq.; note also that Orgoglio is finally defeated by the dazzling light of Arthur's shield). Interestingly enough, as a graphic example of the way, in *The Faerie Queene*, apparently independent events and plots advance each other, it is Una who, on hearing of his downfall, makes explicit the very visual nature of his plight:

> Ye dreary instruments of dolefull sight,
>   That doe this deadly spectacle behold,
>   Why do ye lenger feed on loathed light,
>   Or liking find to gaze on earthly mould,
>   Sith cruell fates the carefull threeds unfould,
>   The which my life and loue together tyde?
>   Now let the stony dart of senselesse cold
>   Perce to my hart, and pas through euery side,
> And let eternall night so sad sight fro me hide.
>
> O lightsome day, the lampe of highest *Ioue*,
>   First made by him, mens wandring wayes to guyde,
>   When darknesse he in deepest dongeon droue,
>   Henceforth thy hated face foreuer hyde,
>   And shut up heauens windowes shyning wyde:
>   For earthly sight can nought but sorrow breed,
>   And late repentance, which shall long abyde.
>   Mine eyes no more on vanitie shall feed,
> But seeled up with death, shall haue their deadly meed.
>
> [1.7.22–23]

And of course Una redeems him from this darkness by equally visual remedies, beginning at the House of Holiness with Fidelia, who "taught celestiall discipline,/And opened his dull eyes, that light mote in them shine" (1.10.18), and culminating in the hermit Contemplation's showing him "The new *Hierusalem*" (1.10.49ff.). After this, Red Crosse suffers once more from blindness, but this time for far different reasons than before:

> This said, adowne he looked to the ground,
>   To haue returnd, but dazed were his eyne,
>   Through passing brightnesse, which did quite confound
>   His feeble sence, and too exceeding shyne.
> So darke are earthly things compard to things diuine.
>
> [1.10.67]

Red Crosse Knight receives his final visual revelation and reward, of course, when he at last beholds the "celestiall sight" (1.12.23) of Una's face, an image that is compounded in the action of the poem by the immediate appearance and unmasking of Archimago. The poem's initial hero and heroine can now see through the worker of the poem's initial false vision.

Spenser quickly undercuts that hopeful ending: Red Crosse must leave Una and return to the world, Archimago in short order escapes, and Duessa although exposed earlier in Book 1 is still very much at large. However dazzling the vision of Jerusalem or Una, mortal sight cannot sustain it, and Book 2 finds Archimago, "That cunning Architect of cancred guile" (2.1.1), preparing the first of the delusions that Guyon will have to encounter. I cannot exaggerate the strongly visual nature of the Book of Temperance: Ruddymane, Phaedria, Braggadocchio and Trompart, Mammon, his Cave and his daughter Philotime, the Castle of Alma, Maleger, the Bower of Bliss, Acrasia and Verdant—all exist in our memories of the text primarily as images. Spenser appropriately emphasizes the visual nature of each. Guyon's reply to each of Mammon's exhibitions of what "liuing eye before did neuer see" (2.7.38) is always something like "Another blis before mine eyes I place" (2.7.33). Acrasia fixes Verdant with her "false eyes . . ./And through his humid eyes did sucke his spright" (2.12.73). Philotime's:

> broad beauties beam great brightnes threw
> Through the dim shade, that all men might it see:
> Yet was not that same her owne natiue hew,
> But wrought by art and counterfetted shew.
>
> [2.7.45]

In that last respect she resembles the Bower of Bliss itself, where art and nature strive to ensnare human sense—first through the eyes, of course. To this wealth of visual enticements Book 2 offers no honorific counterpart; its response, as Guyon's, consists in either denial or destruction. The whole question of vision becomes intensely complicated in Book 2 because of what it is that Spenser is making us look at. We move through a much more recognizably human landscape here, and the villains Guyon encounters, however mysterious their origins, all wear a human shape. Hypocrisy and deceit are no longer represented semi-abstractly by Archimago alone: the all-too-human Braggadocchio and Trompart here enter the poem. Guyon struggles against the seduction of his bodily eye, not the blinding of his spiritual (although one does in fact depend upon the other). Art enters the poem at this point for the same sorts of reasons. It too is a mode of vision, and the wrong kind of art constitutes, for Spenser, a particularly pernicious way of making us see the wrong things. That is the peculiar danger of Acrasia and her Bower: her artistry is an adornment of the physical, an elaboration of the sensual. In Platonic terms, it is the imitation of an imitation. It does not point to the noumenal or partake of the spiritual, but stops the physical eye at the phenomenal world and prevents any kind of passage to the realm of ideas or spirits. That is why, in a nice irony, neither Acrasia's Circean art nor the palmer's hermetic staff affect any more than the bodily appearance of her victims; they have chosen their own mindlessness:

> But one aboue the rest in speciall,
> That has an hog beene late, hight *Grille* by name,
> Repined greatly, and did him miscall,
> That had from hoggish forme him brought to naturall.

> Said *Guyon*, See the mind of beastly man,
> That hath so soone forgot the excellence
> Of his creation, when he life began,
> That now he chooseth, with vile difference,
> To be a beast, and lacke intelligence.
>
> [2.12.86–87]

Acrasia's enchantments extend and elaborate in the world of *The Faerie Queene* the kind of confusion and blurring of vision begun by Archimago and Duessa. The third book of the poem presents us with the triumph of that confusion as, at the deepest point of the descent, in the world of quasi-flesh-and-blood reality, illusion and deception replace vision and sight. The one-eyed Malbecco stands as emblem of this world and its vision, where even Arthur becomes benighted and lost, soliloquizing the darkness that hides Florimell—and Gloriana—from him. The heroes themselves become sources of false vision: Britomart's armor, for instance, masks her true identity and causes subsequent difficulties with Malecasta and for Amoret and Scudamor. The transformations of love, and the transformations caused by love, all display themselves in an almost exclusively visual mode, from their first appearance on the tapestries in Malecasta's Castle Joyous, through Proteus's various shape-shiftings, to their climax in the tapestries of Busirane's castle and the illusions of the Masque of Cupid. The latter are crucially important to this process insofar as they are completely illusory: all are conjured up by Busirane, and all disappear when he is controlled. This differs radically from the Guyon's razing the Bower of Bliss. Acrasia's false art misled the senses, but it was nevertheless a real thing; it misled the eye, but it actually existed. That is why it had to be destroyed. Busirane's spells are unreal; they are the imposition of the mind upon the physical eye—delusions pure and simple. The facts of Amoret's imprisonment by them and Scudamor's inability to penetrate them define exactly where we are in our descent into matter: we have entered so deeply into the illusions of the corporeal world that they have made a house of bondage, a prison so close that the characters of the poem have lost sight of the real world of spirit and idea that sustains the material one. In this respect Britomart's quest both resolves the problems of Book 3 and epitomizes the whole of the poem. She enters Faeryland in response to a vision, seeking the bodily reality corresponding to the ideal vision she has seen in Merlin's magic glass; what she finds is not reality but illusions, illusions to which she unwittingly contributes, and illusions which it finally devolves upon her to dispell, first by freeing Amoret and later, through her love and her own appearance, by forcing Artegal to put off his disguise and ultimately to conform himself to the ideal knight she has seen and sought. The force of love and chastity in Britomart and the quality of her vision are the pivots of the poem, liberating its personae from the power of illusion and moving them back toward the sight of reality. This process begins with the conquest of Busirane and gathers momentum in Artegal's first look at Britomart's face; it makes quantum jumps in the account of what Scudamor encountered in the Temple of Venus (despite the fact that that happened "in the past," for the reader it occurs after those other events) and vicariously for all the characters in the pageant of the marriage of the Thames and Medway, which presents an ennobling masque of love in response to Busirane's debasing one. Both are creatures of the mind, but one of the mind of a poet, the other of the mind of a sorcerer. Busirane's masque projects the fears and suffering of a soul subject to and intimidated by the demands of its body; Spenser's, in the tableau vivant of the wedding of rivers, embodies an archetypal vision of chaste and fertile union. Thus the lustless meeting of Florimell and Marinell follows immediately upon it, and immediately upon that the resurrection of Marinell,

> Who soone as he beheld that angels face,
>   Adorn'd with all diuine perfection,
>   His cheared heart eftsoones away gan chace
>   Sad death, reuiued with her sweet inspection,
>   And feeble spirit inly felt refection;
>   As withered weed through cruell winters tine,
>   That feeles the warmth of sunny beames reflection,
>   Liftes vp his head, that did before decline
> And gins to spread his leafe before the faire sunshine.
>   [4.12.34]

Progress toward true vision is not all as orderly and straightforward as that description may make it sound, however. Book 4, after all, witnesses the false knight Braggadocchio's receiving the prize of the Tournament of Beauty, the False Florimell. Ate and Duessa succeed in afflicting Scudamor with jealous rage, in part at least because Britomart's knightly armor still disguises her true sex; at this point in the poem, hardly anyone has yet seen her face. Here too Artegal's appearance at the Tournament of

Beauty disguised as the Salvage Knight helps compound its confusions and disorder. Some of these sources of mistake and deceit persist into Book 5: there, for instance, Artegal repeats with Radigund the action which, with Britomart, had seemed a sign of progress; that is, upon sight of her beauty, he ends his anger and his fighting. With Radigund that is a disaster, and his submission to her leads initially to Britomart's own misunderstanding and jealous rage. Moreover, it is not until Book 5 that Braggadocchio's boasts are definitively exposed, and it is significant that this inadvertently results from Artegal's once again fighting in disguise, this time bearing Braggadocchio's shield. At this same tournament too the False Florimell and the true at last appear side by side, with the consequent disappearance of the illusion—but not before Florimell has suffered some embarrassment from her and Braggadocchio.

For all that, the Book of Justice marks the ending of the power of illusion and delusion in *The Faerie Queene*. Braggadocchio is exposed, the False Florimell evaporated, the true Florimell restored to the world, Duessa is executed, and Artegal eventually achieves the ideal knighthood posited of him by Britomart's initial vision in Merlin's glass. Once again, Britomart plays a crucial role in this process; as she purges her own vision, Spenser restores true sight to Faeryland. Summoned by Talus, she proceeds—after a proper temper tantrum—to Artegal's rescue; she is almost immediately led off course and, in an episode in some particulars reminiscent of her adventure at Castle Joyous, lodges for the night with Dolon. Here, however, she neither sleeps nor removes her armor, "Not suffering the least twinckling sleepe to start/Into her eye" (5.6.24). She does something far more important than merely stay awake: she begins to come, through her grief, to self-knowledge, and she identifies for herself, and the other characters, and for us, the root source of all our woe:

Ye guilty eyes (sayd she) the which with guyle
  My heart at first betrayd, will ye betray

My life now to, for which a little whyle
Ye will not watch? false watches, wellaway,
I wote when ye did watch both night and day
Vnto your losse: and now needes will ye sleepe?
Now ye haue made my heart to wake alway,
Now will ye sleepe? ah wake, and rather weepe,
To thinke of your nights want, that should yee waking keepe.

[5.6.25]

What the eye sees keeps the heart awake; deceived and misled by sight (as Britomart is at this very moment deceived and misled by Dolon), her "feeble vessell" still tosses on the "Huge sea of sorrow, and tempestuous griefe" (3.4.8–9) that has been the course of her adventures thus far. Spenser links this self-treachery with Peter's denial of Christ in order to stress its importance:

What time the natiue Belman of the night,
The bird, that warned *Peter* of his fall,
First rings his silver Bell t'each sleepy wight,
That should their mindes vp to deuotion call,
She heard a wondrous noise below the hall.

[5.6.27]

The cockcrow warned Peter of his treachery; here, it warns Britomart of Dolon's (the bed on which she should have been sleeping at this point sinks into the floor). More important, Spenser's comparison makes it clear that the ultimate source of this treachery is Britomart herself: the cockcrow points to her as a traitor just as it did to Peter. Dolon has sought to entrap her because—once again—her outward appearance deceived: he took her for Artegal. Britomart herself embodies the dissonance between inward and outward, between physical body and spiritual reality, that is the ultimate source of Faeryland's disorder.[23] Her eyes are false watches because they watched the wrong things, and Spenser makes this clear too when he has Britomart reprove her eyes for their failure to watch "a little whyle." In the biblical episode on which Spenser is drawing for his resonances, Christ, shortly after predicting that Peter will deny him thrice before cockcrow, reproves him as follows: "What, could ye not watch

70

with me one hour? Watch and pray, that ye enter not into temptation: the spirit indeed is willing, but the flesh is weak" (Matthew
26.40–41; see also Mark 14.30–38). *The Faerie Queene* has been
working with the realization of the flesh's weakness and the manner of its weakness for some books now, and while that realization
is in fact Spenser's point, it is not nearly so simplistic, nor so
simply made, as it may seem. The poetic situation, culminating in
the betrayal of Britomart, parallels the biblical situation, culminating in the betrayal of Christ—but in each plot there are two
betrayals and two betrayers, both identified in both texts. In the
physical betrayal, Judas betrays Christ and Dolon attempts to trap
Britomart. In the moral treachery, Peter fails Christ and
Britomart's eyes betray her. In the physical plot, she was Christ's
counterpart; in the spiritual, she analogizes both Christ and
Peter—and precisely that, I think, is Spenser's real point. Our
erected wit may pull us to the *imitatio Christi*—our spirit is
willing enough—but our infected will and concupiscible flesh
more often than not betray us into the imitation of Peter, if not of
Judas. We are all self-traitors, all locked in the underworld of our
own beings, until we see clearly, until we learn to control the focus
of our vision. This is what Britomart is beginning to learn here, and
consequently Spenser has her advance directly from Dolon's castle
to Isis's Church, where she receives a dream vision that complements and confirms her initial sight of Artegal and Merlin's predictions about their linked fates. She sees the truth, and even though
it presents itself to her in a symbolic visual mode that demands
explication, the explication lies ready to hand. Her dream vision
produces a twofold effect: it not only reveals the truth to Britomart,
it also reveals the truth *about* her. It functions as a step toward
reestablishing the consonance between physical embodiment and
spiritual essence that was upset in *The Faerie Queene* the moment
Red Crosse Knight stopped being an abstract symbol and acquired
humanity—erroneously and errantly. In fact, the priest of Isis
reveals Britomart's identity and nature before he says anything at
all about her dream:

Magnificke Virgin, that in queint disguise
Of British armes doest maske thy royall blood,
So to pursue a perillous emprize,
How couldst thou weene, through that disguized hood,
To hide thy state from being vnderstood?
Can from th'immortall Gods ought hidden bee?
They doe thy linage, and thy Lordly brood;
They doe thy sire, lamenting sore for thee,
They doe thy loue, forlorne in womens thraldome see.

[5.7.21]

The priest goes on from this to explain to Britomart what she has just seen, which is the visual confirmation of what, several books previously, she had been told by Merlin: image ratifies language, even if it must in turn be explained by language. Further ratification of this growth in self-knowledge is provided by Artegal's concomitant increase in self-awareness and self-control as he resists in prison both Radigund's crude and Clarinda's subtler lovemaking. The most telling evidence for it, of course, can be found very obviously in Britomart's defeat of her own shadow self, Radigund. After that, Spenser can treat in an almost casual manner the condemnation and death of Duessa in the trial at Mercilla's court: he can apparently trust that the implications of that act are clear and concentrate instead of the roles of Artegal, Arthur, and Mercilla in shaping the final judgment. So too then Spenser does not have to emphasize the structural parallels that link Arthur's and Artegal's final victories over the forces of injustice with the similar simultaneous victories of Arthur and Guyon at the end of Book 2. The pulling down of the Bower of Bliss stands as an unstressed but very real analog to the erection of the palace of justice: both acts constitute the right ordering of an art.

The purgation of the social arts leads directly in Spenser's treatment to an image of true art, Colin Clout's piping to the Graces on Mount Acidale. The Book of Courtesy depicts the restoration of sight and vision. Both Colin Clout and Calidore, as I have said before, actually see the Graces. Arthur twice in the course of the book sees and recognizes Timias, which he was unable to do in

Book 4. Even Cupid here unbinds his eyes and changes his nature from the deity who delighted in cruelty (cf. the Masque of Cupid) to a compassionate justice who extracts condign punishment for the suffering of his devotees (6.7.32ff.). The definitive images of this reestablishment of true vision are, however, Calidore's cognate harrowings of Hell: the restoration of Pastorella "to the ioyous light,/Whereof she long had lackt the wishful sight" (6.11.50) and his Herculean capture of the Blatant Beast, which, like Cerberus,[24] he:

> did . . . compell
> To see the hatefull sunne, that he might tell
> To griesly *Pluto*, what on earth was donne,
> And to the other damned ghosts, which dwell
> For aye in darkenesse, which day light doth shonne.
>
> [6.12.35]

That ascent from those two hells returns the poem to the full light of day and frees the protagonists of *The Faerie Queene* from the dominion of darkness. The shadows of the underworld have lengthened through the poem from the moment Red Crosse Knight entered Error's cave. Calidore's triumphal emergence from these shades constitutes, at least momentarily, at least metaphorically, the purgation from the world of the last dark taint of Error.

2

Milton:

PARADISE LOST

Paradise Lost begins in a manner conceptually quite like the opening of *The Faerie Queene*, with the initiation of motion out of stillness.[1] The first act of the poem, the first declarative sentence of the poem, presents Satan aspiring and falling, "cast out from Heav'n"(1.37),

> Hurl'd headlong flaming from th' Ethereal Sky
> With hideous ruin and combustion down
> To bottomless perdition.
>
> [1.45–47]

Spenser's beginning recreates a universal moment, the emergence of an idea or a soul from the stillness of the One and its gradual acquisition of concreteness and specificity as it penetrates the sublunary world of phenomena. Milton's beginning describes the archetypal moment of Christian history, the falling away from God which is the origin of motion, time, and change as we know them. Satan's defection and fall, which are simultaneous and identical in the eternity and unity of God, constitute the first separation from divinity, the first extrusion, if one may so speak, outside of God. Satan wished to be God, to rule, to create: what he creates is himself as non-God. There, for the human mind and for Milton's poem, the world begins: before that is stillness and oneness, indescribable and therefore incomprehensible, beyond words and therefore beyond poetry, as it was for Dante. The moment of Satan's fall and separation from divinity, the instant of his differentiation from God, is the beginning of motion and action in the cosmos in the only terms the human mind can grasp. Motion is a consequence of imperfection, of finitude: Satan's defection from God is therefore motion, is fall, is the calling into being (or nonbeing?) of what is radically not-God. The only way back to God is consequently the retracing of that motion: the way up and the way down are the same because only one way exists; other than the way, all is God, and of God no poems can be made (no history either; without Satan's fall, nothing happens, and it requires a profound readjustment of our sense of things to realize that, for Milton at least, that is good).

So then: *Paradise Lost* begins with the first act (in our sense of act) which will define all other subsequent acts: defection, fall, privation, separation, and differentiation from God. Adam's and Eve's only other choice is non-act, abstention from acting: not to eat the fruit, not to disobey, not to separate themselves from divinity. Of that too no poem could or need be made—as we understand poem. God creates the world, but Satan recreates the world as we know it; he becomes, ironically, the ground of our knowledge as he is the ground of Milton's poem. We know God, Creation, Adam and Eve first through Satan; only later do we approach them "independently." Satan's mode of existence defines and delimits our mode of knowing and the poet's mode of speaking. For Milton and for us, God can only be presented in terms of what is not himself: this is why the poem begins with Satan and only much later—and briefly—"shows" us God. The poem is

called *Paradise Lost* because, however efficacious the divine redemptive plan may be, the initial unity of the cosmos with God is
lost forever with Satan, and although it may return again at the end
of time when "God shall be All in All" (3.341), that is a phenomenon (or noumenon) not realizable by human minds as they are now
constituted: Satan wins that much.

❦

Within the framework of those limitations on our knowledge and our mode of knowledge, Milton's poem works insistently
to allow us glimpses beyond to the imageless truth. He can only
approach God by a kind of poetic *via negativa*, but to do so he
exploits all of the richness and complexity of epic tradition, as if by
balancing one finite mode against another he can somehow induce
them to cancel each other out and leave us, for a moment at least,
with a clear view of what lies outside and around our mere history.
Even his treatment of Satan evidences this. The *descensus ad
inferos* forms, as I have previously argued, a mainstay of the epic
poem: a narrative action of central importance, a miniature of epic
as a whole, a symbolic account of individual lives and national
destinies, and a philosophic explanation of the human lot as well
as, in itself, one way of learning and coming to terms with the
conditions of that lot. *Paradise Lost* opens unequivocally with a
descensus ad inferos, with the unique and archetypal descent to
Hell which, for Christians, provides that phrase with its profoundest and most unsettling meanings. And yet, for all that the event is
literally *there* in the poem, there in its utter and irreducible actuality, the descent is not present in the poem in the Neoplatonic
guise it customarily wears in epic. Rather, that is implicitly present in Satan's fall as a parody of itself, its usual particulars all duly
present and accounted for, but this time turned against themselves, working against the reader's expectations and forcing him
one by one, step by step, to jettison the impedimenta of a tradition
of *fallen* knowledge if he wishes to come to unfallen truth. (That is

one significant way the reader is genuinely "surprised by sin" in *Paradise Lost*.)[2]

Satan falls to Hell through Chaos, and bears the marks of Chaos upon him there. (If Satan is the ground of knowledge in *Paradise Lost*, Chaos is the medium of it; after his fall, all things pass through Chaos on their way to completion. I will discuss this more fully later.) His descent is then, in a crude approximation of Neoplatonic orthodoxy, through matter, through the *silva* that confuses the Red Crosse Knight, into a place formed out of matter which constitutes, again in orthodox Neoplatonic fashion, his "Prison ordained/In utter darkness" (1.71–72), the darkness of the soul separated from the one and immersed in the prison of matter. He even feels the appropriate drunkenness and confusion consequent upon this descent as he "Lay vanquisht, rolling in the fiery Gulf/Confounded though immortal" (1.52–53). But Satan has not descended into a body; he remains a spirit, however impure, and he retains, to his greater torment, clear memory of his origins:

> the thought
> Both of lost happiness and lasting pain
> Torments him.
>
> [1.54–56]

He now perceives, however, *fallenly*: that is, he sees vaguely, generally, confusedly. He attempts to apprehend as angels do, unitively, inclusively, and intuitively, but that no longer works for him: it returns him only vague, general information:

> round he throws his baleful eyes
> That witness'd huge affliction and dismay
> Mixt with obdurate pride and steadfast hate:
> At once as far as Angel's ken he views
> The dismal Situation waste and wild,
> A Dungeon horrible, on all sides round
> As one great Furnace flam'd, yet from those flames
> No light, but rather darkness visible
> Serv'd only to discover sights of woe,
> Regions of sorrow, doleful shades, where peace

And rest can never dwell, hope never comes
That comes to all; but torture without end
Still urges, and a fiery Deluge, fed
With ever-burning Sulphur unconsum'd.

[1.56–69]

Satan now apprehends not merely affectively—even the unfallen
angels do that—but sequentially: he must now gather information
step by step, piece by piece, more like man than angel.

There the companions of his fall, o'erwhelm'd
With Floods and Whirlwinds of tempestuous fire,
He soon discerns, and welt'ring by his side
One next himself in power.

[1.76–79]

While not corporeal, Satan in passing through Chaos has picked up
the taints of corporeality, and the first of these is number: just as
the Red Crosse Knight moved from the realm of Una to the land of
Duessa, Satan fallen has crossed the border from unity to sheer
multiplicity, and now must know and act sequentially rather than
instantaneously. Thus he "distinguishes" Beelzebub first, then the
promiscuous throng of his followers, whom Milton describes, in a
series of marvelous similes, as multiplicity itself—they are like the
autumn leaves in Vallombrosa, like scattered sedge, like the
wreckage of Pharaoh's army, like the plague of locusts, "so thick
bestrown . . . covering the flood" (1.311–12), "innumerable"
(1.338), "numberless" (1.344). At Satan's signal they alight upon
the plain and promptly become:

A multitude, like which the populous North
Pour'd never from her frozen loins, to pass
Rhene or the *Danaw*, when her barbarous Sons
Came like a Deluge on the South, and spread
Beneath *Gibraltar* to the *Lybian* sands.

[1.351–55]

From a multitude, their number becomes increasingly more
specific and they in turn become more finite, more enmeshed in

number. At the sight of "Th' Imperial Ensign" (1.536), "Ten thousand Banners rise into the Air" (1.545), and thick phalanxes range before Satan: "Thir number last he sums" (1.571). After this, both Milton and Satan assign them finite numbers:

> Millions of Spirits for his fault amerc't
> Of Heav'n
>
> [1.609–10]
>
> O Myriads of immortal Spirits
>
> [1.622]
>
> they anon
> With hunderds and with thousands trooping came
> Attended.
>
> [1.759–61]

Within this entrance into number and corollary to it, the devils grow as well in specificity and individuality as Milton's verse enacts the increasing differentiation and fragmentation that their initial separation from God imposes upon them: first Satan himself, of course, identified as fallen leader and pseudo-hero, then Beelzebub, the loyal lieutenant, and then, emerging one by one from the "promiscuous crowd" (1.380), Moloch, Chemos, the Baalim and the Ashtaroth, Astoreth/Astarte, Thammuz, Dagon, Rimmon, "Osiris, Isis, Orus and thir Train" (1.478), Belial—"All these and more came flocking" (1.522). Two Miltonic sentences trace their decline and fall from unity in God to multiplicity in the created world, from true unitary identity to false and multiple corporeal masks:

> Forthwith from every Squadron and each Band
> The Heads and Leaders thither haste where stood
> Thir great Commander; Godlike shapes and forms
> Excelling human, Princely Dignities,
> And Powers that erst in Heaven sat on Thrones;
> Though of thir Names in heav'nly Records now
> Be no memorial, blotted out and ras'd
> By thir Rebellion, from the Books of Life.

80

Nor had they yet among the Sons of *Eve*
Got them new Names, till wand'ring o'er the Earth,
Through God's high sufferance for the trial of man,
By falsities and lies the greatest part
Of Mankind they corrupted to forsake
God thir Creator, and th' invisible
Glory of him that made them, to transform
Oft to the Image of a Brute, adorn'd
With gay Religions full of Pomp and Gold,
And Devils to adore for Deities:
Then were they known to men by various Names,
And various Idols through the Heathen World.

[1.356–75]

Those two sentences also trace the path of the devils' parodic descent, conversion, and ascent from the loss of their heavenly names, through the temporal/spatial "nor . . . yet . . . till wand'ring o'er the Earth" construction, to their uncertain new identities as "various Idols." That process exactly reverses the orthodox pattern of the descent, wherein the emergent soul, confused by its entrance into matter, forgets its heavenly identity for a time and, "wand'ring o'er the Earth," is only gradually reawakened to its true nature and origin. Indeed, the allegorical understanding of the descent to Hell offers the exact pattern of that reawakening: the slowly rousing soul extends itself in contemplation of the sublunary world in which it finds itself, realizing in that act both the limitations of corporeal things and its own basically spiritual nature, and thus illumined begins its return to its true home and its true selfhood in the spiritual unity of the One. The devils, however, have accomplished a literal descent to Hell, and they have there found their eternal home in Pandemonium. They change as well from "Godlike shapes and forms" to "the image of a Brute" because their passage through Chaos has also tainted them with mass. This is implicit in Milton's first unspecific account of Satan and Beelzebub "welt'ring" in the fiery sea, and it becomes more explicit in his subsequent description of:

81

> Satan talking to his nearest Mate
> With Head up-lift above the wave, and Eyes
> That sparkling blaz'd, his other Parts besides
> Prone on the Flood, extended long and large
> Lay floating many a rood, in bulk as huge
> As whom the Fables name of monstrous size.
>
> [1.192–97]

Milton continues to apply to the devils generally and to Satan particularly a series of abstract words denoting mass—"So stretcht out huge in length the Arch-fiend lay"(1.209); "His mighty Stature" (1.222); "the dusky air/... felt unusual weight" (1.226–27). After this, Milton gives us details of Satan's apparently corporeal paraphernalia, "his ponderous shield" (1.284), "His Spear" (1.292), "Th' Imperial Ensign . . . With Gems and Golden lustre rich imblaz'd" (1.536–38). Concurrent with these details, Milton catalogs the various devils and their future earthly guises, linking them all with more and more physical attributes and climaxing this process of increasing corporealization with the construction of the physical Pandemonium. The entrance of the devils into that building presents their definitive entrance into matter: they throng the hall, "Thick swarm'd, both on the ground and in the air,/Brusht with the hiss of rustling wings" (1.767–68)—a direct Miltonic description that anticipates and already incorporates the debasing corporeality of the marvelous simile of the bees that follows it. The final actions of Book 1, the reduction to minuscule size of the "Throng numberless" (1.780), whom Satan has already numbered, and the assembly of their chiefs, confirm even while they seem to deny the captivity of the demons to number and to mass:

> Thus incorporeal Spirits to smallest forms
> Reduc'd their shapes immense, and were at large,
> Though without number still amidst the Hall
> Of that infernal Court. But far within
> And in thir own dimensions like themselves
> The great Seraphic Lords and Cherubim
> In close recess and secret conclave sat

A thousand Demi-Gods on golden seats,
Frequent and full.

[1.789–97]

   This physical declension parallels and results from the
moral descent of the devils, and it is perceived as such by Satan. He
and his fellow demons consistently use the language of the conventional descent-conversion-ascent pattern to palliate their condition and thereby provide the most important parodic version of
that pattern in the poem. Almost all of the imagery of rise and fall,
all of the language of ascents and descents, in the poem can be
brought to bear upon the touchstone of the Platonic *descensus*.
This is true, for instance, of Satan's most casual and his most
calculated utterances.

For who can yet believe, though after loss,
That all these puissant Legions, whose exile
Hath emptied Heav'n, shall fail to re-ascend
Self-rais'd, and repossess thir native seat?

[1.631–34]

For this Infernal Pit shall never hold
Celestial Spirits in Bondage, nor th' Abyss
Long under darkness cover.

[1.657–59]

   Powers and Dominions, Deities of Heav'n,
For since no deep within her gulf can hold
Immortal vigor, though opprest and fall'n,
I give not Heav'n for lost. From this descent
Celestial Virtues rising, will appear
More glorious and more dread than from no fall.

[2.11–16]

Satan is by and large correct in his general propositions and wrong
in their particular applications. As we know from the dialogue in
Heaven in Book 3, if from nowhere else, the devils are past help:
they will never reascend to Heaven, certainly not "self-rais'd." But
the proper motion of spirits *is* upward: Heaven is their home and
ascension their proper activity. The entire fabric of the Platonic
descensus is based upon that premise: birth, the entrance of the

soul into the body, constitutes exile from its proper home, to which, unless hopelessly mired in corporeality, it naturally desires to return. Orthodox Christianity, however, very explicitly denies the soul the ability to do so by its own powers—and in this respect at least Milton is firmly orthodox. Reascension takes place through the medium of grace, not by man's—or demon's—own efforts. Satan, in positing the possibility that the devils will rise by their own powers to Heaven, is recreating a late humanist version of the *descensus* pattern, one similar to that posed by Cristoforo Landino, whose interpretation of the *descensus* argues that the attainment of the contemplative state and the possession thereby of the *summum bonum* is a human achievement. Landino's syncretist habits equate the journey of Dante with the journey of Aeneas, subtracting grace from the *Commedia* and from the genre of epic.[3] Both Spenser and Milton by their poetic practice sharply disagree with that emphasis: Milton particularly leaves me with the impression that he has devised Satan as a figure (among many other purposes) explicitly to play off against the Landinesque "exceptional man" who achieves the *summum bonum* by his own powers. That is, I think Milton has Landino's sort of humanistic reading of epic very much in mind, and I see that sort of understanding of the epic descent and the epic hero as providing foil and pattern for Satan: they are the path he follows and the background that readers of epic should see him against, and they form a condemnation of him as much as he of them. The Satanic assumption of self-sufficiency leads to the fall of the demons; the epic hero's assumption of self-sufficiency leads to the demise of epic[4]—and both those statements seem to me to be contained, the one explicitly, and other implicitly, in *Paradise Lost*.

Milton's poetic orthodoxy indicts Satan on at least one other important epic count. The Landinesque version of Virgilian (and Dantean) epic argues for the superiority of the contemplative life to the active, the priority of retirement to action: this sums up the whole thrust of the *Camaldulensan Disputations*. In terms of earlier understandings of Virgil's poem, this is in itself a poetic heresy: what Aeneas learns in Book 6, while it is indeed a sort of contemplative wisdom, finds its natural completion not in itself, as Landino proposes, but in the action of the remaining six books of Virgil's poem. The hero, armed with his new understanding and his new knowledge of his goal, must return to active life, to life on this earth, and there use his new knowledge to defeat the enemies to whom he has previously fallen victim. This provides the significance, in both the *Aeneid* and the earlier commentators' explanation of it, of the Sybil's warning to Aeneas about the familiar dangers he must yet face: a new Achilles, a new Helen, another Simois, another war for a foreign bride (*Aeneid* 6.83–97). And this also explains why, in Landino's comments on the *Aeneid*, he scarcely mentions the last six books of the poem; for him it effectively ends at the close of Book 6, since the last half of the poem is a practical refutation of his theses about the first half. Milton's Satan offers himself to the reader and to his fellow demons as Landino's Aeneas, with the added defect of hypocrisy, to be sure, but nevertheless he does present himself to them and to us as a hero of the contemplative life and a Stoic champion of imperturbability:

> Is this the Region, this the Soil, the Clime,
> Said then the lost Arch-Angel, this the seat
> That we must change for Heav'n, this mournful gloom
> For that celestial light? Be it so, since he
> Who now is Sovran can dispose and bid
> What shall be right: fardest from him is best
> Whom reason hath equall'd, force hath made supreme
> Above his equals. Farewell happy Fields
> Where Joy for ever dwells: Hail horrors, hail
> Infernal world, and thou profoundest Hell
> Receive thy new Possessor: One who brings
> A mind not to be chang'd by Place or Time.
> The mind is its own place, and in itself
> Can make a Heav'n of Hell, a Hell of Heav'n.
>
> [1.242–55]

All of Satan's plans and resolutions flow from this pose: God has conquered by force; he, the master of mind, will triumph by guile.

And—in one of Milton's sharpest ironies—all of his plans and apparent triumphs will also be vitiated by the nuclear truth of this pose: the mind *is* its own place, unchanged by the circumstances of apparent victory as little as by the fact of defeat:

> Me miserable! which way shall I fly
> Infinite wrath, and infinite despair?
> Which way I fly is Hell; myself am Hell;
> And in the lowest deep a lower deep
> Still threat'ning to devour me opens wide,
> To which the Hell I suffer seems a Heav'n.
>
> [4.73–78]

The entrance of the demons into the underworld is only the "external" cognate of their fall into the Hell of themselves, from which they can never hope to escape: they have placed themselves outside the world wherein it is natural for spirits to ascend because the only possible goal of that ascension is God, to whom they will never wish to return. So for them, all of the Neoplatonic apparatus of descent, illumination, and ascent is inapplicable and irrelevant: by their defection, they have made descent their natural motion and a self-destructive fixity their only possible intellectual stance, "darkness visible" the absolute limit of their physical and spiritual illumination. The demons embody Milton's vision of a spiritual and epical dead end.

Despite all that, it is important to realize how closely Satan's actions mimic the conventional pattern of the Neoplatonic descent. Exactly as his attempts to reproduce God's grandeur end in a sad travesty of it, his efforts at leadership result in a diabolical parody of formulaic epic heroism. Some of this we have already seen, and some of it is quite clear in the text: the contrived council, for instance, climaxing in his pawn Beelzebub's calling for a volunteer for the perilous mission of exploration, Satan's assumption of that labor and his immediate adjourning of the council lest others "stand/His Rivals" (2.471–72). But the bulk of the parody is borne by Milton's reproduction, in Satan's actions, of the externals of the

Milton: *Paradise Lost*

threefold pattern of descent, illumination, and ascent. All these are approximated more or less physically in the expulsion and nine-days' fall of Satan and his crew, their revival and council, and Satan's bursting the bonds of Hell, crossing Chaos, and reaching earth: Satan fell through Chaos and reascends through Chaos, armed with a new plan, new knowledge about his limitations and his opponent's powers. But he has the wrong plan and the wrong knowledge: restoration and restitution are the tasks of the epic hero, not revenge and the replication of one's own faults:

> This would surpass
> Common revenge, and interrupt his joy
> In our Confusion, and our Joy upraise
> In his disturbance; when his darling Sons
> Hurl'd headlong to partake with us, shall curse
> Their frail Original.
>
> [2.370–75]

Odysseus must restore proper order to his own kingdom. Aeneas must refound Troy. Satan seeks only to bring forth another lost kingdom, more exiles. In that very profound sense, in this single action which lies at the very heart of epic, God and Christ are the only epic heroes in *Paradise Lost*: Satan here falls so far below them that he cannot even achieve parody of them. In this crucial and definitive aspect of the matter of the epic poem, he reveals himself as not epic at all, as simply having no place in the true epic poem. Rather, in his plan to reproduce in others his own fall, to impose on man his own exile—

> League with you I seek,
> And mutual amity so strait, so close,
> That I with you must dwell, or you with me
> Henceforth.
>
> [4.375–78]

—in this attempt he defines himself as a mock epic hero, as a partial and inadequate creator doomed by his own devices—and so indeed, in the fullness of poetic justice, Milton renders him,

87

transformed into a serpent, "punisht in the shape he sinn'd" (10.516).[5]

The underworld, in both the narrative and the allegory of epic, is the place of coming to self-knowledge, of confrontation with the ghosts and selves of the past and learning from them. Satan passes through the forms of this confrontation without ever actually learning anything from them and without ever changing in any way but "physically." This process begins almost with the poem itself, in Satan's hailing Beelzebub with words that recall Aeneas's address to the shade of Hector:

> If thou beest hee; But O how fall'n! how chang'd
> From him, who in the happy Realms of Light
> Cloth'd with transcendent brightness didst outshine
> Myriads though bright.
>
> [1.84–87][6]

From this point the poem proceeds to the council of the demons, which reproduces the form of deliberation without any true content, the balloting being effectually rigged and Satan having already decided what the demonic course of action shall be. Satan's real confrontation with himself, from which he could learn, if he were capable of learning, what he is, takes place when he encounters Sin and Death at Hell Gate. This passage is widely and rightly read as an anticipatory parody of the dialogue in Heaven, in Book 3, between the Father and the Son, and the constellation of Satan, Sin, and Death is equally correctly regarded as an infernal trinity corresponding to Father, Son, and Holy Spirit. It is both these things, and more; its deepest roots grow from epic tradition, from the meetings in Hell, for instance, between Aeneas and Dido or Aeneas and Deiphobus or Aeneas and Anchises. It resonates all of Dante's encounters with the damned, and sums up in one episode all of their parallel and complementary notions of the process and nature of damnation and all of their uses as foils and steps for the self-knowledge of the epic wanderer. Sin and Death are what Satan has accomplished: they are the external manifestations of what Satan is, and Sin at least has been so from her very beginning:

> familiar grown
> I pleas'd, and with attractive graces won
> The most averse, thee chiefly, who full oft
> Thyself in me thy perfect image viewing
> Becam'st enamor'd, and such joy thou took'st
> With me in secret, that my womb conceiv'd
> A growing burden.
>
> [2.761–67]

Satan's failure to recognize Sin constitutes the crucial factor of Milton's presentation of this scene. In failing to know her, Satan fails to know himself, and he fails moreover to grasp the constant to which he is now paradoxically committed: change. This will be made absolutely explicit in Book 4, when Ithuriel and Zephon do not recognize the fallen angel, and Satan replies to their question about his identity with some of Milton's heaviest irony:

> Know ye not then said *Satan*, fill'd with scorn,
> Know ye not mee? ye knew me once no mate
> For you, there sitting where ye durst not soar;
> Not to know mee argues yourselves unknown,
> The lowest of your throng.
>
> [4.827–31]

Zephon's answer of course points out to Satan the obvious fact of his change, a fact that echoes all the louder to the reader for Satan's recent rapid series of metamorphoses and disguises—"Stripling Cherub" (3.636), cormorant, toad. Satan's fall has committed him to an endless declension, the "physical" correspondent to the "lower deep" that always opens within him. Having left God, he has abandoned rest and stability and is now embarked upon an endless process of mutation, from which he will never achieve rest. By his contradictory failure of self-knowledge and simultaneous attempt to redo Heaven and earth in his own image, he has barred himself forever from that Spenserian Sabbath which is the final goal and resting place of all epic journeys.

Satan's reaching at least one of his goals, the earthly paradise of Eden, and the temporary rest he gains there, sitting "like a Cormorant" (4.196) on the Tree of Life, provide the final Miltonic perspective on Satan as epic hero and epic wanderer in this portion of the poem. After his soliloquy to the sun, he has wandered on until he encountered "a steep wilderness, whose hairy sides/With thicket overgrown, grotesque and wild,/Access deni'd" (4.135–37). Milton emphasizes the wildness and complexity of the wood that surrounds Eden:

> Now to th' ascent of that steep savage Hill
> *Satan* had journey'd on, pensive and slow;
> But further way found none, so thick entwin'd,
> As one continu'd brake, the undergrowth
> Of shrubs and tangling bushes had perplext
> All path of Man or Beast that pass'd that way.
> [4.172–77]

Within the context of epic, this forest looks and sounds very familiar. It is the same "selva oscura," the "selva selvaggia e aspra e forte" that confuses Dante the pilgrim, and from which he seeks escape; it is the same Wood of Error which so perplexes Una and Red Crosse Knight with its "so many pathes, so many turnings seene." This is the forest of *silva*, of *hyle*: matter itself, the entrance to which and immersion in which provide the narrative beginning of Dante's and Spenser's epics and the thematic initiation of their heroes into the difficulties of human life in the corporeal world. That is to say, Satan in reaching his goal and entering Eden has arrived at the beginning point of the epic journey for human beings. That he, as spirit, although fallen, can still "At one slight bound high overleap['d] all bound" (4.181) only compounds Milton's irony: his goal is, in complex ways that the rest of the poem must explain, our starting point.

Milton: *Paradise Lost*

Satan's awesome leap into Eden, terrifying as it is in the context of *Paradise Lost,* vibrates with other contexts and other epics, other beginnings and some endings. If the beginning of *Paradise Lost* conceptually resembled the beginning of *The Faerie Queene* by initiating motion out of stillness, it also through its imagery resembles the opening of the *Aeneid.* The storm at sea that scatters Aeneas's fleet and begins the human action of the poem echoes direly in the storm of fire that confounds Satan and his crew, in the "hideous ruin and combustion" (1.46) with which they fell, in the "fiery Deluge" (1.68) and the "Floods and Whirlwinds of tempestuous fire" (1.77) that lash them as they welter on the burning sea. But this storm of fire is a double-edged reference, as is Satan's overleaping the forest that girdles Eden: the fiery defeat of Satan's legions also prods us to think of the chronological beginning of the *Aeneid,* the flaming destruction of Troy. In the same way, Satan's entrance into Eden, by virtue of the presence of the forest, connects us with the conceptual beginnings of Dante's poem and Spenser's and with the allegorically under-stood beginning of Virgil's; by virtue of the presence of "The verdurous wall of Paradise" (4.143), it links us once again with the breaching of Troy's walls, its subsequent fall, and the exile of Aeneas. For the reader of epic, these moments reverberate each other, lifting us out of the confines of the single moment before us or the single action unfolding, playing both action and moment back against the iterated falls and exiles of epic and human history and demanding that we see in Satan's high bound both an end and a beginning.

Paradise Lost is a poem of beginnings: the beginning of motion, the creation of the world and man, the beginning of human sin and human history and time, the new beginning in Noah, the new covenant with Abraham and Moses, the new Adam, the new heavens and new earth that will close the cycle, the new human lot which closes the poem. Each one of these beginnings is also an ending, each ending a beginning: all turn into each other to form the endless round that is Milton's poetic image of God, "All in All"

91

(3.341). So Satan's entry into Eden: for him it is an ascent, his last and highest leap from the gulf of Hell. It completes his false performance of the epic pattern of descent-conversion-ascent, all of which he has performed "physically" rather than intellectually or morally: descent into Hell, conversion in his release from the fiery gulf and subsequent deliberations, ascent in his passage through Chaos to earth. But his climactic moment is also, in the moral and allegorical understanding of that epic pattern, a descent—ironically, into matter and physical nature. Even though Satan overleaps *silva*, his entry into Eden immediately subjects him to its laws, and as soon as he enters Eden he assumes corporeality, a corporeality fully recognizable to us. He is no longer a being who can be described only by the abstract language of physical properties—stature, dimension, etc.—rather, he now dons bodies, sitting in the tree of life "like a Cormorant" (4.196), then:

> Down he alights among the sportful Herd
> Of those fourfooted kinds, himself now one,
> Now other.
>
> [4.396–98]
>
> A Lion now he stalks with fiery glare,
> Then as a Tiger.
>
> [4.402–3]

He ends, of course, for the moment at least, "Squat like a Toad, close at the ear of *Eve*"(4.800). So Satan's ascent ends in the descent from which human epic begins, ends with the beginning of epic as epic pertains to us.

Yet paradoxically, that beginning is no descent for Adam and Eve, and Milton is at pains to make this clear. For them—before the Fall—the body is not privative; corporeality does not cloud the soul nor confuse it. Their creation is an ascent:

> needs must the Power
> That made us, and for us this ample World
> Be infinitely good, and of his good
> As liberal and free as infinite,

That raise'd us from the dust and plac't us here
In all this happiness.

[4.12–17]

Adam's natural motion *is* upward, a telling physical comment on
Satan's claims for demonic nature:

> rais'd
> By quick instinctive motion up I sprung,
> As thitherward endeavoring, and upright
> Stood on my feet.
>
> [8.258–61]

Moreover, a moral motion and direction parallel these bodily ones;
unlike Satan, who argues he is self-created and eternal, and unlike
the Neoplatonic paradigm of the soul newly immersed in the body
and forgetful of its origins, Adam recognizes his contingent nature
and turns naturally to his maker:

> Thou Sun, said I, fair Light,
> And thou enlight'n'd Earth . . .
> Tell, if ye saw, how came I thus, how here?
> Not of myself; by some great Maker then,
> In goodness and in power preeminent;
> Tell me, how may I know him, how adore,
> From whom I have that thus I move and live,
> And feel that I am happier than I know.
>
> [8.273–74, 277–82]

If it doesn't sound tautological to put it so, Adam unfallen is Adam
undescended. Despite the fact that entering Eden is clearly presented in the poem as a new beginning, it is nevertheless still not a
beginning for us, and still not a beginning in the conventional epic
sense.

Milton's structural use of the threefold movement of the
descensus is more elaborate and more complicated than Spenser's
(in part at least because he had the advantage of Spenser's example
before him). While Spenser uses it to show the pattern of providential history, Milton turns it aside from its traditional human

orientation and employs it primarily—though by no means exclusively—as a structural analog for the divine being. His premise is, implicitly, that earth is but the shadow of Heaven; his argument is the poem itself, and his conclusion is the justification of the ways of God through the structural embodiment of those "ways" within the poem itself. By means of the synecdochic relationships set up between the whole and the parts of the epic poem by the allegorical readings of the poem and the *descensus*, Milton can demonstrate in the very organization of *Paradise Lost* both *that* and *how* "God shall be All in All" (3.341). On the simplest level, he accomplishes this by encapsulating the whole poem within a single overarching and symmetrical structural pattern, the pattern of descent-conversion-ascent. He then echoes that pattern both structurally and thematically in all of the smaller units of the poem, so that the whole of *Paradise Lost* is latent in each book of the poem. In the same way, the fall of man is latent in Satan's fall, and the redemption of man implicit in the triumph of the Son in the war in Heaven and explicit in the Son's offer of expiation in the dialog in Heaven in Book 3 (Milton could also, of course, have learned this technique from Dante; whether he in fact did so is probably forever unknowable). It is easiest to clarify such a structure by looking first at its center and then moving concentrically outward.[7]

Books 6 and 7 provide a pivot point for all of *Paradise Lost*, moving the action of the poem irrevocably out of the spiritual sphere and into the corporeal. These books mirror each other exactly: in each, the same characters—Adam, Eve, and Raphael—figure in the same situation—Raphael is instructing Adam and Eve about events in Heaven before their creation. In 6, he describes the war in Heaven, the Son's entrance into the struggle, the defeat and expulsion of Satan's legions, the Son's triumphal return, and the heavenly jubilation. Book 7 parallels and antithesizes that by presenting the work of creation rather than destruction. Raphael describes God's intention to repopulate the heavens with a new race, the Son's entrance into Chaos, its replacement by the newly

94

created universe, and, once again, the Son's triumphal return and the heavenly jubilation. The other books arrange themselves like types and antitypes around these two. Book 5 opens with Raphael's arrival in Paradise: 8 closes with his departure. Both books contain his crucial warnings to Adam about Satan's plans. Book 5 also recounts the beginnings of Satan's rebellion against the dominion of God and the kingship of his Son; 8 nicely counterpoints that with Adam's account of his own beginnings and his immediate recognition of the necessity of "some great Maker" (8.278; compare particularly 5.852ff.). To move further outward: in Book 4, Satan adopts the form of a toad, in 9 that of a serpent. In the earlier book he discovers the prohibition placed upon the fruit of the tree; in the later book he utilizes that knowledge. Book 4 contains the first temptation of Eve, in her dream; 9 contains the successful temptation in actuality. Both books close with a quarrel: 4, between Satan and Gabriel; 9, between Adam and Eve. More examples:

Book 3	Book 10
Prediction that man will sin	Announcement that man has sinned
The Son offers to satisfy divine justice	The Son judges the sinners
A heavenly council, ending triumphantly in hosannahs	A hellish council, ending in hisses

Book 2	Book 11
	Heavenly council
Council of demons	
Satan meets Sin and Death; sees consequences of his own sin in his son	Sentence of death pronounced on Adam and Eve; Adam sees consequences of his sin in his son Abel's death
Satan's first glimpse of newly created world	Adam's first glimpse of new world he has made

Books 1 and 12 complete the process and round the poem: 1 begins with the expulsion of Satan and 12 ends with the expulsion of Adam and Eve. Babel, Nimrod, and the blasphemous city dwellers of 12 correspond to Pandemonium and its inhabitants. The catalog of patriarchs and prophets in the last book answers the catalog of devils and false gods in the first. The demonic speculation about Adam and Eve in Book 1 is confuted by the announcement of the advent of the second Adam in 12. Earth is "but the shadow of Heav'n" (5.575), and the poem ends as it began with the near-total defeat of Satan.

Within this overall structure, the two halves of the poem also break down into repetitions of this pattern, Books 1 through 6 and 7 through 12 constituting smaller repetitions of the original structure. I will list the parallels briefly (and no more exhaustively than this view of the entirety of the poem has been). Book 1 opens, as 6 climaxes, with the fall of Satan, thus enclosing the purely spiritual half of the poem. Somewhat informal Satanic councils take place in each book, and the demonic artifacts, associated in both cases with wind, match each other—Pandemonium in 1 and cannon in 6. The Son's triumphal entry into the heavenly court at the end of the sixth book counterpoints the entry of Satan into council at Pandemonium. Both Books 2 and 5 contain formal demonic councils, but beyond this the correspondences exist more as antitheses than parallels: Satan leaves Hell to attack Adam and Eve, and this is counterpointed in Book 5 both by Raphael's departure for earth to warn them and by Abdiel's leaving the rebel camp to warn God. Raphael's flight through creation to earth answers Satan's journey through Chaos to earth in the same manner that Adam's and Eve's prayers and tasks in Book 5 correspond to the diversions of the demons in Book 2. At the center of this, in 3 and 4, we have the same sort of mirroring that we saw more grandly in 6 and 7, and the same sort of cross-over from Heaven to earth, also less grandly. Satan seen approaching the earth in 3 is counterbalanced by Satan captured in Paradise in 4; the revelation of the second Adam in 3 anticipates the appearance of the first Adam in 4; Satan's use of the form of a lesser angel in 3 prepares for his diminishment into the shapes of cormorant and toad in 4—even his dialogue with Uriel about the wonders of God's new creation anticipates his monologue of self-doubt and wonderment at his first sight of Adam and Eve in 4.

So also in the unit formed by Books 7 to 12, which encloses the corporeal half of the poem. I will only list the parallels:

Book 7	Book 12
Creation of new world to replace loss of Satan and his followers	New beginning of the human race from Noah
Sabbath of Creation	The Second Coming
Opening of Paradise	Closing of Paradise

Book 8	Book 11
Adam denied knowledge of physical heavens	Adam gains knowledge of life on earth
Creation of Adam and Eve; their dominion in Paradise	Announcement of the expulsion of Adam and Eve from paradise
Departure of Raphael from earth	Arrival of Michael on earth

Book 9	Book 10
Adam and Eve discuss their labors	Adam and Eve discuss penitence
Satan tempts Eve in form of serpent	Satan forced into form of serpent
The Fall and the sympathetic fall of earth	Sin and Death start toward earth
Adam and Eve clothe themselves	The Son clothes Adam and Eve

Smaller and smaller units within the poem employ the same basic structure in relatively similar manners. Books 1 to 3 show the physical descent of the demons to Hell, their deliberations and their leader's journey through the middling region of Chaos, and his final escape to light that the poet Milton so joyfully hails, a false ascent which he nevertheless depicts himself as performing vicariously with Satan, though more orthodoxly:

Thee I revisit now with bolder wing,
Escap't the *Stygian* Pool, though long detain'd

97

In that obscure sojourn, while in my flight
Through utter and through middle darkness borne
With other notes than to th' *Orphean* Lyre
I sung of *Chaos* and *Eternal Night*,
Taught by the heav'nly Muse to venture down
The dark descent, and up to reascend,
Though hard and rare.

[3.13–21]

Books 4 to 6 show the moral descent of the entrance of Satan, bearing sin, temptation, and Hell itself into God's new creation; the elaboration of that in Raphael's account of Satan's first sin in Heaven and the initial countering of it by the faithful Abdiel; and moral reascension by the purgation of Heaven and the expulsion of Satan into that hell he discovered within himself at the beginning of Book 4. Books 7 to 9 slightly alter the pattern of 1, 2, and 3 by showing a physical descent *in bono* in the Son's creation of earth out of the materials of Chaos; Book 8, recounting Adam's own creation and the creation of Eve, provides the point of conversion, showing in Adam's adoration of his creator and his equal adoration of Eve the possibilities of moral ascent or descent open to him; and Book 9 the false ascent to godhead that constitutes a real moral descent. Books 10 to 12 show the physical descent of the whole created world through the introduction of Sin and Death, followed by the beginnings of conversion and illumination in the action of grace and Adam's and Eve's repentence. The action of grace is then elaborated universally in Michael's account of the working of providence, culminating in the nullification of Satan, Sin, and Death, and individually and morally; in the possibility of attaining "A paradise within thee, happier far" (12.587).

So pervasive is this pattern that it informs even individual books of *Paradise Lost*—for example, the last book, which begins its descent with the corruption of government and religion among men after the Flood, proceeds through a converting series of precursors of the Messiah to his actual appearance and then completes its ascent with our future, his final victory, and the total purgation its ascent with our future, his final victory, and the total purgation of earth. This can be demonstrated for any book of *Paradise Lost*, though I do not propose to do so here. It will probably be objected ~~Yes~~ that, by a judicious selection of incidents, anything can be made to fit this pattern, and I grudgingly admit there is a kernel of truth in that—but I firmly deny that the objection applies at all to *Paradise Lost*. Putting aside all of the *a priori* reasons for the importance of the *descensus* to such a poem, putting aside even the importance of the Virgilian commentary tradition and the prestige of Spenser's and Dante's precedents, we are still left with a poem in which not a randomly selected group of episodes but every significant event relates directly to this pattern, a poem moreover which by its language, its imagery, its allusions to, and recollections of previous poems in the same genre—particularly the *Aeneid*—constantly calls our attention to the presence of this pattern. The conclusion seems to be inescapable that Milton built the poem out of this pattern and its thematic appurtenances, that the poem is, if you will, "a continued Allegory, or darke conceit,"[8] the solution to which is God. After all that I have said about the pattern of descent-conversion-ascent, there still remains to be pointed out the fact that, with slight changes of language and emphasis—very slight, and of a nature to appeal to what we know of John Milton— that pattern can very adequately be used by orthodox theologians to describe the relationship of the three persons of the Trinity.

❧ *Pattern is becoming so ubiquitous as to be meaningless*

Milton's subject matter and theme lead him logically to rearrange the relation to each other of the structural units of the *descensus* triad. As discussed so far, the pattern consists of a processional series of events leading up to a point of conversion, a nexus, which capsulizes and alters them and leads in turn to a recessional series of events which mirror the first—the Red Crosse Knight fights the dragon Error badly, is enlightened at the House of Contemplation, and fights the great dragon well. This still remains at least partially true in *Paradise Lost*: God's Providence in capturing Satan at Eve's ear is matched in the Providential working out of the historical process of redemption, and both relate to God's bringing good out of evil by his creation of the world. But in *Paradise Lost* those first and last events do not so much reflect each other as they mirror the central unit of the *descensus*, the phase of conversion. That central unit is God and God's works, which can be adequately mirrored only by his Son, the Logos, and not by the human word. He is the source and end of all the reality that art is supposed to mirror, and so cannot reflect anything but himself: all other things reflect him. So the real mirrors of *Paradise Lost* are the first and last units of the poem, and what they mirror is the center. Satan, of course, is a distorting mirror. His attempts to emulate God become a travesty of him: darkness visible is not the equivalent of light invisible. In that sense, Satan and Hell are high burlesque; they are the possibility and the direction of mock epic contained within the epic itself. Adam and earth are the legitimate mirrors of the poem; created in God's image and bearing his impress, they are the high art which our "erected wits" still let us reach to, though our "infected wills" will not let us attain them. This is why, I believe, *Paradise Lost* ends at a point which corresponds to Book 6 of the *Aeneid*: Adam has been illuminated, his goal has been explained, and his real epic works—and ours—are about to begin. Everything before has been prologue; what follows is "the better fortitude/Of Patience and Heroic Martyrdom" (9.31–32) and the "argument/Not less but more Heroic than the wrath/Of stern *Achilles*" (9.13–15).

What all of this structural play derives from, it seems to me, is Milton's allegiance to native English tradition and his earlier consideration of the possibility of Arthurian material as the subject of his epic. In *Paradise Lost*, Milton modestly proposes to encompass everything, and he comes very close to doing so. The overt use of the threefold *descensus* pattern alines his poem with the mainstream of orthodox epic; his elaborate rearrangement of those triadic components provides him with structural access to the other great divergent epic tradition (diverging since the *Odyssey*, perhaps), the romance, and thereby with his great English predecessor and teacher, Edmund Spenser. It is a simple fact that, if *The Faerie Queene* is more regular and orthodox in its structure than has been believed—and I hope I have shown that it is—then *Paradise Lost* is far more akin to romance than has yet been realized. Indeed, a good many of the arguments about who is the hero of *Paradise Lost* can be ultimately resolved by the recognition of the fact that *Paradise Lost*, like conventional medieval romance, has several heroes, performing parallel actions in separate stories. Milton has very simply used the three motions of the *descensus* to allow himself three protagonists engaged in three distinct actions, and has thereby incorporated into the structure of *Paradise Lost* the romance principle of *entrelacement*. (It should be superfluous to point out that, once again, he had here not only the example of Spenser to guide him, but the even more clear-cut cases of the *Commedia* and the *Odyssey*, where the adventures of Telemachus stand in the same relation to those of Odysseus as Adam's and Satan's do to Christ's in *Paradise Lost*.) This means simply that Satan, the Son, and Adam act respectively as the protagonists of parallel but separate plots encapsulated in separate four-book units of the poem—and as such, indeed, we have to this point been speaking about Satan and his role in the first four books of the poem. Those form a single action, conceived within the framework of and bearing an ironic relation to the pattern of descent-conversion-ascent, climaxing in the merely physical ascent of Satan to earth, and ending there tragically—for him—in the frustration of his plans and his (momentary) exile from Eden. Put in that bald form, the similarities to Adam's own four-book *agon* leap to the eye (I will speak more of this later). That leaves the central four books, the scene of the Son's *aristeia*, and it is these I now propose to discuss.

In regular Aristotelean fashion, one single day of Milton's and Raphael's narrative relates the events of the Son's transcendant glory, even though the action of that *aristeia* is in fact spread over many days "such . . . As Heav'n's great Year brings forth" (5.582–83). But Books 5 through 8 of *Paradise Lost* transpire in one day, from the "rosy steps" of morning (5.1) to the "thick shade" (8.653) of evening. Within that single day, Raphael tells of numerous other mornings and evenings, the risings of the Son and the fallings of Satan, all bearing that same imagistic significance, the daylight brightness of God opposing the midnight darkness of Satan.[9] Raphael's arrival itself encapsulates the story of the Son in much the same fashion. Journeying downward from Heaven, sailing "between worlds and worlds, with steady wing" (5.268)—and thereby providing a heavy contrast with Satan's upward voyage through Chaos—he arrives on earth like the phoenix and seems to Adam "another Morn/Ris'n on mid-noon"(5.310–11). This frames the account of the Son's glory with an orthodox *descensus*: the descent of a spiritual being from his heavenly home to earth, where he partakes of corporeal nourishment, speaks of spiritual matters in corporeal terms, describes to Adam his possible refinement from matter, and finally reascends "up to Heav'n/From the thick shade" (8.652–53). Other versions of *descensus* serve as prologue also to the angel's narrative: the false ascent contained in Eve's dream, which is in reality a moral descent,

> Forthwith up to the Clouds
> With him I flew, and underneath beheld
> The Earth outstretcht immense, a prospect wide
> And various: wond'ring at my flight and change
> To this high exaltation; suddenly
> My Guide was gone, and I, methought, sunk down,
> And fell asleep.
>
> [5.86–92]

the poem's own ascent to God (5.219–45), the contemplative ascent of Adam's and Eve's prayer,

> These are thy glorious works, Parent of good,
> Almighty, thine this universal Frame,
> Thus wondrous fair; thyself how wondrous then!

Unspeakable, who sit'st above these Heavens
To us invisible or dimly seen
In these thy lowest works, yet these declare
Thy goodness beyond thought, and Power Divine.

[5.153–59]

the contemplative ascent Raphael describes to Adam,

the scale of Nature set
From centre to circumference, whereon
In contemplation of created things
By steps we may ascend to God.

[5.509–12]

and man's potential physical and spiritual ascent,

And from these corporal nutriments perhaps
Your bodies may at last turn all to spirit,
Improv'd by tract of time, and wing'd ascend
Ethereal, as wee, or may at choice
Here or in Heav'nly Paradises dwell.

[5.496–500]

Even the image of the phoenix elaborates this emphasis, trailing as it does its associations with Christ's crucifixion, death, and resurrection, his ascending the cross, descending into the grave, and rising again to glory.

With all of this as prologue, it is—from my point of view at least—striking, and obviously important, that the actions performed by the Son in Raphael's saga depart from this traditional pattern of the *descensus* in order to emphasize its central phase. The task of the Son, as Raphael describes it, is the process of differentiation—the separation of the sheep and the goats, if you will—and the corollary works of inclusion and exclusion. Thus the promulgation by the Father of the kingship of the Son constitutes (to use human language to describe a divine plan) the first step toward the time when God will be "All in All," and angelic allegiance to or disaffection from him form the first movements of inclusion or exclusion:

103

> Under his great Vice-gerent Reign abide
> United as one individual Soul
> For ever happy; him who disobeys
> Mee disobeys, breaks union, and that day
> Cast out from God and blessed vision, falls
> Into utter darkness, deep ingulft, his place
> Ordain'd without redemption, without end.
>
> [5.609–15]

This Abdiel clearly recognizes, when he argues with Satan that the Son, by his kingship, has become "One of our number" (5.843), and that consequently "all honor to him done/Returns our own" (5.844–45). The Son too confirms this:

> Sceptre and Power, thy giving, I assume,
> And gladlier shall resign, when in the end
> Thou shalt be All in All, and I in thee
> For ever, and in mee all whom thou lov'st.
>
> [6.730–33]

The divine dialectic is an intricate one, and in this respect can be best clarified for us through Heaven's shadowy likeness to earth. On earth, motion and process are the roads back to the divine stasis, and descent provides the readiest form of ascent. In Heaven, differentiation from God will, if properly conducted, lead to unity with God; so the angels, created beings distinct from God, will through the intermediary of the Son, whose kingship apparently distances them still further from the Godhead, ultimately achieve total union with divinity: "I in thee/For ever, and in mee all whom thou lov'st." This dialectic provides as well the base, the touchstone, against which to weigh the diabolical process of differentiation which Milton portrayed in Hell. There are true differentiations and false differentiations, true unities and false unities: Heaven is the home of the true, Hell the place of the false, and earth the meeting and testing ground of both. So it is—to get a bit ahead of myself—that the temptation of Adam and Eve takes the form, simultaneously, of a false ascent and a false unity, both with divinity and with each other (it follows from this, of course, that the temptation itself is subtle, intricate, of far more profound intellectual content than its surface vehicle: I will discuss this later).

Raphael's story begins with the earliest "chronological" event contained in *Paradise Lost*, the "begetting" of the Son as "Head" of the angels. Prior to this (please understand the usual apology for using temporal terms to speak of eternal and instantaneous events), the Son has apparently existed in total union with the Father: "By [him] in bliss imbosom'd" (5.597) is the closest hint the poem provides about his mode of being, and "imbosom'd" appears to carry its full literal force—particularly when contrasted with the Son's position "At my right hand" (5.606) immediately after his begetting. This begetting then, this creation of the Son as Head of the angels, acts in the poem as a differentiation of the Son from the Godhead, an extrusion of him from the unity of the deity or an elaboration of unity into multiplicity. The angels may not ascend to divinity by their own power (that is one of Satan's many heresies), therefore divinity will descend to them. Put it another way: as finite created beings, they are other than God, who is eternally the same. For God to be all in all, otherness must somehow be incorporated into sameness, and only omnipotent Sameness can accomplish that by transforming itself into the paradox of Sameness and Otherness eternally and simultaneously subsisting. The Son is the agent of that transformation, the means by which Sameness will metamorphose itself into simultaneous Sameness and Otherness: thus his work is the task of inclusion and exclusion, and the first "sequential" action of the poem is God's construing his Son as Other and Same: head of the angels, vice-gerent, seated at God's right hand rather than "imbosom'd" in him, yet unifier of the angels "as one individual Soul" (5.610), still "Second Omnipotence" (6.684) and "Image of [the Father] in all things" (6.736). The Father persists, motionless and immutable; the Son goes forth, the agent of destruction and creation. More: he dons otherness, becomes angel—"he the Head/One of our number thus reduc't becomes" (5.842–43) as Abdiel says—becomes man, and thereby enfolds these orders of being in God. To use some of the language I employed in talking about a similar process in *The Faerie Queene*, the Son explicates God in creation and complicates creation into God. He is the unfolding of Sameness and the infolding of Otherness.

Accordingly, he ends the first half of the poem by rising "From the right hand of Glory where he sat" (6.747) and driving the rebel angels from Heaven, thereby bringing the first six books of the poem full circle and restoring Heaven to unity once again— and he does this by motion (the chariot) and by change:

> into terror chang'd
> His count'nance too severe to be beheld
> And full of wrath bent on his Enemies.
>
> [6.824–26]

He separates the sheep from the goats (the demons flee "as a Herd/Of Goats or timorous flock together throng'd" [6.856–57]), or rather, the demons choose exclusion: "headlong themselves they threw/Down from the verge of Heav'n" (6.864 – 65)—appropriately, since they have elected a false sameness, rejecting the "strange point and new" (5.855) at which Satan scoffs, and opting for a false unity among themselves, outside of God. Their exclusion is therefore a settled matter, and their fall from Heaven, self-propelled, is both the logical culmination of their choice and the logical refutation of their claim, in Moloch's words,

> That in our proper motion we ascend
> Up to our native seat: descent and fall
> To us is adverse.
>
> [2.75–77]

With equal consonance and appropriateness, the Son begins the second half of the poem with the works of inclusion, the imposition of the divine image upon the principle of change itself, the formless Chaos outside Heaven. The divine plan, as announced by the Father, will culminate in unity:

> Another World, out of one man a Race
> Of men innumerable, there to dwell,
> Not here, till by degrees of merit rais'd
> They open to themselves at length the way
> Up hither, under long obedience tri'd,
> And Earth be chang'd to Heav'n, and Heav'n to Earth.
> One Kingdom, Joy and Union without end.
>
> [7.155–61]

To accomplish this task of infolding, the Son does not change his countenance, but rather bears the full image of the Father—"all his Father in him shone" (7.196)—who works jointly with him in creation:

> for he also went
> Invisible, yet stay'd (such privilege
> Hath Omnipresence).
>
> [7.588–90]

Up to this point, God's creative acts have confined themselves to the purely spiritual realm of Heaven, however mysteriously that realm may encompass a kind of matter (the materials of the Satanic guns, for instance). Now God furthers the work of inclusion and extends his creative fiat into matter, calling into being material creatures made in his own image. They too will yet further extend his creative work in number and time, producing "out of one man a Race/Of men innumerable" and ultimately *by their agency* sublimating the material world into the spiritual. Thus each apparent further step away from God, each seeming step downward on the ladder of created being, becomes in actuality an extension of the being of God: the way up and the way down are in this sense too the same. This point Adam instinctively grasps and about it he even presumes to lecture his creator:

> To attain
> The highth and depth of thy Eternal ways

All human thoughts come short, Supreme of things;
Thou in thyself art perfet, and in thee
Is no deficience found; not so is Man,
But in degree, the cause of his desire
By conversation with his like to help,
Or solace his defects. No need that thou
Shouldst propagate, already infinite;
And through all numbers absolute, though One;
But Man by number is to manifest
His single imperfection, and beget
Like of his like, his Image multipli'd,
In unity defective, which requires
Collateral love, and dearest amity.
Thou in thy secrecy although alone,
Best with thyself accompanied, seek'st not
Social communication, yet so pleas'd,
Canst raise thy Creature to what highth thou wilt
Of Union or Communion, deifi'd.

[8.412–31]

God has made man his tool for conquering and incorporating multiplicity and matter, two entities seemingly outside of and alien to his spiritual unity; man's fall, far from undoing this plan, merely extends it in another direction and—still through the agency of man—provides God the means by which he can make time part of his eternity. All of this, of course, we have already seen, grotesquely shadowed, in Hell, and will see again, mirrored darkly, in Michael's foretelling of human history; here, in the center of *Paradise Lost*, we are allowed to glimpse it all in its true dimensions as the works of the Son.

All this reveals to us the true nature of the Son's *aristeia*. His work of inclusion and exclusion parallels and indeed sets the pattern for the rhythms of complication and explication which dominate the Platonic emanating triad,[10] and by that same token provides the basal pattern for the movements of the *descensus*. The expulsion of the demons from Heaven forms a descent: the Son leaves the Father, changes himself in encountering the devils, who are Hell, and returns to the Father. The creation is likewise a descent: the Son leaves Heaven, enters and alters matter, which is an *inferos* in itself, and reascends to the Father. Moreover, these are the archetypal actions of the descent: the purgation of spirit (expulsion of Satan) and the conformation of matter to spirit (the creation in the divine image). That is, the Son acts as the central converting unit of the triad, halting the motion of descent, transforming it and redirecting it into the movement of ascension. He, eternally embraced within the immutable sameness of God, enacts and becomes the principle of otherness, the source of transformation. As such, in the central four books of the poem, he performs the poem's primary act of transformation and its major extension of divinity, the transformation of Chaos into form, of matter into the vehicle of spirit. For this reason, the incarnation—which we would normally regard as the basic and most important instance of the *descensus* pattern and of the Son's work of inclusion and exclusion—has no place in this central portion of *Paradise Lost*, but belongs rather to the poem's earlier and later portions describing the movements of falling and arising. Here the Son establishes his nature and deeds as essentially transformative; in that light, his incarnation, death, and resurrection are merely logical extensions in time and space of what he has already performed in eternity and spirit. They are the completion in humanity of an act that originates in divinity. In this sense too, the entirety of *Paradise Lost* forms a perfect Platonic emanating triad, of which these central four books are the nuclear converting unit: in them a fall which begins in the realm of eternal spirit is metamorphosed, by the agency of the Son, into a rise which will complete itself in the realm of temporal matter. So the Son, who is the perfect mirror of the Father, also offers the poem the source image of what is distortedly mirrored in Satan and dimly reflected in Adam, the encounter of spirit with nonspirit and the taming of matter to conformity with divinity. Last, in this same sense, the central four books of the poem are the perfect image of the Son and are coextensive with him: both are conversion and transformation, both the center of the triad. This is one of the ways—perhaps the major way—Milton makes his poem mirror and reproduce God, and thereby not merely justify but literally embody God's ways to man.

At the end of Book 6 of *Paradise Lost* one phase of the poem's action closes. Satan falling from Heaven loops back upon the beginning of the poem, Satan descended into Hell, closing the circle of eternity upon those events which happen solely in the realm of spirit. With Book 7 and Raphael's account of creation, the poem enters a new sphere and a new cycle, those of time and matter, which will end only in Michael's later prediction, in Book 12, of the events of apocalypse and the new heavens, new earth, and "new" eternity which will succeed them. Between those points exists the world we know, the *inferos* of time and matter, of spirits imprisoned in bodies, of souls drunk with corporeality, all the result of Adam's moral descent to sin.

Book 9 opens the section of the poem devoted to Adam's *agon*. Milton takes pains to locate us precisely at this point, not only in terms of the action of his own poem but in terms of the stages of the descent and of the progress of classical epic as well. Even though Adam's sin is for the reader yet to happen, Milton's prefatory remarks deal with a descent already accomplished:

> No more of talk where God or Angel Guest
> With Man, as with his Friend, familiar us'd
> To sit indulgent.
>
> [9.1–3]

Already passed too is the stage of conversion:

> I now must change
> Those Notes to Tragic; foul distrust, and breach
> Disloyal on the part of Man, revolt
> And disobedience: On the part of Heav'n
> Now alienated, distance and distaste,

110

Anger and just rebuke, and judgment giv'n,
That brought into this World a world of woe.
[9.5–11]

Placed thus as preface to the Fall, these lines mean that even the Fall itself is to be construed as part of the rising action of the poem, as indeed even the crudest analysis of the poem's movement indicates: Books 1 to 4, Satan's *aristeia* and the motion of descent; Books 5 to 8, the Son's *aristeia* and the action of conversion; Books 9 to 12, Adam's *aristeia* and the movement of ascent. Milton leaves no doubt of this; he explicitly compares the events he is about to describe in these last four books with the final, ascending actions of the *Iliad* and the *Aeneid*:

> Sad task, yet argument
> Not less but more Heroic than the wrath
> Of stern *Achilles* on his Foe pursu'd
> Thrice Fugitive about *Troy* Wall; or rage
> Of *Turnus* for *Lavinia* disespous'd.
> [9.13–17]

Those events constitute the acme of achievement for their now illuminated and informed heroes, and it is as an achievement transcending them, an achievement more truly heroic, that Milton is directing us to read the final events of his poem. This whole introductory section (9.1–47) serves in fact as a quasi-invocation in close parallel to that which opens Book 3: both begin by remarking a sudden change in scene and tone, both compare Milton and his poem with their epic predecessors, both turn to the poet's "Celestial Patroness" (9.21) and both credit her, the "heav'nly Muse" (3.19), with enabling the blind poet of "an age too late" (9.44) to overcome the difficulties which both catalog as afflicting him. The invocation of Book 3 detailed an ascent which we as readers encountered in the middle of the descending movement of the poem: this introduction to Book 9 correspondingly asks us to witness a descent which is paradoxically but crucially central to the rising action of the poem, a fall that is fortunate in far more profound

111

senses than the easy theological paradox implies. The way up and the way down are the same, and both must be travelled. Motion is the way back to the divine stasis, but outside of that divinity all motion is downward. It follows then—and I do not think Milton shrinks from this conclusion—that the first steps toward God must be directed away from him. Adam's *aristeia* is his fall: to initiate the motion that will ultimately bring him to participate in Godhead.

It is important to realize that Adam, howevermuch "fondly overcome with Female charm" (9.999), falls from perfectly respectable motives—and I do not mean by that merely humanly understandable desires. I mean precisely motives that, in the poem, God could respect—and in fact has. Adam sins, as Milton makes clear, in full knowledge that he is sinning, and, as Milton makes equally clear, he sins in the name of union:

> some cursed fraud
> Of Enemy hath beguil'd thee, yet unknown,
> And mee with thee hath ruin'd, for with thee
> Certain my resolution is to Die;
> How can I live without thee, how forgo
> Thy sweet Converse and Love so dearly join'd,
> To live again in these wild Woods forlorn?
> Should God create another *Eve*, and I
> Another Rib afford, yet loss of thee
> Would never from my heart; no no, I feel
> The Link of Nature draw me: Flesh of Flesh,
> Bone of my Bone thou art, and from thy State
> Mine never shall be parted, bliss or woe.
>
> [9.904–16]

Howevermuch he may later try to rationalize the probable results of eating the fruit, Adam still essentially realizes the sinfullness of his action and accepts fully the consequences and motivation of it. After some thirty lines of rather wishy-washy equivocation about the innocence of eating the forbidden fruit, he concludes quite simply:

112

However I with thee have fixt my Lot,
Certain to undergo like doom; if Death
Consort with thee, Death is to mee as Life;
So forcible within my heart I feel
The Bond of Nature draw me to my own,
My own in thee, for what thou art is mine;
Our State cannot be sever'd, we are one,
One Flesh; to lose thee were to lose myself.
[9.952–59]

Surely it can be no accident that Adam here insistently anticipates the language of the Book of Genesis: however wrongly he may be applying his knowledge, he is completely correct in his perception of the relation of man and wife. So correct is he, in fact, that he anticipates not merely Genesis but also St. Paul, who will use this same language and these same concepts to explain—or to shadow—the marriage of Christ and his church.

So ought men to love their wives as their own bodies: he that loveth his wife, loveth himself. For no man ever yet hated his own flesh, but nourisheth and cherisheth it, even as the Lord the Church. For we are members of his body, of his flesh, and of his bones. For this cause shall a man leave father and mother, and shall be joined unto his wife, and they two shall be one flesh. This is a great mystery: but I speak concerning Christ and the Church. [Ephesians 5.28–32]

To grasp the full importance of this, we must look back to Eve's sin and to Satan's and to the events of the third book of *Paradise Lost*. Eve acts solipsistically, by herself and for herself. She thinks of Adam only after eating the fruit, and even then her reasoning remains selfish; her first impulse is even to exclude him from partnership with her:

But to *Adam* in what sort
Shall I appear? shall I to him make known
As yet my change, and give him to partake
Full happiness with mee, or rather not,

113

> But keep the odds of Knowledge in my power
> Without Copartner?
>
> [9.816–21]

Even her final decision, to involve Adam in her act, is selfishly motivated:

> This may be well: but what if God have seen,
> And Death ensue? then I shall be no more,
> And *Adam* wedded to another *Eve*,
> Shall live with her enjoying, I extinct;
> A death to think. Confirm'd then I resolve,
> *Adam* shall share with me in bliss or woe:
> So dear I love him, that with him all deaths
> I could endure, without him live no life.
>
> [9.826–33]

Eve sins essentially against union, against her unity with Adam, and the union she finally proposes to herself is a false one, motivated by a fear of Adam's survival without her. Satan's sin too was a sin against union, against the inclusion of the angels in the headship of the Son—against, basically, the kind of incorporation into Christ of which St. Paul speaks in language that echoes Adam's reasons for sinning with Eve. The unity the demons achieve in Hell is also essentially a false one, of the same order Eve proposes, a unity of common guilt and common suffering, in their case further cemented by politics and demagoguery. Opposed to that stands the union the Son proposes and St. Paul describes, an organic unity of the parts of a single body with one another. This, is course, delineates as well as human language can the ultimate reach of the Son's task of inclusion, the transplantation of other lives to his, the engrafting of humanity into his divinity. The Father perceives it and accepts it as such:

> Thou therefore whom thou only canst redeem,
> Thir Nature also to thy Nature join;
> And be thyself Man among men on Earth,
> Made flesh, when time shall be, of Virgin seed,
> By wondrous birth: Be thou in *Adam's* room

The Head of all mankind, though *Adam's* Son.
As in him perish all men, so in thee
As from a second root shall be restor'd,
As many as are restor'd, without thee none.
His crime makes guilty all his Sons, thy merit
Imputed shall absolve them who renounce
Thir own both righteous and unrighteous deeds,
And live in thee transplanted, and from thee
Receive new life.

[3.281–94]

Hell then provides a map of false unity just as it does of false differentiation, mere multiplicity. Heaven embodies—if one can say that—true union and true differentiation, number contained within and comprehended by unity. A small clarification of what I mean. The demons all possess marked personalities and differ from each other in character, style, goal, etc. They are "innumerable," though Satan counts them, and they are united only in hate and by guile. The unfallen angels have no personality and are distinguished within their union of love only by their tasks: Raphael is "sociable" because of his errand, Michael warlike because of his. All are subsumed within the Son King. Earth then is the field where these adversaries clash, where they can become confused both in themselves and in the perceiver of them. When requesting a companion of God, Adam had described fully and realized fully his own and mankind's deficiency, specifically in terms of number:

But Man by number is to manifest
His single imperfection, and beget
Like of his like, his Image multipli'd,
In unity defective, which requires
Collateral love, and dearest amity.

[8.422–6]

God approves of this and gives him Eve, "Thy likeness, thy fit help, thy other self" (8.450). Union with Eve is then natural to Adam; their conjugal bond is "the Bond of Nature" which draws him to follow her in sin. For him, solitude is an unnatural state. (It is

115

probably worth remarking here that God equivocates a bit when talking to Adam about this: even he is not quite as alone as he leads Adam to think he is [8.398–411], and he certainly knows one "Second to mee or like" [8.407] as Adam too learns from Raphael's story.) This means that by successfully seducing Eve, Satan has presented Adam with a far more complex temptation than that to simple disobedience, or to *luxuria*, or to pride. Those may perhaps sum up Satan's own self-temptation, or what he offers Eve, but they in no way approach the intricacy of the puzzle that Adam confronts or that we as readers must work through. Adam rightly understands his quandary as involving a choice—for him an excessively cruel one—between differentiation and unity. What he perhaps does not realize (I say "perhaps" because, before his intellect is darkened as a result of his sin, there are some indications that he does realize this, and even, indeed, that this realization, disregarded, *is* his fall) is that both alternatives are false. Satan presents him with a Swiftian dilemma, deceiving him into choosing between being a fool or a knave, a Yahoo or a Houyhnhnm, as if there were no other alternatives. Adam must choose between solitude without Eve or union with her, between what he already knows is an unnatural condition for him and what must be a disastrous condition for them both. Further, he must elect either differentiation from her, who has been made in his image, not God's, or differentiation from God, in whose image he was made. He must discriminate unities and differentiations, and the only evidence he can bring to bear on his choices are what he knows of God and God's commands and what he knows of himself without Eve. He opts for the human half of the equation, thereby creating humanity as we know it, calling into being our fallen state—but he does this in the name of a unity which God himself has sanctioned and which the Son will emulate. Adam's choice—his fall—is the same as the Son's choice—his heroism. Adam elects death with Eve; the Son offers himself to death with man. Adam's sin and the Son's *aristeia* share the same form, and that one is in any sense the consequence of the other is irrelevant both to *Paradise Lost*'s point

116

and its time scheme. Of course Adam's choice is erroneous, sinful, romantic in the most pejorative sense, at its most extenuated the substitution of a lesser good for a higher. But, and this is an enormous but, it is also a choice that is constitutive, definitive, and creative—of the world as we know it, if of nothing else. And it is a choice ratified at least in form by the Son's assumption of mortal (and therefore fallen) humanity. By opting for human love Adam enables God to incorporate that love within himself through the agency of the Son, who is the image of divine love, mercy, and grace—all of which are more or less cognate terms. Adam's choice, while not entirely definitive of human heroism in itself, lays the groundwork of that heroism and creates the possibility of "the better fortitude/Of Patience and Heroic Martyrdom" (9.31–32). It also makes possible, through the agency of the second Adam—and the emphasis in that phrase must fall on Adam, not on second—the inclusion of humanity within the being of divinity.

Adam's act, of course, also creates "a world of woe" for himself and his progeny, and for that reason if for no other remains an action of extreme ambivalence. That ambivalence marks every step of the Fall. Satan seduces Eve from her loyalty to Adam, and she in turn seduces Adam from his loyalty to God, or rather, since Eve in fact says and does very little to Adam, he seduces himself from his loyalty to God. Both events employ and exploit the language of love. Adam's case of course we have been discussing in just these terms: he persuades himself that his love for Eve demands his repudiation of God. In Eve's case, Satan approaches her as the most courtly and Petrarchan of lovers, lost in admiration of his beloved and dazzled by her perfections.

> Wonder not, sovran Mistress, if perhaps
> Thou canst, who are sole Wonder, much less arm
> Thy looks, the Heav'n of mildness, with disdain,
> Displeas'd that I approach thee thus, and gaze
> Insatiate.
>
> [9.532–36]
>
> Faires resemblance of thy Maker fair,

Thee all things living gaze on.

[9.538–39]

But all that fair and good in thy Divine
Semblance, and in thy Beauty's heav'nly Ray
United I beheld; no Fair to thine
Equivalent or second.

[9.606–9]

Her fall is in every sense a seduction, a violation of her marital and psychological union with Adam, and it follows logically from the form of her fall that the first consequences of it, after she has eaten the fruit and it has begun to intoxicate her, should suggest to her first the exclusion of Adam from her new state and second the collateral corruption of her union with him. Adam accomplishes this for her and for Satan by in effect seducing himself: he chooses to view his act as a kind of *Liebestod*, a choice of union with Eve in death rather than life without her. We as readers tend to respond more negatively to Eve's act than to Adam's, seeing in hers a basic selfishness and in his a kind of nobility. This ignores, of course, Milton's iterated reminders of the gross egoism of Adam's act with respect to his as yet unborn descendants—ourselves, in short—and it ignores as well the simple but decisive fact that both acts are the same, and that both boil down to breaking the single injunction laid upon them. One of the most significant aspects of Milton's presentation of the human fall lies in the extreme complexity of motive and choice that precipitates it. The form of the temptation becomes so complex that the content of it is almost lost sight of, as much by the readers as by the participants. The content of the temptation, stripped of all the rhetoric and all the psychological ramifications that surround it, is simple disobedience, therefore sin—but it is exactly those ramifications, that rhetoric, and the confusions of the basic issue that they give rise to that distinguish man's fall from Satan's and allow man to return to grace. In the Satanic fall, motive and act were identical; Satan falls the instant he thinks of not serving (thus God knows of his rebellion as rebellion before Satan has even announced it to his own followers

[5.720ff.]). Angelic reason, which is intuitive, differs from human discourse in precisely this way, and the discontinuities of discursive reason—the disjunctions between motive and act, between apprehension and reality, that discourse permits—provide the ground for the ambiguity of Adam's and Eve's fall. The form of the human act can for this reason be heroic—can in fact resemble the form of the Son's heroism—while its content is unalterably sinful. Thus the parallels between Adam's sin and the Son's sacrifice, the willingness of the two to endure death for another, can never be only ironic: they too must remain fundamentally ambivalent, and that very ambivalence in turn must be seen as informing in the profoundest senses the role of the Son as the second Adam. To borrow a phrase from John Donne, we think that Christ's cross and Adam's tree stood in one place, and we do so for reasons more convincing than symmetry.

I have remarked before that *Paradise Lost* is a poem of beginnings, and the moment of the Fall is one of the most crucial of them. In terms of the epic pattern which interests me in this essay, the moral descent which is the Fall calls into being as its consequence the intellectual and spiritual descent which is the core of the traditional understanding of epic, the descent of the soul into the body and its immersion in matter. Before the Fall, Adam's and Eve's lives in their bodies were in no sense privations: their intellects were clear and their wills strong, their bodies subservient to their minds. The immediate consequences of the Fall reproduce—or set the pattern for—the symptoms of the soul's entrance into the body as the series of privations that Neoplatonic theory posits. Drunkenness takes place first, and carnality quickly follows it:

> now
> As with new Wine intoxicated both
> They swim in mirth, and fancy that they feel
> Divinity within them breeding wings
> Wherewith to scorn the Earth: but that false Fruit
> Far other operation first display'd,

Carnal desire inflaming, hee on *Eve*
Began to cast lascivious Eyes, she him
As wantonly repaid; in Lust they burn.

[9.1007–15]

After that succeed remorse, regret, and shame. Adam turns then to
what has now become his natural element, the darkness of *silva*, in
which both he and Eve seek to obscure themselves:

O might I here
In solitude live savage, in some glade
Obscur'd, where highest Woods impenetrable
To Star or Sun-light, spread thir umbrage broad,
And brown as Evening: Cover me ye Pines,
Ye Cedars, with innumerable boughs
Hide me, where I may never see them more.

[9.1084–90]

Adam urges them to cover their shame with leaves, and so they do:
"both together went/Into the thickest Wood" (9.1099–1100). There
they discover the fig tree whose habit of growth Milton so splen-
didly describes:

[she] spreads her Arms
Branching so broad and long, that in the ground
The bended Twigs take root, and Daughters grow
About the Mother Tree, a Pillar'd shade
High overarch't, and echoing Walks between.

[9.1103–7]

This is a wonderful example of the richness of Milton's symbol-
making: the tree whose leaves provide the covering of Adam's
shame becomes the badge of his shame. The tree which from one
multiplies herself into a whole forest tokens Eve, from whom will
grow the whole fallen human race. The single tree from which
ramifies an entire grove signifies the tree of knowledge of good and
evil, from which sprouts the whole forest of *silva* in which man
will henceforth wander, whose darkness is now his home. As Satan
is punished in the shape he sinned, so Adam and Eve: by a tree they

fall, among trees they will live, clothed in the leaves of those trees they will move and have their being, by a tree they will be saved again. The world as we know it has begun.

The world of epic, as we more usually know it, also begins here. Among the many strands of temptation that make up the Fall, Adam's and Eve's presumption to divinity also plays its part. Like Satan, they think to raise themselves, by their own efforts, to the heavenly sphere; like Satan, they too stumble and fall in that proud ascent. That entire aspect of the Fall seems geared to, and a direct refutation of, any Landinesque notion of the epic hero's or the average human's ability to win salvation or the *summum bonum* on his own: if not Adam, how much less so we, his even more fallen descendants? Yet Adam's fall, in all its complexity, creates what will become the true epic goal and the traditional epic state. Adam by his fall remakes himself as *Adamus Exsul*: he banishes himself from innocence, from eternity, and from Eden, creating himself and his descendants anew as exiles from their spiritual homeland, to which it is their task ever to strive to return. That, both narratively and allegorically, has been the burden of epic for its greatest practitioners before Milton. Exile, return, and restoration constitute the narrative of the *Odyssey* as they do that of the *Aeneid*, the *Divina Commedia*, *Gierusalemma Liberata*, and *The Faerie Queene*, just as those same motions, spiritually understood, constitute the archetypal pattern of the *descensus* and the heart of the allegory of epic. Descent, illumination, and ascent reveal themselves as hieroglyphs for exile, discovery, and restoration; Odysseus and Aeneas and Dante are all children of Adam. Adam's sin exiles them and us, but it also endows us with privileges: it makes Everyman a potential epic hero and holds out to him the possibility not merely of a return to Eden but of the attainment of "A paradise within thee, happier far" (12.587). Just so, Milton's very unconventional poem describes the beginning of conventional epic: after Adam, every epic hero must undergo his own exile, his own illumination, his own restoration of his home or reestablishment of it until the divine providential plan has exhausted the possibilities of time, until number is filled up, and the divine hero restores them all to the new heavens and new earth that will end the possibility and the necessity of human heroism.

Adam himself even comes to share this conventional epic pattern. Before his physical exile from Eden, he is already exiled within Eden. When the Son descends to judge Adam and Eve, they "from his presence hid themselves among/The thickest Trees" (10.100–01); they witness the changes taking place in nature from their covert "hid in gloomiest shade" (10.716). The internal correlative of this is the darkening of intellect and obscuring of vision they endure, the weakness to the assaults of passion they now feel. For Adam and Eve, the epic journey has already begun, and they are embarked—"in a troubl'd Sea of passion tost" (10.718)—upon the dark journey of their own individual *descensus*. That journey will not be completed in *Paradise Lost*: Milton brings them only to the point at which so many commentaries on the *Aeneid* so significantly end, the moment of illumination about their true goal and the ways to it. There, descending (yet again) from the mount of speculation, Milton and the poem dismiss them, their epic labors like the world "all before them" (12.646). What they have learned in the interval remains for us to discuss.

❧

Book 10 marks the lowest point of the descent in this final phase of *Paradise Lost*. The Son pronounces sentence upon Adam and Eve, binding them who sought falsely to rise tightly to the physical earth:

> Curs'd is the ground for thy sake, thou in sorrow
> Shalt eat thereof all the days of thy Life;
> Thorns also and Thistles it shall bring thee forth
> Unbid, and thou shalt eat th' Herb of the Field,
> In the sweat of thy Face shalt thou eat Bread,
> Till thou return unto the ground, for thou
> Out of the ground wast taken, know thy Birth,

122

For dust thou art, and shalt to dust return.

[10.201–8]

Satan, Sin, and Death too reach their nadir here at the moment of their apparent triumph. When Satan greets his progeny upon the bridge that they have built and sends them on their mission, Milton quietly but significantly indicates that for them, at this point, all directions are downward: Satan will "Descend through Darkness" (10.394), while they will "right down to Paradise descend" (10.398). For all three of them this final descent takes place not merely in direction but in being: all three, like Adam tied to the material world, find themselves constrained into bodies and afflicted with corporeal privations. Satan's punishment in the shape he sinned and the marvelous verses in which Milton depicts it are of course familiar to every reader of *Paradise Lost* and need no repetition here. Simultaneously, a similar process is taking place with Sin and Death:

> Meanwhile in Paradise the hellish pair
> Too soon arriv'd, *Sin* there in power before,
> Once actual, now in body, and to dwell
> Habitual habitant; behind her *Death*
> Close following pace for pace, not mounted yet
> On his pale Horse.
>
> [10.585–90]

Although not yet on horseback, Death already holds the form of "this vast unhide-bound Corpse" (10.601), the physical form in which he will manifest himself in so many illustrations and sculptures. This does not only mean that in moving to earth Sin and Death move into allegory: it also means exactly what it says, that they are also moving into the realm of body, and that they now exist corporeally. To paraphrase St. Paul, they reign in our members. Milton insists on this aspect of their transformation and reinforces it by his juxtaposition of the hunger that afflicts the metamorphosed demons—"parcht with scalding thirst and hunger fierce" (10.556)—and sends them climbing for the fruit of the

123

illusory tree of life with the insatiable hunger of Death, who begins his feast with the "Herbes, and Fruits, and Flow'rs" (10.603) of Paradise. Earth may be the kingdom of allegory, in which we see but the shadowy forms of truth, but it is also a corporeal kingdom, and all who enter it must obey the laws of the body—thus Sin's and Death's transformations here, thus Satan's frequent theriomorphisms and his punishment as a serpent, thus too the reversal of these in the Son's incarnation.

That incarnation, or rather, the implicit promise of it, provides for Adam and Eve the pivot around which they arrest the motion of their descent and move toward their illumination by penitence and prayer. Book 11 opens with a succinct *descensus*, complete in all its phases, describing those motions within them and their effects:

> Thus they in lowliest plight repentant stood
> Praying, for from the Mercy-seat above
> Prevenient Grace descending had remov'd
> The stony from thir hearts, and made new flesh
> Regenerate grow instead, that sighs now breath'd
> Unutterable, which the Spirit of prayer
> Inspir'd, and wing'd for Heav'n with speedier flight
> Than loudest Oratory.
>
> [11.1–8]

The result of that prayer and of the Son's intercession for them is yet another *descensus*, in which prevenient grace in the form of Michael comes down from Heaven to tell them that their sentence of death has been deferred and to illuminate their minds about the divine providential plan. The process of that illumination, which in itself corresponds to the central stage of the *descensus*, takes up the remainder of the poem. Several factors complicate it. Most simply, it involves a physical ascent (the verb *ascend* is repeated three times in twelve lines) up "a Hill/Of Paradise the highest" (11.377–78), which Milton connects with part of Christ's temptation in the wilderness. Second, the process of illumination itself culminates in a moral, spiritual, and intellectual ascent for Adam, despite the fact that the actual physical performance of his tasks still lies before him. Michael tells him:

> This having learnt, thou hast attain'd the sum
> Of wisdom; Hope no higher . . .
>   only add
> Deeds to thy knowledge answerable, add Faith,
> Add Virtue, Patience, Temperance, add Love.
>   [12.575–76, 581–83]

Third, the vision in itself describes a complete descent, conversion, and ascent in the continuing workings of sin, the redemption, and the final purgation of creation. The basic synecdochic relationship between the *descensus* and the entirety of the epic poem is nowhere shown more clearly than in this final segment of Milton's poem. This moment of *Paradise Lost*, which corresponds to Aeneas's descent to Hell, Milton presents as a physical ascent which culminates in an intellectual ascent which in turn encapsulates the movements of descent, conversion, and ascent worked out over the entire range of human history, and which yet bears an analogical and metonymic relation, narratively, thematically, and structurally, to the entire poem of which it is a part. All of that is why, at the end of the poem, Milton leaves Adam in a state that corresponds to Aeneas's both at the beginning of the *Aeneid* and at the end of its sixth book: exile and illumination are simultaneous for Adam, as they are for all who with him learn:

>   that suffering for Truth's sake
> Is fortitude to highest victory,
> And to the faithful Death the Gate of Life;
> Taught this by his example whom I now
> Acknowledge my Redeemer ever blest.
>   [12.569–73]

For all those so equipped, descent into the world—"down the Cliff. . . /To the subjected Plain" (12.639–40)—to work out the remainder of their lives also forms their ascent to eternal truth. In that sense, the ending of *Paradise Lost*, despite the fact that it depicts another exile like that of Satan from Heaven which began the poem, constitutes a rising action that completes the motions of the *descensus* that have impelled the poem as a whole and were synopsized in the opening of Book 11: what descends from God is transformed on earth, in space and time, and returns to him again. And in that sense too, the way up and the way down are once again shown to be the same.[11]

Book 12 completes another cycle in the poem, one which began in Book 7 with the Son's irruption from Heaven into Chaos. That creation in the image of God marked, in *Paradise Lost*, the extension of spiritually existent divinity into space and matter, a plastic creation which Adam's sin wrenches out of eternity—he and it were created immortal—and into time. The divine redemptive plan which Michael describes and of which the Son is also the agent impresses the divine likeness upon time as well, bringing it also into God. The sequence here is clear and important: God first begets his own image, the Son, and then creates, purely spiritually, the angels, who are to be incorporated within him by the kingship of his Son. Next he creates physically and spatially, through the Son, in his own image. Finally he creates temporally, in human history, once again by the agency of the Son. Human history, as Milton here conceives it, is nothing more or less than the explication of the Word in time, the unfolding of the eternal and simultaneous in the temporal and sequential. It is also the explication of the Word in the more literary critical sense of the demonstration of just what the Word means. For this reason, this process of explication begins in the poem with Adam's attempts to puzzle out the meaning of "Part of our Sentence, that thy Seed shall bruise/The Serpent's head" (10.1031–32) and his cognate attempt to understand God's image in the Son,

> in whose look serene,
> When angry most he seem'd and most severe,
> What else but favor, grace, and mercy shone?
> [10.1094–96]

Michael, whose mission is to announce the mitigation of man's punishment and to comfort and encourage Adam and Eve, attends to the latter of these first. He brings Adam to the mount of speculation and cleanses his vision—"the Film remov'd/Which that false Fruit that promis'd clearer sight/Had bred" (11.412–14)—and then proceeds to show him the lot of his progeny down to Noah. Adam's visual education follows a carefully graduated sequence. At first, he does not even recognize death, the punishment he himself has merited and which he has introduced into the world; he has no notion of what has taken place before his eyes:

> O Teacher, some great mischief hath befall'n
> To that meek man . . .
> But have I now seen Death? Is this the way
> I must return to native dust? O sight
> Of terror, foul and ugly to behold,
> Horrid to think, how horrible to feel!
>
> [11.450–51, 462–65]

The next vision, of death in all its forms, leads him to question Michael about the divine image: Can it be so debased? Why shouldn't man be freed from such sufferings for the sake of "his Maker's Image" (11.514)? Michael discriminates pointedly in his reply: that divine image "Forsook them, when themselves they vilifi'd/To serve ungovern'd appetite" (11.516–17); thus they disfigure not God's image but their own, since they failed to reverence God's image in themselves. He then shows Adam the pleasanter vision of the people of the plain (11.556–97), to which Adam responds with misplaced enthusiasm, which in turn calls forth rebuke and clarification from Michael. By the end of the next scene, of "oppression, and Sword-Law/Through all the Plain" (11.672–73), Adam is beginning to understand enough of the true content of what he has seen to be able to inquire about details of it. In this case he asks about Enoch, and receives in reply an explanation of true and false heroism (an explanation that Milton has

127

already profited by and used at the opening of Book 9). When scenes of peace and of the flood succeed this vision of war, Adam's analytic powers have sharpened sufficiently for him to draw the correct conclusions: "now I see/Peace to corrupt no less than War to waste" (11.783–84). And when, after this, he sees the ark grounding and the rainbow hung in the sky, he has learned even to read symbols:

> But say, what mean those color'd streaks in Heav'n,
> Distended as the Brow of God appeas'd,
> Or serve they as a flow'ry verge to bind
> The fluid skirts of that same wat'ry Cloud,
> Lest it again dissolve and show'r the Earth?
>
> [11.879–83]

"Dext'rously thou aim'st" (11.884), as Michael tells him, but this symbol-reading forms the farthest reach of Adam's visual education; he is after all, fated by his sin to live where he will see as through a glass darkly, and he has surrendered his right, even his ability, to see God face to face. For this reason Michael now turns to the first form of Adam's own attempts at understanding and proceeds to explain the divine plan to him verbally rather than visually.

Noah acts as the hinge between "the world destroy'd and world restor'd" (12.3). The rainbow that ends the deluge only distantly reflects "the Brow of God appeas'd" (11.880), a beatific vision that Adam and mankind will not attain until "fire purge all things new" (11.900) at the final coming, to which Michael fittingly and briefly refers at the end of Book 11. Noah serves as a sort of second Adam, "a second stock" (12.7) from which mankind begins anew, and as corollary to this second racial beginning, Michael opens a new phase of Adam's education: the world destroyed gives place to the world restored, vision gives place to speech. The account that Michael now begins constitutes the explication of the Word in time, both the gradual explanation of the promise made to Eve that her seed should bruise the serpent's head and the unfolding of the divine image in human time. Human history is divine rhetoric; the burden of that rhetoric, as Milton presents it, is the Word.

Appropriately, this second history begins with a second fall. Nimrod, "Of proud ambitious heart" (12.25) destroys the concord which followed the flood, "in despite of Heav'n" (12.34). This second fall results in the corruption of language, just as the first had produced the corruption of Adam's sight: Babel is its product and its metaphor—"a jangling noise of words unknown/ . . . and the work Confusion nam'd" (12.55, 62). And just as the first half of Adam's education traced the gradual purgation of his vision, this second half will outline the gradual restoration of language, until the final return "In glory of the Father" (12.546) of the Word, "obscurely then foretold,/Now amplier known thy Saviour and thy Lord" (12.543—44). Between these points, Michael step by step clarifies for Adam the promise made to Eve. The word *promise* itself becomes the major vehicle of Adam's education, as he is slowly instructed in both its senses: what it means, implicitly and explicitly, as a verbal contract, and what it means etymologically as that which is "sent forth." Adam's knowledge will be complete, filled with "what this Vessel can contain" (12.559), when those two meanings once again coincide on earth as they always have in Heaven.

Adam's response to Nimrod and the building of Babel seem singularly obtuse: true, he rebukes Nimrod's "Authority usurpt" (12.66), but he concludes his reflections more than lamely by wondering what the tower-builders ever intended to eat up there at the top. Michael ignores that last effusion and uses the example of Nimrod to instruct Adam about inward and outward liberty and the effect of his fall on both. From there he picks up the "one faithful man" (12.113) theme, already announced in Enoch and in Noah and in Book 12 to climax in the Christ. Mention of Abraham naturally introduces the promise made to him and offers the first clarification of the promise made to Eve:

> This ponder, that all Nations of the Earth
> Shall in his Seed be blessed; by that Seed
> Is meant thy great deliverer, who shall bruise
> The Serpent's head; whereof to thee anon
> Plainlier shall be reveal'd.
>
> [12.147–51]

Michael, now embarked upon the history of the chosen people, recounts their fortunes down to Moses and the imposition of the Law. The concept of the Law also introduces the notion of the multiple functions and significances of language: the Law does not merely denote, but also connotes, pointing beyond itself to realities larger than the words themselves:

> God from the Mount of *Sinai*, whose gray top
> Shall tremble, he descending, will himself
> In Thunder, Lightning and loud Trumpet's sound
> Ordain them Laws; part such as appertain
> To civil Justice, part religious Rites
> Of sacrifice, informing them, by types
> And shadows, of that destin'd Seed to bruise
> The Serpent, by what means he shall achieve
> Mankind's deliverance.
>
> [12.227–35]

Adam responds to this information more acutely, inquiring about the relation of the Law and sin, and thus providing Michael the opportunity of anticipating St. Paul and of instructing Adam further in the necessity and complexity of spiritually understanding the words of God:

> So Law appears imperfet, and but giv'n
> With purpose to resign them in full time
> Up to a better Cov'nant, disciplin'd
> From shadowy Types to Truth, from Flesh to Spirit.
>
> [12.300–303]

David next appears in Michael's account, and with him more elaboration of the promise: his throne "For ever shall endure" (12.324), and from his line shall spring the promised seed, to reign forever. This "Cov'nant sworn/To *David*" is "stablisht as the days of Heav'n" (12.346—47), and it will reach fruition in the Son of a virgin and of God, who will "ascend/The Throne hereditary" (12.369–70). Again, Adam grasps only part of Michael's meaning. He understands now why the promise should be couched in terms of "The seed of Woman" (12.379), but he still takes literally the promise of the serpent's bruise, and asks where and when that struggle will take place. Michael answers this by explaining the spiritual meaning of that promise, the undoing of Satan's work in man, and by further elucidating for Adam the nature of the Law and its spiritual fulfillment in love. After this he emphasizes the teaching mission of the Messiah's disciples and their task of promulgating the Word:

> All Nations they shall teach; for from that day
> Not only to the Sons of *Abraham's* Loins
> Salvation shall be Preacht, but to the Sons
> Of *Abraham's* Faith wherever through the world;
> So in his seed all Nations shall be blest.
>
> [12.446–50]

While the disciples discharge this task, the Son shall reascend to Heaven where, as the Word of God, he will be "exalted high/Above all names" (12.457–58) and where he will await the time of his second coming. Adam's understanding of all this consitutes his most acute response so far: he apprehends through it the full dimensions of the paradox of the fortunate fall and all of the ways in which his *culpa* can finally be construed as *felix*. Moreover, the question he eventually asks is a shrewd and realistic one; rather than being overwhelmed by the wonder of it all, he worries about the fate of the followers the Messiah leaves behind. This leads Michael to the climax of his history and of his exegesis: he shifts his attention to the promulgation of the Word on earth and in a parallel manner shifts his emphasis from the promise as spoken contract to the promise and the gospel as written words, both of which are now "sent forth" on earth. A "Comforter . . . /The promise of the Father" (12.486–87) will dwell within the disciples; he "upon thir hearts shall write" (12.489), and they will evangelize all nations, speaking all tongues, and eventually leave "Thir doctrine and thir story written" (12.506) to their successors. Even this language, however, will be corrupted by avarice and ambition, since "those written Records pure" can be "not but by the Spirit understood" (12.513–14). The result will be the reversal of Mosaic law, which by carnal laws tried to point to spiritual truths: now spiritual laws will be enforced by carnal power and "outward Rites and specious forms" (12.534) will satisfy the name of religion. So shall matters continue, despite "what the Spirit within/Shall on the heart engrave" (12.523–24), until the Word is once more sent forth and the promise finally and fully redeemed:

> at return
> Of him so lately promis'd to thy aid,
> The Woman's seed, obscurely then foretold,
> Now amplier known thy Saviour and thy Lord,
> Last in the Clouds from Heav'n to be reveal'd
> In glory of the Father.
>
> [12.541–46]

This completes Adam's epic education, and he draws the proper epical lessons from it, the content of which is always the same, both in the poem and the allegory: self-knowledge, specifically knowledge of one's limitations, whether they be intellectual, physical, or historical. The epic hero is always at the center of vast historical processes which depend not on his transcending his humanity but on his accepting it. The former is precisely what caused Adam's fall, and only acquiescence to his lot with full knowledge can begin to undo that fall:

> Greatly instructed I shall hence depart,
> Greatly in peace of thought, and have my fill
> Of knowledge, what this Vessel can contain;
> Beyond which was my folly to aspire.
>
> [12.557–60]

He has learned too to understand the promise spiritually and all
other things as corollary to it,

> with good
> Still overcoming evil, and by small
> Accomplishing great things, by things deem'd weak,
> Subverting worldly strong, and worldly wise
> By simply meek.
>
> [12.565–69]

To this knowledge Michael can only urge him to join fitting practice, reminding him yet again of the promise and urging him to
unity with Eve, "both in one Faith unanimous though sad"
(12.603). Eve also has learned much during this time, not the least
of which is her large advance in dream psychology ("For God is also
in sleep, and Dreams advise" [12.611]). She too has learned of the
promise and her role in it:

> Such favor I unworthy am voutsaf't,
> By mee the Promis'd Seed shall all restore.
>
> [12.622–23]

But most important, she has relearned her union with Adam, and it
is she who initiates the process of undoing the Fall by sharply
reversing the rhetoric of their conjugal quarrel on the fateful
morning:

> In mee is no delay; with thee to go,
> Is to stay here; without thee here to stay,
> Is to go hence unwilling; thou to mee
> Art all things under Heav'n, all places thou.
>
> [12.615–18]

So in their expulsion from Paradise, Adam and Eve reknit the
union with God and with each other that they violated in their fall
and whose violation *was*, in many senses, their fall. The epic work
of restoration has begun: all that Michael has predicted is contained implicitly in their entry into the world, as they "Through
Eden took their solitary way" (12.649). Their way is solitary be-

cause it is unitary: they are one, and of their now true union will eventually flow, after they "by number . . . manifest/[their] single imperfection, and beget/Like of [their] like" (8.422–24), the ultimate and greater union of manhood with godhead.

The events of Book 12 round Milton's narrative upon itself in many particulars, but none more pertinently than this unitary departure of Adam and Eve from their former home. *Paradise Lost* began with Satan's motion away from God and ends with man's motion away from God: the first of those motions plummeted straight downward in a single act as much physical as moral or spiritual; the last moves downward and away physically only to rise upward and draw near spiritually and morally. Satan's fall has been recast and redirected in Adam's and Eve's fall; his attempt to replicate himself in man has been transformed by the Son into a recreation of the divine image. Satan, solitary at the beginning of the poem, unique in his sin and his exclusion from God, rapidly divides and multiplies till he becomes the whole host of demons, numerically finite though "numberless," each individually trapped in the solitary hell of his own personality and the eternal hell that is spiritual existence outside of God. Adam and Eve, "hand in hand" taking "thir solitary way," have already conquered number for God and through the Son as well as through each other. This is the last and most important reason why the form of their sin cannot be anything but ambivalent: their union, which motivated it, provides the model, the prototype as it were, of their and all humanity's union with the Son, the form who will enwrap personality, finitude, and number within limitless unity. And in the same way, their exile from Eden offers the model for mankind's return to God. Satan's way down is man's way up: motive, act, and form are identical for spiritual beings, but man's radical imperfection—his even greater than angelic finitude—permits the disjunction and disconnection of the three. Ergo Adam's sin: motive laudable, act sinful, form ambivalent. And his exile: motive noble, act honorable, form lamentable. So for man the form of exile and descent can hold an actual content of restoration and rising, descent can in fact constitute an ascent—and that realization, for the reader as much as for Adam, provides *Paradise Lost*'s last and fullest definition of the "promise" and of who and what has been "sent forth." In the identity of their exiles and the inevitability of their returns, the Son, Adam, and Eve form one last trinity which extends the divine activity of transformation and divinity itself into the fallen world of space and time, ultimately to transform that world and bring it home to God.

⚘

Book 12 has also closed the second six-book unit of *Paradise Lost*, its second complete *descensus*: the descent into the *inferos* of matter described in the account of creation and Adam's account of his own creation, the pivotal conversion effected by human sin and divine justice and mercy, and the reascent to spirit narrated by Michael's preview of human history and divine providence. The first six books of the poem functioned in a similar manner: the descent to the literal and moral *inferos* of Hell, the central arresting and conversion of the descent through divine foreknowledge, angelic guardians, and still inviolate human innocence, and the reascent, through Raphael's narrative, to Heaven and the expulsion of the demons. Those simple patterns share points of basic significance, chief among which is the *locus* of conversion: in both cases it is earth, and in both cases the work of conversion is shared by man and the Son. That the Son should be the agent of conversion is only logical: that is his being. But that man and earth should so share does not follow of necessity, but by divine choice: both, after all, bear the image of the Son, impressed on them in their creation, and thereby distantly reflect his nature; both are the middle ground of matter and spirit, and both consequently are contingent beings, informed beings whose existence (to be scholastic) is not identical to their essence. They are, in short, the only creatures (once the angels have made their eternal choices) in existence capable of changing: they are, almost by definition, the instruments fashioned by eternal immutability to incorporate time and change within itself. God is pure being, in which (to continue the scholastic terminology) essence and existence are coextensive. The angels, as purely spiritual contingent beings, chose once and forever their mode of existence, thereby expressing ineluctably their essences. Outside of them, "in the beginning" was only Chaos—unformed matter, pure, passive existent, inert yet constantly changing, dead but eternal: the logical contrary of God, so to speak. God's own epic task has been to incorporate his contrary within himself, to make himself "All in All." In this respect, *Paradise Lost* is a cosmogony just like Dante's poem, divided into three hierarchical planes: the moral and physical (it too is carved out of Chaos) hell of demonic defection; the moral and physical middle ground of earth; and the moral and physical heaven of the conclusion of Michael's prophecies, which will include the "purg'd and refin'd" (12.548) earth, whether:

> New Heav'n and Earth shall to the Ages rise,
> Or down from Heav'n descend.
>
> [10.647–48]

By that point, of course, there will be neither up nor down, body nor spirit, earth nor Heaven: "God shall be All in All" (4.341). Satan will be then excluded forever from, man included eternally into, the being of God, and matter complicated into spirit, all through the agency of the Son, whose own *descensus* and epic tasks these are.

From this follows the paramount structure of *Paradise Lost* and its most important modification of the orthodox arrangement of the units of the *descensus*. Rather than a central unit which in miniature encapsulizes and reflects the sections before and after it, *Paradise Lost* builds itself around a nuclear four books describing the works of the Son (inclusion and exclusion, complication and explication: transformation) which are, as I argued earlier, constitutive of the Son in the poem, and the two wings which surround this nuclear unit reflect it rather than it them. Those four books are the linchpin of the entire poem, ending the cycle of Satanic rebellion and beginning the cycle of material creation, each action shadowing the other: the Son's expulsion of Satan from Heaven predicts his final defeat in time; the entry of the Son into Chaos and his creation there in God's image recalls Satan's plunge through Chaos to Hell and God's own begetting in his own image that spurred the Satanic rebellion. All creation mirrors God, as all creation is enveloped in the Son, and the structure of Milton's creation reflects that order in exactly that order: the Son is central to the poem as he is to the universe of which the poem is a miniature model.

This leaves one last epic hero and one last epic task as yet undiscussed: the poet and his poem. Milton himself implicitly recognizes his task as heroic when he applies to himself the Sybilline description of the difficulty of visiting and returning from Hell:

> Taught by the heav'nly Muse to venture down
> The dark descent, and up to reascend,
> Though hard and rare.
>
> [3.19–21]

That he should choose that particular Virgilian episode and the specific concepts of descent and ascent as the terms by which he establishes his own epic credentials seems not merely consistent with the overall plan and execution of his poem but, to my mind at least, well-nigh inescapable. The Sybil appears to be a sister muse of the Urania he later invokes, both related to "Eternal Wisdom" (7.9) who presided over creation, and thus linked in turn with the "holy Light, offspring of Heav'n first-born" (3.1) and with the spirit that:

> from the first
> Wast present, and with mighty wings outspread
> Dove-like satst brooding on the vast Abyss
> And mad'st it pregnant.
>
> [1.19–22]

137

This sort of syncretism is never casual in Milton, and it is very much of a piece with his distinctions of his muse from that inferior one who inspired, and failed to save, "the *Thracian* Bard" (7.34), Orpheus. The figure of Orpheus of course serves Milton in two capacities, as inspired poet who sang of creation and as at least partially successful pilgrim to and returnee from the underworld. In his invocation to Book 3, Milton explicitly asks us to see himself as an Orpheus, returned from:

> the *Stygian* Pool, though long detain'd
> In that obscure sojourn, while in my flight
> Through utter and through middle darkness borne
> With other notes than to th' *Orphean* Lyre
> I sung of *Chaos* and *Eternal Night*.
> [3.14–18]

His superiority to Orpheus he of course attributes to his "Celestial Patroness" (9.21), at least with regard to his poetry, but he seems to imply as well that he is superior as pilgrim, in the reality of his descent and his rising. When he addresses the light and tells us that "thee I revisit now" (3.13), that return lends at least some of its reality to his descent, just as the inward shining of "Celestial Light" (3.51) lends its authority to his recounting of "Things invisible to mortal sight" (3.55). So emphatic is he on this point that he even casts himself as Satan journeying through Chaos (though, like his comparison of himself to Orpheus, this is a simile with a difference): he revisits the light "with bolder wing" (3.13), having "Escap't the *Stygian* Pool" (3.14) in his "flight" (3.15). With Satan he has fallen, and with Satan he has reascended—but the poet has been "Taught by the heav'nly Muse" (3.19), and he has accomplished his journey properly.

What all this means, I think, is that Milton regards his *Paradise Lost* in the same light and the same manner as the famous letter to Can Grande della Scala regards the *Commedia*: it is a scripture analogous to sacred Scripture, and as such its narrative—its *littera*—is true (or at least, it is the fiction of both

138

poems, as of most other epics, that they are true). In Milton's case, as in Dante's, this results from a profound understanding of the place of the individual poem within the epic tradition. That tradition had always seen the epic as encyclopedic in its narrative (Homer as the source of all knowledge, from tactics to carpentry) and philosophic in its allegory, and had further unified both inner and outer strands of interpretation into a kind of proto-*Bildungsroman* tracing the growth in wisdom of the hero (Everyman or Superman, depending on your critic). The goal of epic, for hero and for reader, was always the *summmum bonum*, felicity, beatitude—again depending on your critic. Milton's great innovation within those spacious confines is really no innovation at all, but a logical extension of Dante's techniques. Dante had gone to the heart of contemporary understanding of epic and made the *descensus ad inferos* the frame of his poem, both narratively and allegorically: what had been at the center of epic he made not merely the heart but also the skeleton of it, and moreover he very boldly did so in the narrative itself. That is, he took what had been the allegory of epic and made it the *littera* of his poem. Indeed, Landino in his commentary on the *Aeneid* praises Dante for precisely this, and seems to regard his practice as a paradigm for literary imitation.[12] Milton has overgone him to the extent that he has completely externalized all of the internals of epic: *Paradise Lost* either contains no allegory or is all allegory. There can be no middle ground between those positions, except perhaps the scarcely less comfortable one (to which I personally incline) of declaring them both true. It is important to remember, in this connection, that the "language of accommodation" is invoked only once in the poem, and not by Milton. Raphael alone complains of the difficulty of relating "To human sense th' invisible exploits/Of warring Spirits" (5.565–66) and says that he will resort to "lik'ning spiritual to corporal forms,/As may express them best" (5.573–74). Milton, with less diffidence, merely states that his "advent'rous Song" (1.13):

with no middle flight intends to soar
Above th' *Aonian* Mount, while it pursues
Things unattempted yet in Prose or Rhyme.
[1.14–16]

As a man speaking to men, Milton does not have to accommodate his perceptions to a foreign mode of speech; he perceives humanly and reports humanly, so that as long as the heavenly muse raises, supports, and illumines him, his language is true, even though his rhetoric may vary. Indeed, even the variations of his rhetoric form a part of the truth of his statements: for instance, the imagery of vastness and wealth, the ornate language of the conventional epic sublime, is largely confined to the depiction of the false heroism of Satan, a conventional rhetoric bearing the burden of and simultaneously exposing the hollowness of a conventional idea of greatness, an argument less heroic than Milton's true subject. By the same token, when the Father and Son converse, their speech is almost entirely free of imagery; instead of figures of speech, they employ figures of thought and devices of amplitude, by which Milton portrays not only their primarily intellectual/spiritual mode of being but also their mutual relation of complication and explication. So too Michael's narrative style is simple and direct (compare his account of the drowning of Pharaoh's host [12.210ff.] with Milton's earlier simile [1.304ff.]), minimizing the importance of individual human events and hurrying over "this transient World, the Race of time" (12.554) to return to eternity and God. Milton claims for his poem precisely the truth of Scripture, nothing more and nothing less. The Muse he invokes is the same one:

that on the secret top
Of *Oreb*, or of *Sinai*, didst inspire
That Shepherd, who first taught the chosen Seed,
In the Beginning how the Heav'ns and Earth
Rose out of *Chaos*.
[1.6–10]

And she it is who "Visit'st my slumbers Nightly" (7.29) and "dictates to me slumb'ring" (9.23); she it is who will raise his name and his poem "who brings it nightly to my Ear" (9.47). These are claims for literal inspiration: "The meaning, not the Name" (7.5) Milton calls upon, and that meaning is the Word, whether one names it Urania, Heavenly Muse, Wisdom, or Light.

Milton's four invocations share many similarities: they always, for instance, associate the creation of the world with the creation of the poem *Paradise Lost*, frequently contrast pagan and Christian muses, reflect on the poet's own debilities or dangers, and all conclude with (it could hardly be otherwise) pleas for or affirmations of illumination. Each of them contains and describes at least one microcosmic *descensus*, the descent of heavenly creative power into the darkness and *inferos* of John Milton, its transformation there, and reemergence as the irradiated language of *Paradise Lost*, equal to "the highth of this great Argument" (1.24). Some contain other brief *descensus* as well (as the first, which moves from the disobedience and fall, to exile—"loss of *Eden*"—to "one greater Man" and the regaining of "the blissful seat," all in a few lines of verse), but all share this one basic pattern, the descent of Urania into the darkness of Milton's slumbers or blindness, the illumination of that darkness, and the production thence of the inspired words of his "unpremeditated Verse" (9.24), which constitute the reascent of the divine creativity. What this makes of Milton is crucial to our final understanding of his poem because it completes in a particular and multivalent way the web of analogies he has already established between the Son, the created world, and man. It makes Milton like earth a *locus* of transformation, like man an agent of change, like the Son himself a nodal point in the triad, a center of explication and complication. What proceeds from God is transformed in him and returns to God and to man, justifying the ways of God to man and incorporating human creativity into God. Milton's role is analogous to the role of the Graces in Spenser's epic: his task, like theirs and the Son's, lies in weaving the rhythms of complication and explication, enfolding and unfolding, by which eternity and time, permanence and

141

change, will be wed to each other.[13]*Paradise Lost* is a Scripture because Milton is an agent of the Word, creating by the word an explication of the Word, following his own dark path into himself and the world that he and we may emerge like Adam and Eve from the darkness, to find a new world and a new poem all before us.

3

Chaucer:

TROILUS AND CRISEYDE

why separate then

w/e somehow

Treating Chaucer's *Troilus and Criseyde* in a study such as this one is made difficult by the general failure of both medievalists and critics to recognize the genre of the poem and its place in the canon of epic poetry. Many, indeed, would probably actively dispute labeling it an epic; most, certainly, prefer to consign it to the scholarly and historical limbo of romance, a kind of catchall non-genre and elephant graveyard of critical conundrums. Fortunately, Chaucer himself was far more explicit than his commentators have been, and he several times and in several ways identifies for us the genre of his poem. The most readily apparent of these, to my eye at least, lies in his adaptation of the structural and thematic apparatus of the *descensus*, which I will discuss later in this essay. Important too in the identification of *Troilus* as epic is the Chaucerian reworking of the Dido-Aeneas relation from the early books of the *Aeneid* (this aspect of the poem will also be discussed later). The most explicit

143

clues can perhaps be found in Chaucer's frequent allusions to or reminders of Statius's *Thebaid*, itself an epic imitative of Virgil's masterwork, and seemingly exploited by Chaucer because of the parallel narrative frames of the besieged and entrapped city and of the prominence in the Latin narrative of Tisiphone and her sister Furies, who analogously preside over Chaucer's tale. The characters themselves frequently call attention to "This romaunce . . . of Thebes" (2.100) of which "been ther maked bookes twelve" (2.108), and throughout the poem cite the examples or actions of Laius, Oedipus, and "bisshop Amphiorax."[1] (Chaucer's simple use of the term *romaunce* to describe the obviously epic *Thebaid* seems to show clearly enough that he—or his characters at any rate—think of epic and romance as identical forms.) In addition, Chaucer has quite gratuitously appropriated a few important names from the *Thebaid* for minor characters of his own invention—notably, Antigone for one of Criseyde's nieces and "Argyve" (Argia) for her mother—thereby reminding his readers again of the *Thebaid* and its narrative. Most explicit of all, of course, is his direct imitation of Statius's coda to his own epic, Chaucer's famous "Go, litel bok" stanza (5.1786ff.). It is not sufficient merely to regard this as a literary *topos*: *topoi* are functional, and this one is no exception. It identifies the genre of the poem and establishes its pedigree, an epic poem by Chaucer out of "Virgile, Ovide, Omer, Lucan, and Stace" (5.1792), the greatest narrative poets of antiquity, two of them, Ovid and Lucan, offering models of the kind of apotheosis and illumination Troilus will very shortly undergo, and the other three the great patrons and exemplars of epic. There can be no doubt that Chaucer saw his poem as epic: the real question is what he meant by that.

❧

Our dealings with *The Faerie Queene* and *Paradise Lost* enable us to abstract some elements of the epic genre as practiced in England after Chaucer; however anachronistic such a procedure may be, we are free to seek for the presence of those same elements or their ancestors in Chaucer's poem. In the same way, we can step back before Landino and extrapolate the elements of the commentary tradition which would have been available to Chaucer and use them to determine the parameters of epic for a medieval poet. And we have a third aid as well: Dante's comments about his own epic in the letter to Can Grande della Scala. Whether Chaucer knew it or not is completely irrelevant: it, and the practice of Spenser and Milton, and the tenets of the commentators, all provide us with valuable information about the genre of epic. Only an examination of the *Troilus and Criseyde* itself will tell us anything about Chaucer's actual exploitation or ignoring of that generic material.

First, then, what do *The Faerie Queene* and *Paradise Lost*, considered on the most abstract level, rarefied from the details of their peculiar narratives, tell us about epic as genre? What are their irreducible common demoninators? The *descensus*, clearly, but the *descensus* most importantly in its moral and intellectual guises, in its broadest application as metaphor for man's state in this world and somewhat more restrictively as gauge, measure, or road map of his spiritual and intellectual success or failure. *De facto*, such use of the *descensus* has also meant that both poets emphasized the concepts of motion and rest—motion through the sublunary world, through the forest of material things, through time itself, to the resting point of God, or Vision, or Oneness. Still proceeding deductively, it is easy to see that such notions in turn dictated the translation in each poem of these concepts into the metaphors of pilgrimage and quest, with all of the attendant apparatus of false goals, misdirections, false resting places, bondage, and captivity: each quest proceeds (archetypally; obviously there are myriads of individual variants) from initiation through errors and mishaps, physical, spiritual, and intellectual bondage to illumination, freedom, and rest. In our two examples so far, that final goal has been expressed by both purged vision and restored language, sight and speech returned as it were to grace. All of this narrative/thematic frame of the *descensus* supports itself on the

145

structural frame of the *descensus*, the tripartite symmetrical skeleton which I have discussed in connection with both preceding poems.

Second, all of these aspects and emphases are already present in the Virgilian commentaries of Fulgentius and Bernardus Silvestris, the major pre-Landinian analyses of the *Aeneid* and through it of epic. Indeed, it is from them that I derived the notion of the centrality of the *descensus* and its concomitants to the genre. In the Fulgentian and Bernardine versions of epic, man's soul descends from eternity to wander and suffer in the corporeal world, to enter deeper into darkness and bondage until, in a paradoxical still deeper descent which is really an ascent, it is illuminated, freed, and at last reascends to light, eternity, spirituality. Even the pseudo-Fulgentian commentary on the *Thebaid* preserves these outlines, however crudely, by making the besieged city of Thebes (man's soul) the hero of the poem for which, in a kind of psychomachia, greed and lust, aided or opposed by worldly philosophy and foresight, struggle and which successive vices dominate after the sacred light (Laius) has been slain: finally the soul of man is freed by humility and "the grace of the goodness of God" in the person of Theseus.[2] Even though it stands in place, Thebes too performs the necessary pilgrimage through sin and bondage into grace and freedom.

That all of this should sound familiar is no accident, since it is of course the abstract pattern of Dante's *Divina Commedia*. Every point I have enumerated tallies with Dante's poem, even to the purgation of speech and sight which concludes that epic. The pattern of the *descensus* is so overt in the *Commedia*, beginning as it does with a narrative descent to Hell, as to call for little comment as a structural metaphor: the three stages of descent, conversion, and ascent correspond exactly to the three great divisions of the poem.[3] But the centrality of the *descensus* to Dante's conception of his poem and the archetypal significance the pattern of the *descensus* seemingly held for him is perhaps less apparent, even though

146

Dante signals it quite clearly in his letter to Can Grande by his choice of scriptural passage with which to illustrate the polysemous nature of this work: "When Israel went out of Egypt, the house of Jacob from a people of strange language; Judah was his sanctuary, and Israel his dominion" (Psalm 113/4).[4] Dante lists for Can Grande the literal, allegorical, moral, and anagogical senses of the verse, offering them as a miniature of the way his far lengthier poem is to be understood. But there is another more literary dimension to the verse he has chosen, about which Dante says nothing—or perhaps felt no need to say anything. That verse from Psalm 113 encapsulates the whole of Exodus; it is shorthand for an entire biblical narrative just as Dante uses it as shorthand for his entire narrative. Those two narratives, the scriptural and the poetic, are identical: beginning in the house of bondage, passing the Red Sea and enduring wanderings and purgation in the wilderness, and at last attaining the promised land. That is, the biblical verse too recreates the pattern of the *descensus* (in its specifically theological, specifically Christian form) and, I think, demonstrates the absolute centrality of that pattern to Dante's deepest thinking about his own poem. Dante has gone to the heart of epic as it could be understood by his culture and in the very basal structure and narrative of his poem has embodied, in their simultaneously strictest and richest forms, its most literal and most elaborate manifestation. The dichotomies set up by the biblical verse provide the tensions which animate Dante's poem and which we have already seen sustaining the epics of Spenser and Milton: the house of bondage as opposed to the promised land, implicitly mediated by the wanderings in the wilderness, translate themselves into the dialectics of captivity and freedom, ignorance and knowledge, pride and humility, part and whole, and all are embraced by and embrace the framework of the *descensus*. Chaucer, in his "Go, litel bok" stanza, when he distinguishes his "litel . . . tragedye" from the comedy in which he may yet figure, is for himself at least distinguishing his poem from Dante's and from Dante's idea of

147

comedy and of epic—but he is doing so in Dante's terms and on Dante's premises, and it is within those grounds that we too must explore his meaning and his choices.

Style

! >

The most significant way Chaucer distinguishes his epic practice from Dante's (for our purposes I must speak of Chaucer as if he were fully aware of Dante's endeavors; an untruth, perhaps, but of such fictions poetry and useful criticism are made) is also, aside from scope, the most obvious: his choice of "classical" setting and subject matter as opposed to Christian. *Troilus and Criseyde* and the *Commedia* in their respective selections of subjects and narratives prefigure one of the major and central controversies of Renaissance epic criticism, i.e., the suitability of Christian themes, stories, and "machinery" to epic poetry, or, conversely, the appropriateness of pagan themes, stories, and machinery to a Christian audience. This conflict must have been latent in the genre from the moment early Christianity ceased to condemn totally all of pagan culture (if it ever did so) and began to carry off the gold of Egypt, to extract the kernel of charity from the husk of lying fable. Certainly the tension between pagan and Christian is quite overt in Fulgentius's treatment of the *Aeneid*: more than once the interlocutor Fulgentius draws a parallel between what his spectral commentator Virgil tells him was his meaning and some specifically Christian or biblical notion; in each case the fictive Virgil is made to deny, emphatically, that Christian truth was known to him. The prolix Virgil that Fulgentius so comically creates leaves no doubt that he is the obtuse Fulgentius's intellectual superior and responds to his frequent Christianizing interruptions with impatient humility:

> "You may see what the true Majesty has taught you, while I can only set forth what I see." [122]
> "I am delighted, little man, with the meanings you have proposed, for even though truth did not provide me with a full account of the good life, yet even over my unillumined mind it scattered its sparks with a sort of groping accuracy. As I started to say. . . ." [123]
> "I would not be a pagan if I did not leaven so many

148

Stoic truths with a pinch of Epicurean foolishness. No one is permitted to know all the truth except you Christians, on whom shines the sun of truth. But I have not come as an expositor well versed in your books of Scripture, in the sense that I should argue about matters I ought to receive with understanding, and not rather throw light on matters I well undersood. Now listen to the rest." [133]

So too in the commentary of Bernardus, citations of scriptural parallels are relatively rare, and the great bulk of Bernardus's interpretation consists of broadly ethical allegorizing of a distinctly "nondenominational" cast. Even the work that is regarded as one of Chaucer's more important "sources" for the *Troilus*, the versified Dares of Joseph of Exeter, resolutely preserves this tension between pagan and Christian poetry and knowledge: at the end of the poem, as at the beginning, Joseph announces his intention of writing a greater poem, about the Crusades. He will tune "the lyre of sacred song;" he will sing "in a grander style." "[A] more glorious Apollo will come down from heaven" to inspire him, and he will labor "to produce that which is worthy of a grander lyre."[5]

This pronounced dichotomy in the epic tradition between pagan and Christian elements endows Chaucer's choice of subject in the *Troilus* with an initial interpretative significance which we would be well advised not to ignore. It means, in effect, that in setting his story in "classical" times and in suppressing most reference to Christianity (the few explicitly Christian references in the poem all occur as oaths or expletives in the characters' speech), Chaucer is deliberately eschewing the polysemousness that Dante prized. He is cutting himself off from the fourfold allegory of Scripture and leaving open to himself and his poem only the sort of loose ethical allegory that we find in Fulgentius and Bernardus. The *Troilus* cannot be read patristically; its subject matter and its genre bar this, and Chaucer makes no attempt—as he would quite overtly have to—to circumvent this limitation. The negative evidence is unanimous; the bulk of the poem and the whole of the story transpire in a non-Christian universe, a world from which the doctrinal content of Christianity is simply absent. It is this absence, this void, that provides both the impetus for and the coherence of Chaucer's concluding address to "yonge, fresshe folkes" (5.1835) to turn to "thilke God that after his ymage/Yow made" (5.1839–40). That explicitly Christian advice Chaucer carefully brackets between two syntactically parallel stanzas that definitively illustrate the exclusively non-Christian context of the rest of the poem:

> Swich fyn hath, lo, this Troilus for love!
> Swich fyn hath al his grete worthynesse!
> Swich fyn hath his estat real above,
> Swich fyn his lust, swich fyn hath his noblesse!
> Swych fyn hath false worldes brotelnesse!
> And thus bigan his lovying of Criseyde,
> As I have told, and in this wise he deyde.
>
> [5.1828–34]

> Lo here, of payens corsed olde rites,
> Lo here, what alle hire goddes may availle;
> Lo here, thise wrecched worldes appetites;
> Lo here, the fyn and guerdoun for travaille
> Of Jove, Appollo, of Mars, of swich rascaille!
> Lo here, the forme of olde clerkis speche
> In poetrie, if ye hire bokes seche.
>
> [5.1849–55]

So too does he offer the book to "moral Gower" (5.1856) and "philosophical Strode" (5.1857) for correction, since ethics and philosophy rather than theology are the appropriate *artes* to be brought to bear upon it. For this same reason, he can list the *Troilus* among the "enditynges of worldly vanitees" at the end of *The Canterbury Tales*, where he also makes explicit the Dantean nature of the comedy that, at the end of the *Troilus*, he hopes "to make in" (5.1788):

> ... and graunte me grace of verray penitence, confessioun and satisfaccioun to doon in this present lyf, thurgh the benigne grace of hym that is kyng of kynges and preest over alle preestes, that boghte us with the precious blood of

his herte; so that I may been oon of hem at the day of doom
that shulle be saved.

All of this means that Chaucer has chosen to locate his poem
outside of Christianity, outside of the dominion of grace and the
intricacies of theology, outside of the realm of fourfold allegory and
patristic exegesis, while briefly contrasting, at the end of the poem,
the scope and possibilities of action available to his characters to
those far different ones available to his audience. He has done a
similar thing before, to a similar end: in the *Book of the Duchess*,
he has so truncated and altered the Ovidian Ceyx and Alcyone
story as to defuse its allegorical possibilities and thereby draw an
important implicit contrast between pagan and Christian. Ovid's
story, in *Metamorphoses* 11, recounts the drowning of Ceyx in a
storm at sea, his wife Alcyone's dream vision of his doom, her
subsequent despair and suicide, and the transformation of both
into seabirds. In the hands of the allegorizers, this became a fable of
salvation, a parable of ultimate Christian resurrection.[6] Chaucer's
version of that tale cuts off all possibility of such an allegorical
reading: as the dream figure of his Ceyx reports, "I nam but ded"
(204), and Alcyone "deyede within the thridde morwe" (214). That
is all: no transformation, no resurrection, no reunited happiness.
Within the framework of the *Book of the Duchess*, with its overall
richness of allusion to Revelations and its progress through the
canonical hours of the ecclesiastical day, the absence of resurrection and transcendence in the "classical" story functions as a vivid
contrast to the implicit promise of such consolation in the contemporary one, forcing the reader to see the barrenness and fragil-
ity of "worldes blysse" (209) in itself. In just the same way, at the
end of the *Troilus*, Chaucer's mention of:

> hym, the which that right for love
> Upon a crois, oure soules for to beye,
> First starf, and roos, and sit in hevene above
> [5.1842–44]

draws the same sharp contrast with Troilus's *Liebestod* and the spiritual poverty of his world and the very limited sort of transcendence it is capable of.

Chaucer's deliberate choice of short-circuiting the allegorical possibilities of his poem offers him corresponding advantages, however. For all its spiritual impoverishment, the world of Troilus and of the *Troilus* is contrastingly rich in psychology and emotion. This seems to have been Chaucer's aim: by eliminating the distractions of allegory, particularly allegory of a scriptural type, with its constant motion away from the text, away from particulars to generals, from psychology to typology, he frees himself to focus on the intricacies of human emotion in a recognizable human landscape. No character has the benefit of any higher knowledge or superior insight; all, like Fulgentius's Virgil, are forced to work out their lot with strictly human equipment, with limited knowledge, abilities, and weaknesses. In effect Chaucer has opted for a protohumanist point of view, making man and man's ways in this world the center of his story. It does not seem to me an exaggeration to say that Chaucer, by freeing himself of what for him was the encumbrance of allegory in *Troilus and Criseyde*, created the possibility of *The Canterbury Tales*, the human comedy that so pointedly balances Dante's divine one at the pinnacle of medieval literary achievement. (Correspondingly, I see no harm in juxtaposing Chaucer's exploration of the psychology of love in *Troilus* with Dante's elaboration of the metaphysics of love in the *Vita Nuova*.) The overarching frame of the pilgrimage encloses Chaucer's pageant of self-revealing and world-exploring characters as surely as it does Dante's. Both poets reach the universal by way of the particular (in contrast to Spenser and Milton, whose poetic practice achieves the particular through the mythic and universal). The vital differences between them lie in their respective foci, in Chaucer's declining—or disbelieving—the option of transcendence. (It is important to note carefully the exact nature of the very limited transcendence Troilus attains after his death: his vision is bounded by "The erratik sterres" [5.1812], his insight limited to a rather vague *contemptus mundi* in the face of the even vaguer "pleyn felicite/That is in hevene above" [i.e., above him still; 5.1818–19]. Even the reader is not allowed any comfortable perch from which to appraise *him*: aside from all the critical controversy about where Troilus is when he looks back to earth, Chaucer deliberately and thoroughly obscures Troilus's final disposition—"And forth he wente, shortly for to telle,/Ther as Mercurye sorted hym to dwelle" [5.1826–27]). That choice necessarily makes fallen humanity and its finite world the appropriate actors and the only possible stage for Chaucer's essentially humanist art. He succeeds, in the *Troilus*, in circumventing allegory, in focussing attention on this world, now, and on a proper human response to it. The relation of the *Troilus* to the epic tradition that Chaucer repeatedly invokes is thus an ironic one, a relation of reversal and frustration. Troilus is not given to us as Everyman, but as a specific historical particular, and Lollius is—fictively—real history. Troilus and Criseyde are negative exempla rather than allegorical figures: they do not perform a meditative descent, but rather live an ethical one.

Troy and its attendant literary history provided Chaucer with a natural setting for such emphases, a setting which in itself facilitated the discarding of allotropic allegory. Troy exists in literature almost as an embodiment of finitude: ringed in by enemies, enclosed within its walls, inescapably doomed to total destruction, it is circumscribed in time and space, confined to its purely material dimensions (the gods too desert Troy, war against it). Its history illustrates the turnings of Fortune's wheel, presents a paradigm of *de casibus* tragedy. Moreover, Troy is a morally questionable entity, and not just in respect to the rape of Helen. Troy has always been ungrateful to the gods, has often affronted them by its pride. Joseph of Exeter's Dares thus apostrophizes it:

> O rich and mighty Troy, o Pergamum, you will never yield quietly to any God! The powers above, the Fates and their strong threads, will not be unjust. The native race is itself forging its own fateful destiny, the Trojans are earning from a once kindly heaven exile, swords, and flames. [6]

153

Later in the poem, when speaking of Priam's rebuilding the city, Joseph makes a particularly charged comparison between Troy and Babel:

> A loftier palace rose, its summit soaring into the clouds above. It would have stood as tall as the line dividing man's world from the Gods', if it had not been so reckless and had been content with its rightful share of space. Instead, it invaded heaven, presuming upon a sphere not its own. It more than Babel's tower deserved the dividing up of tongues, it more than Pelion piled on Ossa deserved the thunderbolts of Jove. [13–14]

In addition, of course, the moral climate of Troy is typified in literature, in Dares as well as in Virgil, by the choice of Paris and its significance and by the installation of Helen as almost the presiding deity of the city. The Virgilian commentary of Bernardus Silvestris realizes the fullest implications of all these notions. From the comments scattered throughout his exegesis of the *Aeneid*, one can extract a coherent and consistent vision of Troy in its allegorical dimensions. Troy is the human body, presided over by the spirit (15, 45, 97).[7] Priam is passion, dominating the body and giving birth to sense and fear (Paris and Deiphobos [99]). Sense prefers the life of pleasure to either theory or action (the judgment of Paris [46]) and consequently is awarded Helen (etymologically, "goddess residing"), earthly riches which dwell and rule on earth (99). The Greeks besieging Troy are vices or necessities vexing the body (99); Trojan women are the frailties of this flesh (26). The Trojan horse represents lechery, and by this vice the city is destroyed (102).Similarly, Chaucer's many allusions, throughout the *Troilus*, to the *Thebaid* point to an almost identical allegorical dimension: a besieged city (man's soul), struggled for by lust and greed (Eteocles and Polyneices), dominated by pride (Creon), and almost destroyed before being liberated by humility and the grace of God (Theseus). Besides sharing a common tenor, these allegories function similarly in their broadly ethical rather than specifically theological focus. Moreover, and to my mind most important, these are autotropic allegories: they move us inward rather than outward by focussing our attention on the psychological processes at work in an individual and by holding us firmly in this material, emotional world rather than sublimating us to any transcendent spiritual or intellectual sphere. The whole allegorical background provided by the Troy setting that Chaucer uses locks us into the corporeal world and denies any access to the workings of grace (the sole exception is the literal *deus ex machina* enacted by Theseus, and he or any equivalent character simply does not exist in *Troilus and Criseyde*). Thus the entire literary background, narrative and allegorical, that provides the setting and the foil for Chaucer's poem works to underline the importance of the poet's final condemnation of "payens corsed olde rites" (5.1849) while forcing us and Chaucer's contemporary audience to jettison the expectations of allegory, at least of the allotropic, spiritualizing variety, and to devote our attention to the complexities and importance of intellectual and emotional responses to a finite corporeal world. The precise point of such allegory as Chaucer employs is not to move us into abstractions but to focus us sharply on this world. What allegory exists in *Troilus and Criseyde* functions as an extension of psychology, giving the reader a grid against which to measure the characters' personal development. Thus, as I hope to show, all of the classical *inferos* imagery of Book 2 serves as an ethical rather than a theological location, just as does the entire pre-Christian setting of the poem. Chaucer is talking about this world, not about Paradise, and talking about it with full awareness of its limitations, even though talking about it exclusively: this is why, among other reasons, *Troilus and Criseyde* is his tragedy and not the comedy he hopes someday to make. That, *The Canterbury Tales* will later create by means of the contrasting (to the *Troilus*) scaffolding of the pilgrimage—while still preserving the quotidian focus and psychological complexity that the deliberate stripping down of his literary tools and resources, which Chaucer practices in *Troilus*, first enables him to call into being.

155

Chaucer makes clear from the outset that *Troilus and Criseyde* is going to be, to understate slightly, an unusual poem. I am hard put to think of another poem, classical or English, that names a Fury as its Muse. The choice is an unlikely one at best and needs serious examination.

are there any?

The mere presence of Tisiphone performs one immediate function, that of location: it tells us clearly that we are already in the underworld, that the descent has already been accomplished—that is, in terms of the threefold motion of the *descensus* proper, that the poem that is to follow this strange invocation will constitute the central portion of that triad, the section of conversion and/or transformation. The end of the poem confirms this concentration on the middle of the *descensus* by depicting in a few brief stanzas (and vaguely, as I have already remarked) Troilus's ascent:

> And whan that he was slayn in this manere,
> His lighte goost ful blisfully is went
> Up to the holughnesse of the eighthe spere.
> [5.1807–9]

We can puzzle out easily enough the nature of this descent: of the four options open to us, we can eliminate right away that of magic (there is no evidence whatever for it) and the moral descent (when, shortly, we first see Troilus, he has as yet done nothing to merit either praise or blame, save militarily). It remains possible that, for the narrator and the reader, this is an intellectual or meditative descent; the rest of the poem does indeed eventually corroborate that suspicion. But for the poem itself, and for its principal characters, the descent that Tisiphone's presence announces functions primarily as a descent into the body. As Bernardus Silvestris remarks, "Before philosophy grew into a state of vigor, the professors of theology denied that the lower regions were anything except

156

human bodies; indeed, they called the lower regions bodies because they had discovered nothing else lower among things" (28). "And, therefore, since nothing is lower than the human body, it is called *infernum*, the lower region. Indeed, we also read that souls are forcibly held in the lower regions as if in spiritual prisons; people say that souls suffer the same thing in the body through vice" (29). Tisiphone then ushers us into the world of the body, of the physical *inferos*, for which, as we already know from Bernardus, Troy is a symbolic equivalent. That the narrator calls upon her to help him "for t'endite" (1.6) "The double sorwe of Troilus" (1.1) strengthens the etymologically inescapable link between Troilus and Troy: "kyng Priamus sone of Troye" (1.2), little Troy, the son of passion, is defined for us as much by the patroness of his tale as he is by his name, birth, and nation. Ostensibly, to judge from the portion of the *descensus* pattern Chaucer is utilizing, Troilus's task will consist of learning the limits of his corporeal nature and moving himself from matter to spirit, transforming the downward thrust of the descent into the upward motion of the ascent. That the narrative movement of the poem, "Fro wo to wele, and after out of joie" (1.4), contradicts this does not necessarily mean that the intellectual and moral ascent is also frustrated—though it certainly casts grave doubt on the possibility of the orthodox completion of the *descensus* pattern.

Indeed, the "double sorwe" itself offers some disturbing ambiguities. Certainly it refers primarily to Troilus's sufferings before he and Criseyde are united and after she has left him—but it is also a very common technical phrase that, in its orthodox usage, has intimate connections with Tisiphone and the underworld, both pagan and Christian. "Duplex poena" describes the torments of the damned:[8] pain of body, sorrow of soul (both of which Troilus endures in his private *inferos*). This is a theological commonplace, as applicable to the Christian Hell as it is to the punishments of the pagan Tartarus (again, Bernardus's commentary on the latter makes this clear). However understressed this connotation of the phrase may be, the narrator's invocation of the "goddesse of tor-

157

ment" (1.8) to help him to help lovers "to pleyne" (1.11) implicates it into the web of notions that the first few stanzas spin out of the touchstones of Furies, underworld, and corporeality. In this same way, the general tendency of the narrator's comments throughout the invocation works to identify love, at least his idea of love, with the underworld and with sorrow, as if loving in itself were one of Troilus's sorrows—as, indeed, it is.

Chaucer's emphasis on sorrow in connection with one of the Furies forms another unusual element in his poem's beginning. While not without classical precedent, the notion of the Furies "sorwynge evere yn peyne" (1.9) is nevertheless extremely rare: far more commonly the Furies cause pain, are cruel and vengeful, as they and Tisiphone in particular are in the *Thebaid*. Be that as it may, the *locus classicus* for the sorrowing Furies has very direct bearing on Chaucer's context here.[9] "Then first, tradition says, conquered by the song, the cheeks of the Eumenides were wet with tears" (10.45–46): the lines are Ovid's, the song Orpheus's, the occasion his visit to the underworld in an attempt to bring back Eurydice.[10] It should scarcely be necessary for me, at this stage, to point out that that episode constitutes a full-fledged *descensus*. Bernardus Silvestris singles out Orpheus as an example of the wise man who virtuously descends to mundane things in meditation in order to turn more clearly to the Creator (30). In the course of his exegesis of Virgil's sixth book he offers an elaborate explication of the Orpheus legend which demonstrates in important detail the kind of significance the Middle Ages attached to it:

> We interpret Orpheus to be wisdom and eloquence. Whence he is called Orpheus, as if *orea phona*, that is, "good voice." He is the son of Apollo and Calliope, that is, of wisdom and eloquence . . . Orpheus has a harp, i.e., rhetorical speech in which diverse rhythms as if rhetorical colors resound. With his soothing remedy he urges sluggards to honest work, calls the unstable to constancy, calms the truculent, and therefore it is said that he draws out rocks, stops rivers, and calms beasts. Eurydice is his

158

wife, i.e., he is naturally joined to natural appetite. For no one is without natural concupiscence. . . . We understand that the natural appetite which dominates human nature is called Eurydice, that is, the appetite for the good, for it is given in order to seek the good. She wanders about through the meadows, i.e., she errs through earthly things which in a way flourish and immediately dry up, and so all the glory of the world is like a flower of the field. While Eurydice wanders, ambling here and there, Aristaeus falls in love with her. Aristaeus is interpreted as divine virtue: *ares*, that is, *virtus*, "virtue," . . .; *theus* indeed means *deus*, "god." This virtue is called divine because man has in himself something divine. The function of a shepherd is given to him since it is the duty of virtue to watch over the flock, that is, the multitude of thoughts, words, and deeds. Aristaeus wishes to join Eurydice to himself: virtue wishes to join appetite to itself so that appetite may seek the highest good and abhor evil. Fleeing Aristaeus, Eurydice treads on a serpent in the fields (in this earthly life she encounters temporal good). The serpent is called temporal good because it crawls through lower things, and, although it appears beautiful, it is deadly. The serpent's bite poisons her: the delight of temporal good infects sense. Having received the cause of death (delight in temporal good), she is drawn to the underworld (she is led away to temporal things and abandons heavenly matters). Moved by desire for his wife, Orpheus goes to the underworld: he descends by thought to temporal matters so that, once he has seen their fragile nature, he may withdraw his appetite from them. He charmed the lords of the shades, that is, the possessors of temporal good. After he has sung for a while (after he has exercised his wisdom and eloquence), he regains his wife (he moves appetite from earthly matters) with the stipulation that he will lose her if he looks back (if he thinks again about the temporal). [54–55]

All of this may seem a very far remove from Chaucer's text, however obviously present in it is the image and concept of the sorrowing Fury. But there is an intermediary for all this which Chaucer knew and medievalists know very well, the account of

Orpheus in Boethius's twelfth meter of the third book of the *De consolatione* (like Bernardus's exegesis, Boethius's narrative draws heavily on Ovid's account). There all that Bernardus says at length is contained *in nuce*. As Chaucer translates it,

> This fable apertenith to yow alle, whosoevere de-
> sireth or seketh to lede his thought into the sovereyn day
> *(that is to seyn, into cleernesse of sovereyn good)*. For
> whoso that evere be so overcomen that he ficche his eien
> into the put of helle *(that is to seyn, whoso sette his
> thoughtes in erthly thinges)*, al that evere he hath drawen
> of the noble good celestial he lesith it, whanne he looketh
> the helles *(that is to seyn, into lowe thinges of the erthe)*.

That this passage was very present to Chaucer as he wrote the opening of the *Troilus*, while not absolutely provable, seems to me strongly indicated by the similarity of the language of the two passages: weeping, pleyning, cruel gods and cruel Fury, torment, pain, sorrowing lovers and compassionate audience (the narrator, in *Troilus*), even the "double sorwe" are present in both texts: Orpheus "sang, with as mochel as he myghte of wepynge, and with as moche as love, that doublide his sorwe." However subliminal this all may seem, it remains nevertheless present in Chaucer's text through the touchstones of the sorrowing Fury (after all, what makes a Fury compassionate?) and the concept of the *descensus*. I think it means that Chaucer from the outset is envisioning his poem in terms of the meditative descent to creatures, the descent into corporeality and temporal good, and is moreover, if the example of Orpheus is at all valid, predicting an unsuccessful descent, one in which appetite will be lost in the *selva oscura* of finite things.

Tisiphone offers one more area of significance to Chaucer's poem that deserves comment at this point: she presents the first of the triadic concepts that will govern the movement of *Troilus and Criseyde*. This she does both by what she is, one of three sister goddesses in the service of one of three brother gods, who govern the threefold division of the universe, and also by what she leads to and is contrasted with in Chaucer's text. While Tisiphone and the story of which she is patroness are firmly locatable in "classical" time, the narrator functions in Christian time, in the poem's present tense. He translates Troilus's story from the fictive Latin of Lollius, from "the forme of olde clerkis speche/In poetrie" (5.1854–55), in both the literal and conceptual senses, turning Lollius's Latin into English and relating the "classical," pagan concepts that underlie the story to the knowledge and attitudes of a Christian audience. Thus, immediately after the two stanzas of invocation to Tisiphone, the narrator describes himself as "I, that God of Loves servantz serve" (1.15), a phrase that recalls the style of the Popes, and goes on to speak what has been identified as a bidding prayer, imploring, among other things, the intercession of the "loveres, that bathen in gladnesse" (1.22) for himself and other despairing lovers. Such a request explicitly emulates the language of orthodox Christianity; it has traditionally been seen as incorporating into the poem the whole matrix of the religion of love, which I for one seriously doubt ever existed other than as a rhetorical device. More to the point, to my mind, is the fact that such language and conceptions implicitly but quite clearly draw into the poem, for its audience if not for its characters, the threefold division of Christianity into the church militant, the church suffering, and the church triumphant (the church on earth, in purgatory, and in Heaven: "loveres, that bathen in gladnesse"). The end of the poem answers this in the same manner as it responds to the descent signalled by Tisiphone with the ascent performed by Troilus; there, the narrator directs his audience to the faithful love of Christ, the true intercessor who "nyl falsen no wight" (5.1845) and prays for himself and us to the true trinity so weakly shadowed in the three Furies and in Dis, Neptune, and Jove.

> Thow oon, and two, and thre, eterne on lyve,
> That regnest ay in thre, and two, and oon,
> Uncircumscript, and al maist circumscrive,
> Us from visible and invisible foon
> Defende, and to thy mercy, everichon,

So make us, Jesus, for thi mercy digne,
For love of mayde and moder thyn benigne.
Amen.

[5.1863–69]

The prominence and the solemnity of such trinitarian conceptions should warn us that, however much Chaucer may be curtailing the threefold structural pattern of the *descensus*, other triadic patterns still have a large part to play in his poem. What they are will not be far to seek, since they too have their roots planted in the epic tradition and in the intellectual motions of the *descensus*. Certainly—as the progression from Tisiphone to Trinity should tell us—growth in consciousness and expansion of awareness provide the basic rhythm of the poem, the pulse to which it moves. Equally certainly, from what we have seen so far and what we all know of the narrative, the characters of *Troilus* do not live to that rhythm. They rather frustrate it, locking their consciousnesses to a single object and viewing it through their desires rather than in itself. We will have to seek that metabolic growth in the narrator and the audience rather than in the actors, in the poem as an entity in itself rather than in its protagonists.

Bernardus Silvestris nicely identifies for us the rhythms of consciousness to which I refer. Near the beginning of his commentary on Virgil's sixth book, Aeneas's literal and meditative descent to Hell, Bernardus names the "three things which furnish perfect wisdom: wit, the instrument of discovering; reason, the instrument of discerning what is discovered; memory, the instrument of retention" (47). He regards Aeneas's tour of Hell as the exercise of these three faculties on corporeal things (their exercise on incorporeals would come in the Elysian fields, i.e., beyond the point at which Bernardus's commentary breaks off). He even goes so far as to identify the Cyclopean gates and arch of *Aeneid* 6.631 as "the vault of the human brain" and the gates as its three chambers:

We come to heavenly contemplation through these
... by exercising wit, reason, and memory. . . . [The Sybil and Aeneas] approach the gates when with wit they dis-

162

cover something, with reason they discern it, and they commit it to memory. . . . Aeneas occupies the entrance (*aditum*) when he exercises wit. . . . "He sprinkles his body with fresh water" when substance refreshes itself with new doctrine. . . . But since committing to memory follows discovery by wit, Aeneas places the branch (*ramum*)—philosophy—across the threshold (*limine adverso*), the rear chamber. [114–15]

Fulgentius's commentary on the *Aeneid* discerns a similar tripartite progression governing Virgil's poem, a "natural order" (122) moving through "a threefold progression" (124): "first, to possess; then to control what you possess; and, third, to ornament what you control" (124). "Think of these three stages," the spectral Virgil tells Fulgentius,

> as arranged in my one verse line, as "arms," "man," and "the first." "Arms," that is, manliness, belongs to the corporeal substance; "man," that is, wisdom, belongs to the intellectual substance; and "the first," that is, a ruler (*princeps*), belongs to the power of judgment; whence this order, to possess, to control, to ornament. Thus in the guise of a story (*historia*) I have shown the complete state of man: first, his nature; second, what he learns; third, his attaining to prosperity. [124]

Bernardus in effect raises Fulgentius's three divisions a notch higher when he substitutes the three faculties, wit, judgment, and memory for man's nature, what he learns, and attainment of prosperity, but the basic rhythm remains intact—and it requires no oversubtle intellect to see in the actions of discovering, understanding, and remembering yet another set of correspondents to our now familiar descent, conversion, and ascent. That is, these consitute yet another way—a specifically psychological way—of construing the threefold motion of the *descensus*, and it is this particular version of the pattern that Chaucer exploits in *Troilus and Criseyde.*

Comic or satiric versions of all these motions abound in the poem; indeed, much of the true nature of the comic elements of

Troilus and Criseyde only becomes visible when placed against the backdrop of the *descensus* tradition. Chaucer uses Troilus as the focal point for most of these frustrated and disrupted patterns, both in their Bernardine and their Fulgentian guises. I cannot overemphasize the ludicrousness of Troilus as an epic hero: in many respects, he prefigures the heroes of mock epic. Looked at as a Fulgentian hero, the young warrior should progress from arms to what should be wisdom to what should be judgment, from corporeal nature to intellectual nature to the achievement of prosperity. In fact, at the beginning of the poem he possesses, in his rather shallow cynicism about love, more wisdom than he is ever again to demonstrate, and small portion though it is he quickly abandons it in his rapid development from warrior to doting lover. Such prosperity as he attains he equally swiftly loses, leaving himself at the end of the poem and of this process somewhat worse off than he was at the start, with only arms—i.e., in Fulgentius's phrase, what "belongs to the corporeal substance" (124)—to comfort him. Even more explicitly does the poem parody the Bernardine pattern of wit, judgment, and memory in Troilus's discovery of Criseyde, his failure to understand her or their love (the full dimensions of his incomprehension reveal themselves in his curtailed Boethian rumination on causality and determinism, 4.953ff.), and the agonies that misdirected remembrance causes him. Chaucer plays so boldly with this that he comes close to violating the fictive historicity of his story by having his character Troilus construe himself literarily: he makes Troilus see himself as an exemplum while still missing the point of his own history:

> Thanne thoughte he thus, "O blisful lord Cupide,
> Whan I the proces have in my memorie,
> How thow me hast wereyed on every syde,
> Men myght a book make of it, lik a storie.
> What nede is the to seke on me victorie,
> Syn I am thyn, and holly at thi wille?
> What joie hastow thyn owen folk to spille?

"Wel hastow, lord, ywroke on me thyn ire,
Thow myghty god, and dredefull for to greve!
Now mercy, lord! thow woost wel I desire
Thi grace moost of alle lustes leeve,
And lyve and dye I wol in thy byleve;
For which I n'axe in guerdoun but o bone,
That thow Criseyde ayein me sende sone."

[5.582–95]

Chaucer even incorporates this frustration of the purpose of memory into the structure of *Troilus and Criseyde*, using the symmetries of the conventional triadic pattern to convey its abortion rather than its completion: the patterns and actions of Books 4 and 5 are ironic repetitions of the patterns and actions of Books 1 and 2 rather than advances upon them. Book 4 opens with the besieging Greeks and the actions of Calkas just as did Book 1, and there follows this the same alternation of narrative attention between Troilus and Criseyde as in the earlier books, the same advisory and consolatory appearance of Pandarus, corresponding uses of him as go-between, a repetition of the earlier exchange of letters, a dream of Troilus's to answer Criseyde's dream in Book 2, the action devolving downward until we are returned to the solitary and despairing Troilus with whom we began. Chaucer extends this repetition to the smallest details—for instance, even to the narrator's declining to tell us of Troilus's battles, since that is not his subject, and urging us to seek such details in Dares (5.1765–71), just as at the beginning he refused to digress into the fall of Troy and directed us for that story to Homer, Dares, and Dictys (1.141–47). Criseyde is handled similarly and even more blatantly, as the process of her surrender to Diomede reproduces—and in its brevity parodies—the steps of her acceptance of Troilus. These structural and narrative repetitions hammer home what transpires psychologically within the characters—or rather, what doesn't happen, for there is no learning process here, no understanding of what happens to them or what they are, except on the most superficial level. Troilus, Criseyde, Pandar, even to some extent the narrator are like the allegory, autotropic, incapable of looking outside or beyond themselves for significance. Their few attempts to do so are ludicrous and ludicrously rendered: Troilus's wrestling with free will and determinism, Criseyde's exclamations about "fals felicitee" (3.814) immediately before she and Troilus commit themselves fully to it. The narrator shares their folly, using their own rhetoric to depict their union as Heaven even though the steady undercurrent of Chaucer's themes describes it as Hell—for the language of descent regularly attaches itself to love in the *Troilus*:

> This Troilus is clomben on the staire,
> And litel weneth that he moot descenden;
> But alday faileth thing that fooles wenden.
> [1.215–17]
>
> But tho gan sely Troilus for to quake
> As though men sholde han led hym into helle,
> And seyde, "Allas! of al my wo the welle,
> Thanne is my swete fo called Criseyde!"
> [1.871–74]

Criseyde, at the moment when Pandar visits her to lead her into love, has just been reading "how the bisshop, as the book kan telle,/Amphiorax, fil thorugh the ground to helle" (2.104–5). Similarly, in his earlier talk with Troilus Pandar has compared the pains Troilus suffers with those of "Ticius in helle" (1.786) and has sworn:

> "To Cerberus yn helle ay be I bounde,
> Were it for my suster, al thy sorwe,
> By my wil she sholde al be thyn to-morwe."
> [1.859–61]

Antigone's response to Criseyde's question—"is ther swych blisse among/Thise loveres [?]" (2.885–86)—reinforces these associations while at the same time making an important distinction:

166

"But wene ye that every wrecche woot
The parfite blisse of love? Why, nay, iwys!
They wenen all be love, if oon be hoot.
Do wey, do wey, they woot no thyng of this!
Men mosten axe at seyntes if it is
Aught fair in hevene (why? for they kan telle),
And axen fendes is it foul in helle."

[2.890–96]

Even the proem to Book 3, which ostensibly celebrates the recip-
rocal love of Troilus and Criseyde as Heaven, warns the reader of
the varieties of love's descents in the example of Jove "amorous . . .
/On mortal thyng," compelled "in a thousand formes down . . . /For
love in erthe" (3.17–32). The frequent association of death with
love—especially because of love— compounds all this and culminates in Troilus's profound swoon immediately before the consummation of his love with Criseyde, immediately after which
both Troilus and Criseyde adopt the rhetoric of Heaven while
belonging (in terms of the metaphorics of the *descensus*) to the
province of Hell, to transitory, corporeal reality, to Criseyde's
declaimed-against "fals felicitee." In Antigone's terms, they claim
that they are experiencing "The parfite blisse of love," but their
own statements and the narrator's give the game away, first subtly
in small reversals of value that could be no more than the excesses
of lovers' rhetoric or poetic convention (for example, when in his
aubade Troilus assigns to day "the peyne of helle" [3.1458]), then
ambiguously, as in:

And verraylich, of thilke remembraunce,
Desir al newe hym brende, and lust to brede
Gan more than erst, and yet took he non hede
[3.1545–47]

and finally quite baldly when Troilus tells Pandar, "Frend, as I am
trewe knyght, . . . /I hadde it nevere half so hote as now"
(3.1648–50). Shortly after this consummation, of course, the narrative turns: news of the exchange of Antenor for Criseyde reaches
the lovers, and with it all of the imagery of the classical underworld

returns in full force to their speech. Two examples of this seem to me particularly revelatory. The first is Troilus's:

> "The deth may wel out of my brest departe
> The lif, so longe may this sorwe myne;
> But fro my soule shal Criseydes darte
> Out nevere mo; but down with Proserpyne,
> When I am ded, I wol go wone in pyne,
> And ther I wol eternaly compleyne
> My wo, and how that twynned be we tweyne."
> [4.470–76]

The second is Criseyde's:

> "Myn herte and ek the woful goost therinne
> Byquethe I, with youre spirit to compleyne
> Eternaly, for they shal nevere twynne.
> For though in erthe ytwynned be we tweyne,
> Yet in the feld of pite, out of peyne,
> That highte Elisos, shal we ben yfeere,
> As Orpheus with Erudice, his fere."
> [4.785–91]

Troilus sees himself, in effect, becoming a Fury "sorwynge evere yn peyne" (1.9), lamenting eternally love's injustices: the language and ideas of his speech are in fact quite similar to those of the opening of Book 1. He sees himself, that is, in the process of becoming a denizen of the underworld; like Proserpina with whom he links himself, not a native citizen, but acclimatized, although carried unwilling from the precincts of light. Chaucer clearly wants us to read the two stanzas in counterpoint (the last line of Troilus's is practically the fourth line of Criseyde's), and the juxtaposition is interesting. Criseyde remains more optimistic in her woe and more circumstantial in some aspects of her imaginings. She minimizes, in her version of their plaint, their separation in favor of an eternal afterlife together, contrary to Troilus's vision of eternal separation. Pain too appears minimally here, banished from the Elysian fields where they will share a twilight eternity. The significance of the Orpheus and Eurydice reference should certainly be obvious, though its ironies are heavy: given his failure to retrieve Eurydice, Orpheus can be viewed as being trapped in the *inferos* of corporeal existence, drawn down to Hell by his devotion to Eurydice. Significant too (I plan to speak more of this later) is the *style* implicit confusion of sexual roles in each passage, Troilus associating himself with Proserpina and Criseyde linking herself primarily—although the reference is ambiguous—with Orpheus. This underworld imagery and its later manifestations bring the poem full circle, to return us to a Troilus whom the narrator this time tells us suffers "cruele peynes . . . /That passen every torment down in helle" (4.1697–98). Criseyde too shares this imagery, praying that if she is false to Troilus:

> Saturnes doughter, Juno, thorugh hire myght,
> As wood as Athamante do me dwelle
> Eternalich in Stix, the put of helle!
>
> [4.1538–40]

(It is a small point, but worth noting, that Chaucer uses the exact phrase "the put of helle" in his translation of Boethius's explana- *cliché(?)* tion of Orpheus's descent: see above, p. 160.) Indeed, the imagery that clings to Criseyde explicitly runs full circle, linking her to that Amphiorax whose fate she mentioned at her first meeting with Pandar: she calls the river Simois to witness:

> That thilke day that ich untrewe be
> To Troilus, myn owene herte fre,
> That thow retourne bakward to thi welle,
> And I with body and soule synke in helle!
>
> [4.1551–54]

Chaucer lets no detail, no implication of this imagery slip unexploited. Even such apparently gratuitous events as, for instance, Troilus's being convinced of the imminence of his death because:

> The owle ek, which that hette Escaphilo,
> Hath after me shright al thise nyghtes two
>
> [5.319–20]

connect coherently with the body of imagery he develops: Ascalaphus was transformed into an owl by Proserpina because he revealed that she had broken her fast in the underworld, and thus thwarted her return to light (Troilus of course has already imagistically identified himself with Proserpina). By means of such imagery Chaucer develops his most important narrative irony: not even the forced withdrawal of Criseyde frees Troilus from his captivity to corporeality. Even the literal removal of the single body that has constituted his snare only works to imprison him the more. The condition of Troilus is exactly the condition of Troy, as Diomede describes it to Criseyde: "The folk of Troie, as who seyth, alle and some,/In prisoun ben" (5.883–84). By means of such imagery also, Chaucer allows himself to show the frustration of the motions of the *descensus*. *Troilus and Criseyde* ends not with the intellectual illuminations or social and moral purgations or symbolic resurrections that close *The Faerie Queene*, but rather with the entrapment of its protagonists in the shortsighted worldliness that has all along enthralled them. Criseyde's change of allegiance nullifies what had seemed most admirable in that worldliness and renders Troilus's devotion completely futile: it ends the poem with a cynical vision of corruption, of a whole world false to the core, from which the wit, understanding, and memory of the reader can draw only the warning of total avoidance. That lesson the poem derives for us when it urges us, in the narrator's new inflections, to turn from the love trinity of Troilus, Criseyde, and Pandar to the trinity of love that "nyl falsen no wight" (5.1845).

Medievalists have made much of the notion of ambiguity in connection with the *Troilus*, seeking sometimes to resolve ambiguities perceived in the poem, sometimes to discover others, sometimes to use the notion as a means of avoiding altogether the real problems raised by the poem. Most of these specific am-

170

biguities that have thus far preoccupied criticism are specious: they constitute a form of metaphysical wit that Chaucer frequently indulges in, wherein correct arguments are drawn to demonstrably false conclusions or left unconcluded (think of Troilus's ruminations of free will and fate, extracted from Boethius, without his solution to them) or perfectly valid insights are given to characters who immediately proceed to ignore what they have themselves just said (again, Troilus immediately before and after seeing Criseyde, in his public pronouncements on love, or Criseyde on the subject of "fals felicitee"). This wit takes many forms. At its simplest, for instance, it resembles what we would call a time gag, a delayed take; Chaucer uses the natural pauses of speech rhythms and verse line closure coupled with a thought that seems complete and comprehensible in itself to set up an expectation or belief in his audience's find which is comically defeated or betrayed by the next syntactical unit. It takes longer to describe than to do:

> Fil Pandarus on knees, and up his eyen
> To heven threw, and held his hondes highe,
> "Immortal god," quod he, "that mayst nought deyen,
> Cupid I mene. . . ."

[3.183–86]

"Cupid I mene" clearly works there as a comic deflation of the meaning established by "Immortal god . . . that mayst nought deyen." Much of the so-called religion of love apparatus functions in the poem in exactly this way on a larger scale: twice, for instance, Troilus goes through the form of a ritual confession (once to Pandar, and once to Criseyde), ending ludicrously in both cases with his conversion "out of wikkednesse" (1.999) and particularly in the second case with even a parodic absolution and remonstrance to sin no more:

> "And if that in tho wordes that I seyde
> Be any wrong, I wol no more trespace.
> Doth what yow list, I am al in youre grace."

171

And she answerde, "Of gilt misericorde!
That is to seyn, that I foryeve al this.
And evere more on this nyght yow recorde,
And beth wel war ye do namore amys."

[3.1174–80]

Such episodes are not ambiguous: they are funny, even if the comedy is touched—as comedy almost always is—with serious overtones.

Such wit does not, of course, explain all of the ambiguities of *Troilus and Criseyde*. Many more are traceable to the role of the narrator: his sympathies, his frequent obtuseness, and his occasional acuteness all consitute a layer of interpretation intervening between the reader and the actions of the protagonists; they frequently redirect the reader's responses, and they always add another element to the complex he must respond to. Perhaps even more important, however, is the central ambiguity of Troilus himself, and this is the point I wish to explore now.

The Troilus of Dares was primarily a warrior, "a man of violent temperament, one who thirsted after war and whose advice was always the sword" (30). After Hector's death, he became the Trojan's rallying point, "the only one whom the Greeks thought worthy of their praises"(72). With his prowess he combined youth and beauty:

Troilus was broad and tall. In spirit he was a giant, but in age he was a boy. He was second to none in venturing upon brave needs. Pride graced his noble features, more pleasing because it was blended with manly vigor. [41]

Little of that Troilus appears in Chaucer's poem, where attention centers upon the romantic Troilus of Boccaccio and Benoît de Sainte-Maure. The only other significant background source for the character of Troilus can be found in a single reference in the *Aeneid*: in the temple at Carthage, where he is soon to meet Dido, Aeneas sees depicted on the walls the various battles of the Trojan

172

War, and among them (1.474–78) Troilus fleeing, his arms abandoned, from Achilles. Virgil calls him *infelix puer atque impar
congressus Achilli*—an unfortunate youth, unequal in conflict to
Achilles. This Troilus, of course, differs greatly from the character
portrayed in all the other sources, and Servius's note on the passage
seems to pick up a possible ambiguity in Virgil's *impar congressus
Achilli* in manner which extends those differences even further:

> The truth, however, is this: that Achilles, led by
> love of Troilus, set doves, which he delighted in, before
> him; when he sought to hold them, he was taken by
> Achilles, and perished in his embraces. But this, which is
> unworthy of a heroic poem, the poet has changed. [*Veritas
> quidem hoc habet: Troili amorem Achillem ductum,
> palumbes ei, quibus ille delectabatur, objecisse: quas
> cum vellet tenere, captus ab Achille, in ejus amplexibus
> periit. Sed hoc, quasi indignum heroico carmine, mutavit
> poeta.*]

This Troilus, I think, became very important to Chaucer's conception of his own protagonist. Certainly some key elements of the
Virgilian-Servian Troilus figure largely in Chaucer's characterization of his unfortunate youth, sexually ambiguous, whose end—
and whose life?—is unworthy of a heroic poem.

　　Troilus's sexual ambiguity, as I see it, arises not just from
his verbal association of himself with the victim of mythology's
most celebrated rape, Proserpina. For that matter, he connects
himself in the same way with another sexually ambiguous character (and one who figures largely in the *Thebaid*), Oedipus:

> Ne nevere wol I seen it shyne or reyne,
> But ende I wol, as Edippe, in derknesse
> My sorwful lif, and dyen in distresse.
>
> [4.299–301]

Troilus's sexual ambiguity, though it is reinforced by such references, arises rather from the unmanly role he plays at key moments in the plot and from his complete and utter passivity. That

last fact is also the most obvious: it requires only reviewing the broadest outlines of the story to realize—with something of a shock, it is true—that Troilus literally does nothing for himself in Chaucer's version of the narrative. Pandarus accomplishes everything for him. Up until the moment, at the end of Book 1, when Pandarus screws Criseyde's name out of him and promises to speak to her on his behalf, all of his torments have been completely self-inflicted and completely pointless: he has not even addressed Criseyde, and she has no reason and no way to know that she even remotely figures in his thoughts. Troilus persists in this line of nonconduct throughout the poem, relying on Pandar to arrange every meeting, to prosecute each further step of his liaison. Troilus's major action in the poem consists precisely in taking no action. Chaucer makes this point crystal clear when, in Book 4, at the receipt of the news that Criseyde will be exchanged for Antenor, he makes Troilus muster a whole battery of reasons for doing absolutely nothing. More subtly, but equally devasting for Troilus's putative heroism, Chaucer has him preserve intact, in his meditations on fate and free will, the example Boethius offers to Lady Philosophy of a completely determined act: a man sitting. That image, it seems to me, functions in Troilus's speech as a metaphysical conceit, encapsulating his condition and his response to it. It would fit the facts of the poem more precisely if it were a man sleeping, since that, or at least lying in bed, forms Troilus's major iterative act in the poem. At every crisis, he goes to bed.

> And whan that he in chambre was allone,
> He doun upon his beddes feet hym sette.
>
> [1.358–59]
>
> Yet Troilus for al this no word seyde,
> But longe he ley as stylle as he ded were.
>
> [1.722–23]
>
> Tyl at the laste he seyde he wolde slepe,
> And on the gres adoun he leyde him tho.
>
> [2.514–15]

It fel that I [Pandarus] com romyng al allone
Into his chaumbre, and fond how that he lay
Upon his bed.

[2.555–57]

With al the haste goodly that they myghte,
They spedde hem fro the soper unto bedde.

[2.946–47]

And Troilus he fond allone abedde,
That lay, as do thise lovers, in a traunce
Bitwixen hope and derk disesperaunce.

[2.1305–7]

Sone after that, down in thi bed the leye,
And sey, thow mayst no lenger up endure.

[2.1517–18]

Lay al this mene while Troilus . . .

[3.50]

And Pandarus, as faste as he may dryve,
To Troilus tho com, as lyne right
And on a paillet al that glade nyght
By Troilus he lay.

[3.227–30]

And for the more part, the longe nyght
He lay and thoughte how that he myghte serve
His lady best.

[3.439–41]

   but certeyn, at the laste,
For this or that, he [Pandarus] into bed hym [Troilus] caste.

[3.1096–97]

Retorned to his real paleys soone,
He softe into his bed gan for to slynke.

[3.1534–35]

Now torne we ayeyn to Troilus,
That resteles ful longe abedde lay.

[3.1583–84]

Departed out of parlement echone,
This Troilus, withouten wordes mo,
Unto his chambre spedde hym faste allone.
But if it were a man of his or two,
The which he bad out faste for to go,
Bycause he wolde slepen, as he seyde,

175

And hastily upon his bed hym leyde.

[4.218–24]

    and tho this sorwful man
Upon his beddes syde adown hym sette.

[4.233–34]

    joie nor penaunce
He feleth non, but lith forth in a traunce.

[4.342–43]

Whan they were in hire bed, in armes folde,
Naught was it lik tho nyghtes here-byforn.

[4.1247–48]

To bedde he goth, and walweth ther and torneth
In furie, as doth Ixion in helle.

[5.211–12]

And Troilus tho sobrelich he [Pandarus] grette,
And on the bed ful sone he gan hym sette.

[5.293–94]

Now ris, my deere brother Troilus,
For certes, it non honour is to the
To wepe, and in thi bedde to jouken thus.

[5.407–9]

And lessen gan his hope and ek his myght,
For which al down he in his bed hym leyde.

[5.1438–39]

Cassandre goth, and he with cruel herte
Foryat his wo, for angre of hire speche;
And from his bed al sodeynly he sterte,
As though al hool hym hadde ymad a leche.

[5.1534–37]

No epic hero will again be so inactive until Colley Cibber takes his place as the hero of *The Dunciad*. Such an overwhelming accumulation of incidents is not merely ludicrous, but works to define Troilus for the reader, to delineate aspects of his character and role. Certainly, the bed is tinged with sexuality, particularly in Book 3—but the vast majority of the incidents I have cited (and they are by no means all I could have cited) take place without Criseyde. Pandarus comes closest to the truth early in the poem when he asks Troilus whether "slombrestow as in a litargie?"

(1.730). Troilus *is* in a lethargy: he passes his days in a cloud of unknowing of his own manufacture and allows himself to become the passive toy of the Fortune he so frequently exclaims against. He makes himself impotent—thus the necessity for Pandarus to prosecute the love affair on his behalf—and he does so to such an extent that at the climax of the affair, in what is to my mind one of the funniest moments in all romantic literature, Pandarus has to dump his unconscious body into bed with his paramour. Such frequent mentions of the bed, in a poem with such a subject, *should* be primarily sexual references, and Chaucer's redirection of that imagery constitutes one of the major elements in his construction of an ambiguous sexual persona for Troilus.

Other aspects of Troilus's conduct confirm the essentially weak, passive sexual role Chaucer creates for him. These also reach their climax in the scene where Pandarus throws him into bed with Criseyde. Troilus has swooned with emotion at Criseyde's bedside (in itself a reversal of sexual roles, at least according to the clichés of romantic writing), and Pandarus is forced once again to take an active hand:

> For this or that, he into bed hym caste,
> And seyde, "O thef, is this a mannes herte?"
> And of he rente al to his bare sherte;
>
> And seyde, "Nece, but ye helpe us now,
> Allas, youre owen Troilus is lorn!"
> "Iwis, so wolde I, and I wiste how,
> Ful fayn, " quod she; "Allas, that I was born!"
> "Yee, nece, wol ye pullen out the thorn
> That stiketh in his herte," quod Pandare,
> "Sey 'al foryeve,' and stynt is al this fare!"
>
> [3.1097–1106]

Troilus's lack of "a mannes herte" transfers the active sexual role to Criseyde, as Pandar's urging her to pull out the implicitly phallic "thorn/That stiketh in his herte" acknowledges. Criseyde's own words and subsequent actions confirm this. When he revives, she addresses him as follows:

"Why do ye with youreselven thus amys?"
Quod tho Criseyde, "Is this a mannes game?
What, Troilus, wol ye do thus for shame?"

And therwithal hire arm over hym she leyde,
And al foryaf, and ofte tyme hym keste.

[3.1125–29]

Criseyde plays the "mannes game," Troilus the woman's. She retains this role to the end of the poem, overriding Troilus's objections to her plans about leaving Troy and returning, and generally dictating the terms of their relationship. Troilus continues to decline the masculine options open to him, spurning, for instance, Pandar's suggestion that he keep Criseyde by force (for which, of course, there is impressive precedent in Troy). All of this is the fruition of a process that began with the poem itself, with Troilus's fear to speak to Criseyde, to mention her name to Pandarus, to approach her on his own: he even considered suicide rather than do that, an act that he subsequently defines to himself, to his shame, as "bothe . . . unmanhod and a synne" (1.824). Pandar has several times had to chide him for his "wrecched mouses herte" (3.736), and Criseyde leaves little doubt who "wears the pants" in their relationship:

"But natheles, this warne I yow," quod she,
"A kynges sone although ye be, ywys,
Ye shal namore han sovereignete
Of me in love, than right in that cas is;
N'y nyl forbere, if that ye don amys,
To wratthe yow; and whil that ye me serve,
Chericen yow right after ye disserve."

[3.169–75]

Such sovereignty is of a piece with all of the inversions of *Troilus and Criseyde*: the parodic religion of love, this upsetting of social hierarchy, the reversals of sexual roles—all mesh to define a Troilus and a Troy in which values are topsy-turvy, all order askew, all energy misdirected or frustrated. At the end of the poem, leaving Troilus and leaving Troy are cognate acts which move Criseyde out of the looking-glass world into the real one. Diomede immediately takes hold of her bridle (a charged conceit, given the long history of the horse and rider as images for reason and passion) and leads her away to restore her to the authority of her father. He will take the lead and vigorously prosecute his suit in the same manner, using all of the submissive language that Troilus uses without ever in fact submitting himself to Criseyde's will; she instead is curbed and reined to his desire. Troy is a woman's town—its presiding deity is Helen—and its analog Troilus a woman's man: the Greek camp provides the only masculine locus of the poem. Just as Troilus has been insistently linked with bed, at key moments in the poem Criseyde also performs significant iterated acts: she feasts. On the evening of her first face to face meeting with Troilus, "She com to dyner in hire pleyne entente" (2.1560) at Deiphebus's palace, where he "fedde hem wel with al that myghte like" (2.1570). "And she to soper com, whan it was eve" (3.595) for her first acceptance of Troilus as carnal lover. She, Calkas, and Diomede drink festively on the day he pushes his suit. All this, of course, stands in marked contrast to Troilus's love pains and constant lack of appetite; appetite, in fact, is what it means.

Let us return for a moment to Fulgentius's neat little triad and its correspondents: arms, man, the first; manliness, wisdom, ruler; corporeal substance, intellectual substance, power of judgment; to possess, to control, to ornament; man's nature, what he learns, his attaining prosperity. Those consitute what Fulgentius's Virgil calls natural order, the complete state of human life. That order is violated, all of the sequences upset in *Troilus and Criseyde*. Chaucer's Troy matches exactly the Troy Bernardus describes: the feminine dominates it, the weakness of the flesh smothers the powers of intellect. Appetite controls reason, which means, in terms of the metaphorics generated by the commentators' equations as well as in Chaucer's metaphors, that the ostensible men are genuinely unmanly, that the intellectual substance submits to the corporeal, surrenders control, that the power of

179

difficult to see how it fits in this book

judgment is suspended, the ruler unseated, nothing learned, and prosperity not attained. *Troilus and Criseyde* depicts the failure of the epic quest, the absence of epic aspiration. It shows us what happens to a perfectly ordinary man without grace, without a goddess mother to guide him, an average human being at home in the world, whose intellectual (and therefore manly) failing is so great that he does not even grasp the first and most fundamental epic truth: that the world is not his home. Perhaps the greatest irony of Chaucer's pervasively ironic poem is that it is Criseyde who leaves Troy rather than the so aptly named Troilus.

All epic heroes must leave their homes in order to find their true homes; all epic heroes must leave their old identities to learn the nature of the new ones that await them. That Troilus does not do so locates him, in the geography of epic, in the precincts of the failed. He is like the Aeneas who wished to fall with Troy: a man wedded to an outmoded idea, fastened to a merely temporal good. That Aeneas is remembered, in Virgil's poem, by an older, maturer Aeneas, who recounts his story to the Carthaginian queen. Interestingly, however, it is not that first Aeneas whose career Troilus's most resembles. Chaucer instead draws heavily upon Virgil's account of Aeneas's sojourn in Carthage and his liaison with Dido: *Aeneid* 4, the *locus classicus* for the meeting of the epic hero and romantic love. That love, as Virgil portrays it, constitutes almost as great a danger for the hero as not leaving home in the first place, since it tempts him to establish himself in the wrong home. Virgil's narration makes this clear: Juno uses Dido as bait to ensnare Aeneas and divert the predestined greatness of his city from Rome to Carthage. The commentators are equally explicit: Book 4 describes the spirit of adolescence or young manhood, freed from parental control and oblivious of God, inflamed by passion and involved in adultery, from which he is withdrawn only by the promptings of Mercury, the god of wisdom (parenthetically, it is worth remarking that Bernardus Silvestris defines the allegorical meaning of adultery to be dereliction of, or inconstancy in, duty [112]).

Chaucer: *Troilus and Criseyde*

Some superficial similarities between this and *Troilus and Criseyde* spring to the eye at once: Troilus is, after all, literally a young man driven by passion into an illicit affair, and he is—in a chillingly mordant fashion—recalled from his obsession and removed from Troy only when Mercury comes for him. (I suspect that touch must have roused a grim little laugh among the more serious of Chaucer's listeners.) Many greater parallels than that exist, however; so many, in fact, and in so many significant details, that I have been forced to conclude that Chaucer is using the armature of Virgil's story to bear the burden of his own narrative. Consider the range of the narrative parallels: Troilus first sees Criseyde in a temple, as Dido first sees Aeneas in the temple of Juno; Dido and Criseyde are both widows; Troilus is incited to love by Cupid, who also pricks Dido to love Aeneas; in both cases the love is almost instantaneous, involving brief reflection before commitment; Dido is urged to love and to overcome scruples about her widowed state by her sister Anna as Criseyde is urged to love and to overcome her scruples about widowhood by Pandarus. In both poems the consummation of the affair takes place during a violent rainstorm; Bernardus's comment on the *Aeneid* passage links it with passion aroused by excessive eating and drinking at feasts of the sort which preceded the union of the lovers in the *Troilus*. In each poem, one of the partners regards the liaison as marriage: Dido refers to Aeneas as husband, and Troilus addresses Criseyde as "fresshe wommanliche wif" (3.1296; see also 3.106), and thanks Cupid, Venus, and—significantly—Hymen for uniting him with Criseyde (3.1254–60). In each case the affair ends with the forced departure of one of the partners, Aeneas and Criseyde, leaving the remaining lovers, Dido and Troilus, frenzied and threatening suicide. Each of the departed lovers will of course eventually choose a new consort, and in each poem the whole incident closes with the death of the forsaken lover. There are even specific verbal parallels between Troilus's lamentations and Dido's, and between Pandar's last interview with Criseyde and Dido's last conversation with her sister Anna (Pandarus even at

181

has he read Filostrato?

one point refers to her as "my suster, ful of discomfort" [4.848]);
even the role of Rumor in spreading the news of Dido's liaison is
paralleled in Chaucer's poem by Fame's announcing Criseyde's
exchange for Antenor.

Fascinating as such similarities are in themselves, their true
importance lies in the use and redistribution Chaucer has made of
them. Crudely put, the roles of Dido and Aeneas reverse themselves in the plot of Troilus and Criseyde: Troilus performs most of
the key functions assigned by Virgil to Dido. He remains the
faithful lover, left behind in a city history is sweeping by, trapped
in mourning for the past and destroyed by the bitterness it engen-
ders. For Aeneas, Carthage is a false refuge, a diversion from the
true home and new empire he must seek. For Troilus, Criseyde is
the same sort of false refuge, the same deceiving resting place. Epic
heroes, forced into motion by their fates, all aspire to rest, to cease
from wandering. Troilus makes the mistake of thinking he has
found that rest in Criseyde. Time and again the poem and its
protagonists return to the concept of the heart's rest; it is almost a
touchstone of the poem. Criseyde initially doubts that she should
"myn herte sette at reste/Upon this knyght" (2.760–61). Pandarus,
at Criseyde's bedside, urges Troilus to kneel "There God youre
hertes brynge soone at reste" (3.966). Criseyde subsequently calls
Troilus "myn owen hertes list,/My ground of ese, and al myn herte
deere" (3.1303–4). Troilus tells Pandar that "Thow hast in hevene
ybrought my soule at reste/Fro Flegetoun, the fery flood of Helle"
(3.1599–1600), after which:

> Pandarus hem two
> Abedde brought, whan that hem bothe leste.
> And thus they ben in quyete and in reste.
> [3.1678–80]

It is only later, after the news that Criseyde must leave Troy, that
Troilus learns that "For, as in love, ther is but litel reste" (4.581).
As might be expected the narrator is the very last to realize that
"Swich is this world, whoso it kan byholde:/In ech estat is litel

182

hertes reste" (5.1748–49). This false rest contrasts sharply with the true refuge from wandering to be found in the fixed love of God, the true home of epic wanderers as of everyman:

> O yonge, fresshe folkes, he or she,
> In which that love up groweth with youre age,
> Repeyreth hom fro worldly vanyte,
> And of youre herte up casteth the visage
> To thilke God that after his ymage
> Yow made, and thynketh al nys but a faire
> This world, that passeth soone as floures faire.
>
> [5.1835–41]

Those directions do not contradict the tenor of the poem that precedes them; rather, they complement and complete it, confirming with the fullness of Christian revelation the belated and partial illumination that Troilus gains after his death. They define, once and for all, the failure of Troilus as lover and hero: he is only Aeneas *manqué*, an Aeneas who never left Troy, who never gave up Dido, who, willing or unwilling, never even began to seek Hesperia, a youth who, in epic terms, never became a man at all. That is his, and the poem's "tragedye."

❧

> Galeotto fu 'l libro e chi lo scrisse:
> quel giorno più non vi leggemmo avante.
>
> [*Inferno* 5.137–38]

Near the beginning of Dante's descent to the underworld, Francesca's words warn him and the reader about the use and abuse of books and stand as a necessary corrective to the exclusively honorific view of literature provided by the poet's earlier meeting with Virgil's companions Homer, Horace, Ovid, and Lucan: "A pandar was that book and he who wrote it: that day we read no further." It is not my purpose here to discuss the complex role that the concept of the book plays throughout Dante's poem, but to call attention to its similar ubiquity and complexity in Chaucer's.

The narrator does not let us long forget "myn auctour called Lollius" (1.394), and we have already remarked on the frequency with which "This romaunce . . . of Thebes" (2.100) is mentioned or alluded to through the *Troilus*. Provocative too is Pandar's conduct during the crucial bedside meeting between Troilus and Criseyde in his house:

> And with that word he drow hym to the feere,
> And took a light, and fond his contenaunce,
> As for to looke upon an old romaunce.
>
> [3.978–80]

Troilus's and Criseyde's own words, however, carry us closer to the heart of the matter: both, as Chaucer's story winds down to its sad denouement, begin to view their lives as the subjects of the book that will be written—i.e., this book that we are now reading. I have already cited Troilus's comment and the literary boldness of its violation of artifice. Criseyde speaks in a similar manner:

> "Allas! for now is clene ago
> My name of trouthe in love, for everemo!
> For I have falsed oon the gentileste
> That evere was, and oon the worthieste!
>
> Allas! of me, unto the worldes ende,
> Shal neyther ben ywriten nor ysonge
> No good word, for thise bokes wol me shende.
>
> [5.1054–60]

Such comments work in multiple ways. They call our attention to the highly literary minds of the protagonists, who already envision their lives as literary exempla; conversely, they also emphasize the verisimilitude of the materials of the book itself, by insisting on a kind of interpenetration between life and art, the materials of each feeding and feeding upon the other. And paradoxically too such comments also direct us toward an awareness of the artifice of the book, of the unreality of what we provisionally accept as real. This is something we are accustomed to think of as a very modern technique, but for all of its putative modernity Chaucer seems fully able to exploit its advantages in engaging the reader simultaneously in following the narrative and in participating in the creation of the work itself. Chaucer's ultimate fiction rests on the fiction of fiction, what Coleridge centuries later was naively to call our "willing suspension of disbelief." Chaucer appears to know that "is it true?" is both the most naive and the most sophisticated question that can be raised about any fiction, and has consequently and deliberately set out to implicate his audience in creating the truth and falsity of his fable.

His mode of so doing is both subtle and devastatingly simple. Much of epic poetry, as I have remarked elsewhere, depends for its success on a kind of internal hermeneutics, a sort of self-referential grid established within the poem itself by parallels and contrasts, relations and disjunctions of event, character, image.[11] In *Troilus and Criseyde*, Chaucer has built an elaborate analogy between the actions of Pandarus and Troilus in the poem and those of the narrator, ostensibly recounting the poem, and the audience outside the poem. The narrator panders to the audience, which stands in the same relation to him as Troilus to Pandarus; the Criseyde he brings them is the book itself, his poem in praise of love. *Galeotto fu 'l libro e chi lo scrisse*.

The narrator's conduct, comments, and attitudes parallel Pandar's in several interesting ways. For instance, right at the outset of the poem, the narrator informs us that he serves the servants of Love and, while he himself is unlikely to win grace from Love, nevertheless:

> if this may don gladnesse
> To any lovere, and his cause availle,
> Have he my thonk, and myn be this travaille!
>
> [1.19–21]

Pandar similarly describes himself as an unsuccessful lover, who has not yet tasted love's grace; nonetheless, he too can help others to the bliss he cannot reach, and his attitude toward this labor is the same as the narrator's:

> "Yef me this labour and this bisynesse,
> And of my spede be thyn al that swetnesse."
>
> [1.1042–43]

Both narrator and Pandar confidently assure us that no one can withstand the power of love (1.232–38 and 1.974–80); both praise Criseyde as the worthy object of Troilus's love, and both share an exalted notion of Troilus's worth. The narrator indeed identifies himself completely with Love's party, sharing fully its value system with his own characters, praising love as an improver of the lover's conduct and character, as the sum of human felicity, and specifically seeing the physical union of Troilus and Criseyde as an unalloyed and supreme good. Later in the poem, when he knows and Pandarus guesses Criseyde's infidelity, both seek as long as possible to deny, obfuscate, and palliate her conduct—Pandarus to shield Troilus from the truth, the narrator to moderate the bitterness of that truth for the reader and himself. And when Pandarus and Troilus finally see undeniable proof of Criseyde's betrayal, the narrator's subsequent confusion, his fumbling with the story (the fits and starts and false conclusions by which he moves himself to his final perspective and his true conclusion) parallel exactly Pandar's psychological state, *his* confusion and fumbling for words (for the very first time in the poem, he doesn't have a ready solution) and disgust with Criseyde (like the narrator's final turning "fro worldly vanyte" to God). Despite his apparently superior knowledge, the narrator seems to subject himself to the flow of his own story and to respond to its vicissitudes vicariously with his own characters; their progress through the story measures his progress through it—with the vital difference, for the audience, that when at the end Pandarus finds himself at a loss for consolation ("Right fayn I wolde amende it, wiste I how" [5.1741]), the narrator, although he is slow to realize it, does have access to a consolation and a solace superior to "payens corsed olde rites" and "what alle hire goddes may availle" (5.1849–50).

What I am implying here is that the narrator of *Troilus and Criseyde* is not a static character whose voice, at the end of the poem, is superseded by Chaucer's. Rather, the narrator is a consistent fiction, just like Troilus or Pandarus or Criseyde. He shares the poem with them, superior to them only in the sense that he learns from and with all of them, vicariously living their lives as he retells them. Thus for instance he learns along with Troilus that desire grows by what it feeds upon, just as he finally learns along with Troilus that "false worldes brotelnesse" (5.1832) is not superior to "Felicite, which that thise clerkes wise/Comenden so" (3.1691–92). He learns slowly, reluctantly, painfully: like Pandarus and Troilus he fights hard to preserve the illusions that give him pleasure, but the nature of the events he describes drives him to his ultimate realizations. Those realizations have been latent not so much in the events themselves but in the language the narrator has used to recount them. Chaucer achieves his final masterstroke of literary propriety by forming the conclusion of his poem and the completion of his narrator's knowledge out of the latter's final awareness of the implications of what he has been saying all along.

Turning once again to the very beginning of the poem will show this most clearly. There the narrator employs, from the third stanza of the poem onward, ecclesiastical language and conceptions, liturgical forms and formulae. He casts himself essentially as the Pope of Love's church and describes the poem he is inditing as essentially a spiritual work of mercy directed toward himself and others:

> For so hope I my sowle best avaunce,
> To prey for hem that Loves servauntz be,
> And write hire wo, and lyve in charite,
>
> And for to have of hem compassioun,
> As though I were hire owne brother dere.
>
> [1.47–51]

187

Pandar too assumes the functions of a priest, hearing Troilus's confession, urging him to amendment, assigning him a penance, celebrating what some critics have taken too seriously as a parodic mass. (By the same token, Pandar reverses the game and usurps some of the narrator's functions, becoming a fiction-maker himself and even reflecting aloud on the purpose and methods of the art of narration, as in 2.255–62 and 2.1610–22.) The narrator truly is the head of Pandar's church, but what is amusing in Pandar is more blameworthy in him, since he could and should know better—as his very ability to appropriate orthodox theological language proves. For Pandarus to celebrate romantic love in the forms of the highest conceivable good provides a kind of mock-heroic comedy for the audience of the poem: Pandarus remains, after all, a pagan, cut off from the fullness of revelation. The narrator does not have that excuse, and his apparent sincerity in applying liturgical notions to the love of Troilus and Criseyde would constitute serious error indeed if he were not so lugubriously solemn about it. He is, in more ways than one, a pontifical ass. Whether one agrees with that assessment of the narrator or not, the fact remains that his use of orthodox Christianity as a referential system leaves the values of Christianity intact and makes them available to the poem for straightforward use at whatever point the corresponding values of the counterculture of romantic love have been discredited—which is exactly what takes place at the end of the poem. Criseyde is the keystone of the narrator's "belief" in love as a system of the highest spiritual good. Her infidelity discredits the system by disproving one of its major tenets—that love ennobles the lover—and by disvaluing the reward that such love offers; her infidelity in effect justifies Pandar's cynicism that so much embarrasses the narrator (4.428–34). Just as Pandarus is driven by the certain knowledge of Criseyde's infidelity to revise drastically his opinion of her and to ultimate silence, so is the narrator driven first to apologies for having to tell of it at all, then to solicitude for his book, then, rather distractedly, back to the final moments of his tale and Troilus's complete disillusionment, when in death he is finally freed from loving Criseyde, which even her falsity did not accomplish. It is only then, when his protagonist learns to condemn "al vanite" in the face of "the pleyn felicite/That is in hevene above" (5.1817–19), that the narrator returns to the language of orthodox Christianity and now uses it as a contrast to rather than a parallel with the values of romantic love. He learns only at the same pace his characters learn, but he is able to carry their pagan revelations to their Christian conclusions. They act as his Virgil, conducting him to the border of the earthly Paradise; beyond that point, he must depend on other guides.

That his own characters guide the narrator may make a fine *Style* irony for Chaucer, but it offers cold comfort to the reader, whom, after all, the narrator in his turn guides. Pandar acts as Troilus's Sybil (or Virgil, if you like; he has some artistic claims, after all) to lead him into the underworld of matter. The narrator, of course, performs the same function for the reader, leading him into the *inferos* of the poem itself as well as that of matter. Both journeys climax, as does that parodic mass whose offertory bell Pandarus hears (3.189),[12] at the deepest penetration into corporeality (I apologize for the unavoidable *double entendre*), the sexual union of Troilus and Criseyde: simultaneous consecration and communion, it sits at the dead center of the poem, a literal incarnation marking the lowest point of the *descensus*. Troilus, of course, misses the direction of his journey in his thanks to Pandar:

> "Thow hast in hevene ybrought my soule at reste
> Fro Flegetoun, the fery flood of helle. . . ."
>
> [3.1599–1600]

The narrator errs in a similar manner, assuring us that they feel "As muche joie as herte may comprende" (3.1687):

> Felicite, which that thise clerkes wise
> Comenden so, ne may nought here suffise;
> This joie may nought writen be with inke;
> This passeth al that herte may bythynke.
>
> [3.1691–94]

He is using, as most readers have recognized, the technical language normally reserved to describe the state of beatitude and the possession of the *summum bonum*: how wrongly both he and Troilus evaluate this situation the end of the poem makes clear.

A non-omniscient narrator presents one kind of critical problem, but a narrator so radically off course, one whose assessment of his tale is so thoroughly wrong, confronts the reader with a far more complicated interpretative situation. Where really do we stand in relation to him? What truly is his role in relation to the poem of which he is ostensible author? These questions cannot be answered simply, but the poem does provide intriguing clues, especially in the particularly rich interweaving of motifs in its opening invocation. I have hinted at part of this solution in my earlier discussion of those stanzas: their submerged reference to the Boethian Orpheus provides the beginnings of an answer, since it implicitly links the narrator and that Orpheus, the wise and eloquent person who descends to matter to withdraw his appetite from it—and who fails in that quest because the attractions of corporeal being draw his gaze back to them. Our poet is, I think, that Orpheus, charming the dwellers in the underworld with his song, but ultimately forced to leave his Eurydice (remember that Criseyde too is associated with appetite) behind in the shades. He visits the *inferos* meditatively, through poetry (remember also that he insists on his lack of actual experience in love), but so allured is he by his own creation that he transposes values and mistakes Hell for Heaven:

> For whoso that evere be so overcomen that he ficche his eien into the put of helle (*that is to seyn, whoso sette his thoughtes in erthly thinges*), al that evere he hath drawen of the noble good celestial he lesith it, whanne he looketh the helles (*that is to seyn, into lowe thinges of the erthe*).
> [*Boece*, 3, meter 12]

That is the narrator's tragedy: the "litel myn tragedye" that he addresses at the end of the poem is both his book and his experi-

ence, and as such provides the logical base from which he proceeds
to hope that he will yet "make in som comedye."

The web of Orphean associations suggests an answer to the
question of the narrator's relation to his own work, but it does not
provide any clarification of the narrator's relation to his audience.
For that we must pick up another aspect of *Troilus*'s opening
stanzas, and return once again to the poem's muse, Tisiphone. For
all the things I have already had occasion to say about her, I have
not yet approached one fundamental question, i.e., why does
Chaucer—or the narrator—single out Tisiphone from the three
Furies? The narrator gives us a part of the answer to that:

> For wel sit it, the sothe for to seyne,
> A woful wight to han a dreery feere,
> And to a sorwful tale, a sory chere.
>
> [1.12–14]

Tisiphone certainly provides an appropriate "feere" for his excursion into the underworld, but Allecto or Megaera would have done
as well. But he specifically calls upon Tisiphone to "Help me, that
am the sorwful instrument,/That helpeth loveres, as I kan, to
pleyne" (1.10–11), and in so doing he distinguishes Tisiphone *by
function* from her sister Furies. All three Furies were begotten by
Acheron on Night; Bernardus Silvestris and most mythologists
agree in interpreting them as the daughters of sorrow out of ignorance of the spirit (69). There is some small disagreement among the
mythologists about the precise equivalents of Allecto and Megaera, though Bernardus lies pretty much in the main stream when
he identifies them as "distorted thought" and "wicked deed,"
respectively. There is only unanimity, however, about Tisiphone.
Her name tells her story: she is, etymologically, *istarum vox*, the
voice of the Furies, "voice resulting from wicked thought, and that
is wicked speech" (69). Bernardus is very illuminating on the
subject of Tisiphone. She is "completely armed, as befits a daughter of ignorance," with false and true accusations in her left and
right hands. She can be said to summon her sisters "when wicked

191

speech provokes them to wicked thoughts and wicked deeds." She presides over "the wicked mouth, the passage away from the peaceful mind" (107). This makes fairly transparent the reasons for the selection of Tisiphone as the muse of *Troilus and Criseyde*, and it should moreover lend some support to the sort of Boethian Orphic role I have posited for the narrator. As the voice of the Furies, Tisiphone is the voice of the underworld in both the moral and the philosophic senses, provoking evil thoughts and deeds and guiding away from peace of mind. She is, simply a kind of infernal muse, and Chaucer and his narrator use her directly as such, invoking her aid at the beginning of the poem and the start of their descent into "lowe thinges of the erthe." The narrator shares her functions: he, by his praise of the love of Troilus and Criseyde, by his celebration of their carnal union, leads at least himself and potentially the reader away from peace of mind and into what Stoics would have called perturbation and Christians temptation—that is, he too provokes wicked thoughts and wicked deeds. The narrator, of course, does not fully realize these implications, even though he later reinvokes Tisiphone and her sisters for what he sees as the falling action of the poem (4.22–28). That he is aware of at least part of her role, however, seems to me fairly clearly shown by his substitution, during what he views as the acme of his story, of Tisiphone's celestial counterpart, Calliope; the etymology and meaning or her name, as given by Fulgentius, Bernardus, and mythologists generally, completes the web of associations linking Tisiphone (their voice), Orpheus (good voice), and herself, Calliope (beautiful voice; she is also Orpheus's mother). All are joined as speakers, as, in effect, poets, and all are thereby fused in the role of the poet-speaker who indites "Thise woful vers" (1.7).

The narrator stands then in this triple relation: to the characters of the poem, the lost souls of this lower world, he is the voice and articulation of their despair; to himself, he is the failing Boethian Orpheus whose vision is held by the allurements of the lower world; to the audience, he is the tempter, the pander who presents the glitter of that world for its delectation. The common denominator is persuasive speech, in which Pandar also shares—and so it is only appropriate that the poem ends in Pandar's baffled silence ("I kan namore seye" [5.1743]), in the narrator's falling back on the authority of "thise olde bokes" (5.1753), and in Troilus's bitter laughter. The poem has exhausted the voices of the underworld, and leaves the narrator, shorn of all his illusions, with nothing left but "to the Lord right thus" to "speke and seye" (5.1862):

> Thow oon, and two, and thre, eterne on lyve,
> That regnest ay in thre, and two, and oon,
> Uncircumscript, and al maist circumscrive,
> Us from visible and invisible foon
> Defende, and to thy mercy, everichon,
> So make us, Jesus, for thi mercy digne,
> For love of mayde and moder thyn benigne.
>   Amen.

❧

Troilus is undone, in Chaucer's poem, by a hollow man, by Diomede's empty armor wearing the brooch that Troilus gave Criseyde. That sardonic comment sums up Troilus's heroism and dismisses it, as it rejects martial heroism as a possible subject for epic poetry. *Troilus and Criseyde*, despite its exploitation of the matter of Troy, of the most conventional of epic materials, remains a poem without a hero in the conventional sense, and it is legitimate to wonder who or what fills that gap. The likeliest candidate, however unorthodox, seems to me the reader. It is the reader, constantly reminded of Lollius and the artifice of the book and the interpenetration of life and literature, the reader alert to the sympathies and naiveté of narrator and protagonists, who is called upon to make the true epic *descensus*, to send his mind and imagination into the *inferos* of Troy and corporeality, to evaluate what he finds there, and to return to the light instructed and illuminated. Chaucer systematically destroys the possibilities of his characters' or his narrator's accomplishing that journey, while just as systematically preserving the referential points of the epic system that demands that the journey be made. He is taking the epic lesson one logical and revolutionary step farther; he is forbidding his audience the luxury, the comfort, of allowing a surrogate, an exemplar, to perform that arduous and painful pilgrimage for them. Each reader of the poem must walk that road himself, each man must become his own epic wanderer, leaving his comfortable home in this world to journey painfully through its darkness to discover his proper place in the sun. Epic, particularly Virgilian epic as construed by its commentators, has always implied that: Chaucer makes the implication explicit.

Troilus and Criseyde forces the reader to do so by insisting on the failure of its protagonists even to begin that journey. The poem establishes a correspondence between Troilus and Troy, Criseyde and Antenor. Antenor is not merely exchanged for Criseyde: his arrival destroys Troilus's happiness just as, the narrator pointedly reminds us (4.197–210), he will betray Troy. Retrospectively we can see shadowings of that fall in the details of Troilus's climactic interview with Criseyde, as he waits, like the Greeks lurking in the Trojan horse, silently "in a stew" (3.601) for Pandarus to release him, and as he is depicted in Pandarus's tale to Criseyde that same evening, arriving "thorugh a goter, by a pryve wente" (3.787), just as the Greeks were similarly admitted by a secret passage into Troy by Antenor in Dares' and Dictys's accounts of the fall of Troy. Chaucer's point is clear, and absolutely consonant with the allegorical values invested in Troy: the moral fall of Troilus corresponds to the physical fall of Troy, the spirit submits to the frailties of the flesh, to appetite, and the body is invaded by vices. There is no need for Chaucer to stress this, since every element of the poem's background and the matrix from which it arises point ineluctably to it. At the center of his poem is a moral descent, a moral betrayal, that the reader is called upon to see and evaluate as such, with understanding and compassion, to be sure—else why such a sympathetic narrator in the first

 Utterly insensitive reading

Crseyde = reason!

place?—but nevertheless clearsightedly and unequivocally. Criseyde's ironic surrender to Troilus narratively counterpoints an almost cliché allegorical submission of reason to passion, and what the reader must see in it is the fall of the citadel of the mind, the bankruptcy of the city of this world, whether it be called Troy, Babel, or Babylon. It is the reader who must perceive this as the nadir of the *descensus*, who must turn from the flesh to begin his gradual extrication from the attractions of the world as Criseyde's weaknesses and Troilus's impotence are gradually made more and more clear to him; it is the reader and the book as an entity in itself, and not the protagonists or the narrator, who must finally leave Troy, free themselves from the house of bondage, purge themselves of the dross of corporeality, as the narrator is forced inexorably by his authorities to recount the whole story, to carry his tale through to its, to him, unsatisfactory conclusion.

At the center of *The Faerie Queene* lies Busirane's house of bondage, through which Britomart, acting for all Spenser's heroes, must pass. Dante the pilgrim and Milton the poet journey through Hell. Adam and Eve leave the prison that they have made Eden to journey through the wilderness of the outside world. Troilus stays in Troy, wedded to the flesh, a prisoner in his own house of bondage. "The folk of Troie . . . alle and some/In prisoun ben, as ye youreselven se" (5.883–84). The reader sees that and the book sees that, and both turn from it to achieve the transcendence that eludes Troilus, the rest that "payens corsed olde rites" cannot provide. The reader and the poem complete the epic journey, carrying the reluctant narrator with them, leaving Troilus still in bondage to go "ther as Mercurye sorted hym to dwelle" (5.1827). All of the characters of *Troilus and Criseyde* somewhere in the course of the poem come to at least a partial realization of the truth about themselves: Troilus and Criseyde in their reflections on their own actions as story, Pandarus earlier in his speech to Troilus about what he has done and become in his service, the narrator late and grudgingly, in his confusion and dismay at the conclusion of the tale he has chosen to tell. The autonomy of events once set in motion, of actions taken, forces the protagonists of the poem to their revelations; the autonomy of the story itself, what "other bokes" (5.1776) say, binds the narrator. Only the reader is free, left after his journey through the shades to look back with Orpheus, if he chooses, to remain in Troy and perish with great and little Troy, losing his Eurydice and his life, or free to repair "hom," as the newly chastened narrator now urges, to him who conquered those shades and performed the epic *descensus* aright, the hero:

> the which that right for love
> Upon a crois, oure soules for to beye,
> First starf, and roos, and sit in hevene above.
>
> [5.1842–44]

Everyman is an epic hero: that is the reverse of the Virgilian commentators' vision of the epic hero as Everyman. Chaucer's own vision embraces that equation and sees further into it. If that is true, then the *imitatio Christi* and the *imitatio Troili* are the two alternative paths that Everyman can walk: into the world or through the world, to the city of man or the city of God, to tragedy or comedy. Chaucer has designed *Troilus and Criseyde* as a roadmap of one of those journeys, to give Everyman a headstart on the pilgrimage he must take, the choice he must sooner or later make.

EPILOGUE

Chaucer's insistent counterpointing of the frustrations of epic expectations against a grid of epic reference-points forms a coherent pattern that critics ought to recognize: it describes the basic pattern of mock epic.[1] Granted, that term may seem a little bizarre when applied to *Troilus and Criseyde* because we primarily associate it with overtly comic and/or satiric poems—but I would maintain that *Troilus* is a comic and satiric poem, and in any event there is no intrinsic reason that a comic pattern cannot be put to serious uses: to select an example within the genre that concerns us, Alexander Pope does just that with mock epic in *The Dunciad*. Chaucer creates in *Troilus* a series of characters who in turn create the entities that are their own undoing. Criseyde becomes the victim of her own prudence and worldly wisdom, Pandarus of his own sophistication. Troilus falls to his own naiveté and misplaced idealism by making of Criseyde and what he feels for her the sole purpose of his existence, so that when she leaves him for Diomede, his self-created value system tumbles to the ground. The narrator almost destroys himself through his own creatures: the pronounced sympathy he feels for them leaves him too a victim of the

197

events he is forced to narrate, of the autonomy of the story over its putative author. Intellect, in the person of Calkas (in traditional fashion of epic exegesis, Chaucer provides an etymological explanation of his name that denotes his function in the poem: he "knew by calkulynge" [1.71]), abandons Troy at the very outset of the poem, never to return. Troilus spends the entire poem in an ironic state of the rest which is the end of epic wandering, tied powerlessly to his bed, never embarking upon the journey that intellect has made and Everyman ought to make. Troy and Troilus, the city and its eponym, are Chaucer's images for man wedded to the world, locked in a self-chosen mindlessness, frustrating both the demands of epic and the stirrings of consciousness. It is not so great a step from that vision to the parallel one of Cibber snoring in the lap of Dulness. Between the two points and the two poets stretches the impressive continuity of the English epic tradition, rephrased and rearticulated for each cultural generation, but anchored always in the bedrock of its preoccupations, the primacy of consciousness.

Epic is the poetry of knowing: at its most fundamental and profound level, it concerns itself with consciousness and the control that flows from consciousness. All epic descents constitute journeys to the world: that is why epic is encyclopedic. All epic descents likewise constitute journeys into the self: that is why epic is epistemological and psychological. Self and world, subject and object—it is tempting to think of them as polar opposites, but they are not so in epic. In epic, "to know" functions as the copula that links self and world, fusing them into identity. The epic hero can internalize the world and just as easily externalize it: he can become the world and he can make the world. Odysseus does this, Aeneas does it; so too do all the heroes of *The Faerie Queene*, so too do Adam and Eve, so does the Son. And so do all epic poets who, in Dante's most profound metaphor, descend to Hell with Virgil for their guide.

It is next to impossible, in writing about a topic as large as epic, not to sound glib and superficial. The subject matter is vast, the lines of argument raised by it important. Poets have never avoided big issues, and epic offered one of their chief means of dealing with them. Even to say that sounds glib, but it remains true: epic constituted an exploratory device, a heuristic tool, by means of which successive generations of poets mapped out the roads linking individual and cosmos for themselves and their audiences. By so doing, of course, they created those roads and thereby shaped both the selves and the worlds they described. Epic poets are, in the very profound sense that the epigraph I quote from Erich Kahler intends, world-begetters: successful epic poetry marks a cultural leap, a maturational stage in the development of human consciousness.[2] It both depicts and performs the process of centroversion: it brings to conscious knowledge the contents of both underworlds, the self and the universe.

I shall have to risk sounding even more glib and superficial in order to say a few things of—I hope— ultimate pertinence for epic. Epic conceives of the relations between self and world more often than not (the epic commentators always) in terms of the familiar mind/body dichotomy. That is, it sets out to explain consciousness and the place of consciousness in the cosmos in terms of the relation of spirit and matter. In so doing, the genre addresses itself to what is perhaps the central philosophic problem of Western culture; individual epics both describe and contribute to the various solutions that have been proposed for that single problem. This has been so, I would argue, at least from Homeric epic onward, with the balance of epic vision seesawing between the primacy of body and the primacy of mind. It can be no accident that the *Iliad* begins and ends with mourning for the dead: the notion of death as the encircler of life constitutes the essential Iliadic vision of man's state. Within the brief time allotted to man, spirit achieves only a few moments of autonomy—Achilles' realization that the brave man and the coward die the same death—in its struggle against the dead weight of the body and the irrational wrath and violence that are its concomitants. Achilles does not make the choice of a short life with glory intellectually: his grief and rage at the death of Patroclus make the choice for him and confront him with a *fait accompli*. The end of the *Iliad* mourns the death of Achilles as much as the death of Hector, the mortality of all men as much as the insubstantiality of the spirit that animates them. The *Odyssey*, whether or not it is by the same Homer, shares that same vision: the shade of Achilles confirms it when he tells Odysseus that the meanest human life is preferable to the overlordship of the disembodied wraiths. Odysseus, whom tradition has so insistently and correctly seen as the man of intellect, must confront and understand what physical death means before he can return and conquer—and conquer as much by physical strength as by intellect. Homer, I think, recognized the paradoxical nature of the connection between mind and body as surely as Heracleitus, and anticipated his formulation of it, when he placed in Odysseus's hands for his final victory the bow (*bios*)—life (*bios*)—whose work is death. The real Odyssean triumph lies in his preservation of the tension between matter and spirit, in his refusal to allow either one to dominate the other. Odysseus is no ascetic, though he is perfectly capable of disciplining his body to the demands of his spirit; conversely, he is equally capable of allowing his mind to play— indeed, he may well be said to be the first to have discovered, in any meaningful sense, what the play of mind means—a fact I find confirmed in the hearty commendation of his deceits and tall tales that Homer puts in Athene's mouth. But for all the intellectual vigor he attributes to Odysseus, Homer carefully preserves the balance between body and mind. The shades that Odysseus must invoke are powerless in themselves, but they possess certain knowledge; Odysseus as a living man wields great power, but even his knowledge is unsure (therefore his repeated lies and disguises and his repeated testing of Penelope).

Plato's anti-Homeric revolution upsets that balance. Banishing the poets from the republic parallels freeing the Greek "curriculum" from Homer: both form part of Plato's attempt to assert the primacy of spirit over body, an attempt which, whatever its philosophic fortunes, left a large mark on subsequent epic. The *Aeneid* shows the effects of this tipping of the beam. Virgil's hero serves an idea which is greater than himself, a concept in the mind of Jove that overwhelms his individual importance. He is allowed no pleasures, lest his body distract his mind from his task; relentlessly Virgil strips him of his wife, his homeland, his identity as a Trojan warrior, any resting place other than the mysterious destiny that commands him. He reduces Aeneas to the bare nub of a will driving a body, in obedience to the sure knowledge imparted by spirits, by—and this is crucial—Platonic spirits who are not merely the insubstantial residue of the past but the powerful shape of the future. Granted that that future depends for its realization upon the efforts of the still corporeal Aeneas, nevertheless Virgil's Aeneas, in his person and in his role, is clearly the ox who pulls the plow of destiny, a body subservient to mind. For subsequent Christian culture, that fact in itself constituted one of the attractions of the *Aeneid*, and—as we have seen—the Virgilian commentators quickly emphasized it and elaborated it with a great deal of Neoplatonic scaffolding. The scholarly tradition that accrues around epic moves inexorably along one line, defining with greater and greater emphasis the dominion of mind over matter: it culminates in Cristoforo Landino, whose commentary flatly equates Aeneas's goal with the contemplative life and thereby completely internalizes and intellectualizes the whole of epic.

The working epic tradition, however, moved in a different direction from the scholarly, however willingly it exploited the materials that the commentators provided. Poets are an ungrateful lot, and not above biting the hand that feeds them (or flatters itself that it feeds them). The epic poetry produced by the scholars themselves, of course, exemplifies fully the control of mind over body (for example, the poems of Bernardus himself, or of Alan of Lille), but few poets who had their bread to earn by their craft could ever long have held that comforting notion. Certainly Chaucer's *Troilus and Criseyde* describes a corporeality powerful enough to overwhelm spirit and to annihilate all logical processes. The coda of the poem presents an alternative to that vision in the love of God that enables frail humans to transcend earthly love, but while that offers the possibility of the triumph of spirit, it does not necessarily imply the victory of mind as well. Rather it seems to point to the harnessing of the irrational force of love to a higher goal, the channeling of emotion toward spirit rather than the rational control of emotion. That this should be done for logical reasons does not substantially alter the nature of the attempt, nor does it seriously modify the distance that separates Chaucer's view of the relations of mind and body from those of Bernardus and his colleagues. Troilus remains trapped in Troy and in his love for Criseyde just as firmly as Palamon and Arcite remain locked in the prison of their love for Emilye even after their release from the confinement of the "real" prison. Dante the pilgrim walks through the realms of spirit, but Chaucer the pilgrim lives, and moves, and has his being in a world of matter. From that matter, release is difficult and hardly won, the struggles of spirit arduous and uncertain: the way back from Hell is hard indeed, as the Sybil says.

This is probably even more emphatically true for Spenser's poem than for Chaucer's. In *The Faerie Queene*, matter dominates the actions of the characters from the confusions engendered by Red Crosse Knight's entrance into the Wood of Error through the attacks of Maleger and his crew upon the Castle of Alma and the metamorphoses effected by Acrasia to the metamorphoses of Proteus and beyond. Shape-shifter matter deflects the aspirations of Spenser's heroes from their goals just as surely as Proteus confines Florimell and holds her from her love. Corporeality pervades the poem, providing the center and circumference of the circle of mutability, from which neither we nor the heroes of *The Faerie Queene* will escape until "all shall rest eternally/With Him that is the God of Sabbaoth hight" (7.8.2). Spirit in Spenser's poem is enmeshed in matter, tied to it, and must work out its destiny in terms of it. Transcendence, here and now, is visionary and fleeting, imperfectly and briefly achieved; real transcendence and the final victory of spirit must await the end of mutability's reign.

Milton's vision in *Paradise Lost* stands at an even greater remove from, for instance, Landino's confidence that man can, unaided, reach the *summum bonum* of the contemplative state. In *Paradise Lost*, matter is basic, chaotic, and eternal, apparently coeval with God. And it is powerful: it can imprison spirits, as Satan and his demons illustrate, and after the Fall it can easily dominate weakened human intellect, as Michael's capsule review of history shows. *Paradise Lost* posits matter as the basic building block of the universe as we know it and moreover implies strongly that it will remain at least co-tenant with spirit in the new heavens and new earth that will succeed the Second Coming. So strong is matter that it forces—and to this extent Landino's interpretation of the *Aeneid* is quite pertinent to Milton's poem—the complete internalization of the epic quest as that quest applies to human beings. What Adam and his descendants have to seek is "A paradise within thee" (12.587), which, although "happier far," does not provide the home they have lost in Eden or the home they will—it is hoped—attain, "From the conflagrant mass, purg'd and refin'd" (12.548), but only the solace of their exile, the consolation of spirit in the wilderness of matter.

This process of internalization had been long growing within the epic tradition, and even a poem like Chaucer's, that stands in so ironical a relation to much of the allegorical tradition, that views so skeptically that tradition's claims for the primacy of mind and spirit, even such a poem still understands its hero's proper goal to be an intellectual and spiritual one, culminating in eternity rather than time. To that extent at least the allegorizations of the *Aeneid* have triumphed over the explicit example of Virgil in English epic practice: Aeneas, it is true, must internalize his goal and the knowledge or foreknowledge needed to reach that goal—but his true epic task, to which Virgil devotes the final six books of this poem, consists precisely in his externalizing that goal, in beginning the work of empire on earth. Spenser's and Milton's heroes also begin the work of empire on earth, but theirs is the empire of the spirit, and in Milton especially all of their actions work toward that end not in the allegory but in the *littera*, in the literal understanding of the narrative. By his choice of subject, Milton has automatically jettisoned the overt subject matter of traditional epic and has made its allegorical materials his narrative frame. The quest for the *summmum bonum* serves as Milton's story, the renewal of empire (spiritual empire) its allegorical or analogical extension. What had traditionally been the tenor of epic becomes in Milton its vehicle: the content of the epic story replaces that story.

Once the significance of epic has usurped the place of its signifiers, there remains little else for epic—at least in its traditional formal guise—to do. The magnificence of Milton's achievement in *Paradise Lost* masks the fact that it represents a dead end for epic, but it remains a dead end nevertheless. His hero satisfies every divergent claim: he is both everyman and exceptional man. His narrative presents the archetypal quest story at the same time that it portrays a quintessentially Christian version of history. His version of the *descensus*, in its barest narrative components, encompasses all of the conceivable applications of that framework—physically in the progression from creation to recreation, metaphysically in the revolt of the demons and their ultimate defeat, morally in the sin and redemption of Adam and Eve, psychologically in their separation and reunion, cosmologically in the overarching mission of the Son. Even his adaptation of an explicitly Christian story puts the finishing touches to the persistent tension in the epic tradition about the relation of Christian ideas to a basically pre-Christian vehicle, and neatly counterpoints Landino's final and complete secularization of the epic allegory in his positing of man's ability to achieve the *summmum bonum* unaided. In the name of the Father, and the Son, and the Holy Spirit, *Paradise Lost* surrenders the world to matter and epic to its own allegory—and does so so successfully that it leaves nothing else for would-be epic poets to say. After such knowledge, what forgiveness? After such a vision, what possible alternatives, save the kind of spinning out of the political analogies inherent in it that Dryden attempts in *Absalom and Achitophel*? Epic can have no more to say until it has a new world to say it for, a new tenor to hitch to its durable vehicle. Milton sums up and finishes an entire cycle of epic tradition as surely as his poem epitomizes the profoundest Christian understanding of the world—and the perfect expression of such concepts *is* their death knell. The paradise that is lost with Milton's poem includes the broad cultural unity that bound together over twenty centuries of Classical and Christian culture and fostered the great continuities of epic tradition. The world that replaces this is a far different one, dominated by matter, geared toward the understanding and manipulation of matter, equipped with a new "scientific" knowledge, a new notion of mind and spirit, and eventually engendering a new kind of epic, commensurate with those changes.

NOTES

PROLOGUE

1. "A Discourse Concerning the Original and Progress of Satire," in *Essays of John Dryden*, ed. W. P. Ker, 2 vols. (New York: Russell and Russell, 1961), 2; 36.

CHAPTER 1

1. Many critics have argued for the unity and completeness of *The Faerie Queene* as we have it. See for example Northrop Frye's "The Structure of Imagery in *The Faerie Queene*," reprinted in *Essential Articles for the Study of Edmund Spenser*, ed. A. C. Hamilton (Hamden, Conn.: Archon Books, 1972): pp. 153–70. My discussion of Spenser's epic is indebted to many critical and scholarly works, most notably the following: Paul J. Alpers, *The Poetry of "The Faerie Queene"* (Princeton: Princeton University Press, 1967); Harry Berger, Jr., *The Allegorical Temper: Vision and Reality in Book II of Spenser's "Faerie Queene"* (New Haven: Yale University Press, 1957); Albert R. Cirillo, "Spenser's Myth of Love: A Study of *The Faerie Queene*, Books III and IV" (doctoral dissertation, Baltimore: Johns Hopkins University, 1964); T. K. Dunseath, *Spenser's Allegory of Justice in Book Five of "The Faerie Queene"* (Princeton: Princeton University Press, 1968); Angus Fletcher, *The Prophetic*

Moment: An Essay on Spenser (Chicago: University of Chicago Press, 1971); Rosemary Freeman, *"The Faerie Queene": A Companion for Readers* (Berkeley: University of California Press, 1970); Thomas Greene, *The Descent from Heaven: A Study in Epic Continuity* (New Haven: Yale University Press, 1963); A. C. Hamilton, *The Structure of Allegory in "The Faerie Queene"* (Oxford: Clarendon Press, 1961); John E. Hankins, *Source and Meaning in Spenser's Allegory: A Study of "The Faerie Queene"* (Oxford: Clarendon Press, 1971); Graham Hough, *A Preface to "The Faerie Queene"* (New York: Norton, 1963); Merritt Y. Hughes, *Virgil and Spenser* (Berkeley: University of California Press, 1929); Thomas P. Roche, *The Kindly Flame: A Study of the Third and Fourth Books of Spenser's "Faerie Queene"* (Princeton: Princeton University Press, 1964); Rosemond Tuve, *Allegorical Imagery: Some Medieval Books and Their Posterity* (Princeton: Princeton University Press, 1966).

2. The text of the *Aeneid* quoted here and throughout this work is the Loeb Library edition, trans. H. Rushton Fairclough (London: William Heinemann, 1960).

3. For a fuller discussion of the medieval and Renaissance commentaries on Virgil, see also my *Epic to Novel* (Columbus: Ohio State University Press, 1974): pp. 26–52. For many other details of that tradition and its dissemination, see especially Don Cameron Allen's *Mysteriously Meant: The Rediscovery of Pagan Symbolism and Allegorical Interpretation in the Renaissance* (Baltimore and London: Johns Hopkins University Press, 1970): pp. 135–62. The most accessible form of Fulgentius's commentary is Leslie George Whitbread's translation of it, "The Exposition of the Content of Virgil," in his *Fulgentius the Mythographer* (Columbus: Ohio State University Press, 1971): pp. 103–154. All my quotations from or citations of Fulgentius are drawn from this volume.

4. See Allen, *Mysteriously Meant*, pp. 141–42. The text of Bernardus's commentary has recently been made available in an important new edition by Julian Ward Jones and Elizabeth Frances Jones, *The Commentary on the First Six Books of the "Aeneid" Commonly Attributed to Bernardus Silvestris* (Lincoln and London: University of Nebraska Press, 1977). My synopses of Bernardus's remarks are based on this text and a translation of it by Earl G. Schreiber and myself, in preparation for publication by the University of Nebraska Press; parenthetical page references are keyed to the Jones and Jones edition.

5. "Cristoforo Landino's Allegorization of the *Aeneid*: Books III and IV of the *Camaldolese Disputations*," trans. Thomas H. Stahel, S.J. (doctoral dissertation, Baltimore: Johns Hopkins University, 1968): "It is with remarkable judiciousness that he expresses the following matters concerning the entranceway to hell [*Aeneid* 6, 274–81]. For if, in accord with

the opinion of him whom he follows (Plato), he is describing the descent of souls into their bodies, it is clear that the soul, which up till now had been separated from all these evils, falls into them now because of the contamination of the body. Thence it is that it feels all those disturbances: it is troubled with cares and mourning; it fears impending events; it experiences illness and hard work; it is vexed by hunger and need; it is pressed with all the calamities which Vergil enumerates. Apart from the body, it had always been free of such" (pp. 222–23). Because there is no modern edition of Landino's commentary, all future quotations from Landino will be drawn from this translation. Page references to Stahel's text will be given in parentheses after the quotations.

     6. Winthrop Wetherbee, *Platonism and Poetry in the Twelfth Century: The Literary Influence of the School of Chartres* (Princeton: Princeton University Press, 1972): pp. 124–25. On Bernardus Silvestris, see also Brian Stock's *Myth and Science in the Twelfth Century: A Study of Bernard Silvester* (Princeton: Princeton University Press, 1972).

     7. Allen, *Mysteriously Meant*, pp. 286–87. For a fuller discussion of Landino's views on epic, see Frank J. Fata, "Landino on Dante" (doctoral dissertation, Baltimore: Johns Hopkins University, 1966).

     8. The text of *Paradise Lost* quoted here and throughout this work is *John Milton: Complete Poems and Major Prose*, ed. Merritt Y. Hughes (New York: Odyssey Press, 1957).

     9. The term *centroversion* I have derived from Erich Neumann's monumental *The Origins and History of Consciousness* (Princeton: Bollingen Books, Princeton University Press, 1970).

     10. For Platonic emanating triads, see Edgar Wind, *Pagan Mysteries in the Renaissance* (New Haven: Yale University Press, 1958): pp. 39–50. For Fulgentius's explicit Platonizing, see Whitbread, *Fulgentius the Mythographer*, pp. 122, 129, 132. Landino prefaces his discussion of the *Aeneid* with a lengthy presentation of Platonic ideas about poetry and the high status it and particularly Homer held among the ancients; he then modulates to Virgil in this manner: "And now something with which I will sum up the rest, for there is nothing that cannot be proved by the testimony of Plato alone; in his book concerning the *summum bonum* he affirms that all the arts, whether divine or human, have flowed together into one of Homer's poems as if into their proper receptacle. Now when Vergil understood that Homer's teaching, taken from sources in the Egyptian priests, was very similar to that of the Platonists (of whom he was very eager to have an understanding), he so admired it that he wished to achieve the same thing in his Aeneas which Homer had fashioned before him in Ulysses.

     "It is for this reason that he shaped that man for us with beautifully poetic figures—a man who, gradually expiated of very many and very great vices and finally adorned with marvellous virtues, achieved in spite of everything his greatest good, a thing which no one can achieve without being wise. Moreover, when he had learned from Plato that the *summum bonum* consisted in the contemplation of the divine, he also learned that that goal is scarcely able to be anticipated before our souls, inwardly cleansed, are brought to those virtues pertaining to life and mores. Because Socrates himself denies that the pure is allowed to have anything to do with the impure, he has not only marvellously expressed the greatest good for us, but has also shown the way and means by which man can finally attain it. And so the part of his philosophy which the Greeks call Ethics (what we call moral philosophy) was not omitted; for in it we study nothing else but, first, the greatest good and the greatest evil, and, finally, the works by which—as if by a kind of road—we may be led to them" (Stahel, "Landino's Allegorization of the *Aeneid*," pp. 52–53).

11. *The Faerie Queene* 7.7.58. The text of Spenser's poems quoted here and throughout this study is *The Faerie Queene*, ed. J. C. Smith, 2 vols. (Oxford: Clarendon Press, 1961), and *Spenser's Minor Poems*, ed. Ernest de Selincourt (Oxford: Clarendon Press, 1960).

12. Pertinent to this aspect of Spenser's allegory is the tradition of *silvae* as the materials of rhetoric (compare Ben Jonson's *Timber, or Discoveries*). Note also that Error herself is chiefly a creature of rhetoric (her vomit is of books), and that Red Crosse Knight and Una have been silent until their approach to Error's cave.

13. Landino's preservation of remnants of the ages-of-man theory underlines this aspect of epic by making Troy, the "first ages" of man, initially innocent sensuality later corrupted by Paris's choice of Venus over Juno or Pallas, an act morally definitive of himself and Troy: "For instance, Aeneas arises out of Troy; and by this city I think we may properly understand that first age of man in which, since all reasoning is still asleep, the senses alone reign. . . . And so no one will say that there is virtue in a boy. But when by the advance of age our minds begin to be illuminated somewhat with the light of reason, then and then only does so much of counsel appear in us that we can distinguish good from evil. . . Because we then do things with a certain sure reason, they are ascribed to virtue if they are right; but if they are not right, they are ascribed to vice. So both Aeneas and Paris grow up in Troy. But because one of them values Venus (that is, pleasure) over Pallas (that is, virtue), it is necessary that he perish together with Troy" (Stahel, "Landino's Allegorization of the *Aeneid*," pp. 55–56).

14. Interestingly too, Bernardus Silvestris in his commentary on the *Aeneid* understands Cerberus as eloquence, a point that dovetails nicely with both Spenser's use of Cerberus as a figure for the Blatant Beast and also as a correspondent to the rhetorical aspects of Error.

15. For other comments on epic structure, with particular reference to *The Faerie Queene* and *Paradise Lost*, see *Epic to Novel*, pp. 91–103.

16. See for example the entry for Adonis in Charles Etienne's *Dictionarium Historicum, Geographicum, Poeticum*. The edition I have used is Oxford, 1671, pp. 25–26.

17. Stahel, "Landino's Allegorization of the *Aeneid*," pp. 187–88.

18. See John 1.38–39. The text of the Bible quoted here and throughout this study is the King James version.

19. On the Graces, see Wind, *Pagan Mysteries*, pp. 31–56.

20. Much of this discussion of Books 3 and 4 derives from A. R. Cirillo, "Spenser's Myth of Love."

21. As Don Cameron Allen noted in "Milton's Busiris" (*Modern Language Notes* 65 [1960]: 115–16), Carion's *Chronicle*, as augmented by Melanchthon (1572), links the Pharaoh who held the Jews in bondage with the legendary Busiris. Later George Sandys, in his *Ovid's Metamorphosis Englished*, ed. K. K. Hulley and S. T. Vandersall (Lincoln: University of Nebraska Press, 1970) is able to treat the connection as a commonplace: "[Busiris] is held to be that king of *Aegipt* who so grievously oppressed the Israelites" (p. 428). The important aspect of this linkage is, I think, that it provides the biblical/classical conceptual base for the House of Busirane's functioning in Spenser's poem as a literal house of bondage.

22. Hamilton, *The Structure of Allegory, passim*. In this connection, see also Joseph B. Dallett, "Ideas of Sight in *The Faerie Queene*," *ELH* 27 (1960): 87–121.

23. It is worth noting here that a specific episode such as this one may serve honorifically in the *descensus*, starting an upward action, and still work pejoratively in the hero's own individual tale, as in T. K. Dunseath's reading of this episode (*Spenser's Allegory of Justice*, pp. 169–70).

24. Also important here is another interpretative tradition attached to Cerberus: Natale Conti, for example, understands him as the grave and by extension, the earth, i.e., the matter from which all things are made and to which they will return (*Mythologiae, sive Explicationis Fabularum Libri Decem* [Frankfort, 1584], p. 205). Spenser's six books then move from the entrance into *silva*, into and out of the prison of Proteus, to end with Calidore's conquest of Cerberus—matter or the grave. Landino differs only

slightly from this, and in ways equally pertinent to Spenser. For him, Cerberus is the earth and his barking "the insatiableness of the body," which must be controlled by the man pursuing higher goals: Stahel, "Landino's Allegorization of the *Aeneid*," pp. 237ff.

CHAPTER 2

1. Principal among the works that have helped shape my thinking about *Paradise Lost* are the following: Don Cameron Allen, *The Harmonious Vision: Studies in Milton's Poetry* (Baltimore: Johns Hopkins University Press, 1954), and especially Allen's essay, "Milton and the Descent to Light," originally published in *Milton Studies in Honor of Harris Francis Fletcher, JEGP* 60 (1961): 614–30, and later reprinted in the revised edition of *The Harmonious Vision* (1970); Albert R. Cirillo, "Noon-Midnight and the Temporal Structure of *Paradise Lost*," *ELH* 29 (1962): 372–95—an essay from which I have profited greatly; Jackson I. Cope, *The Metaphoric Structure of "Paradise Lost"* (Baltimore: Johns Hopkins University Press, 1962); Stanley E. Fish, *Surprised by Sin: The Reader in "Paradise Lost"* (New York: St. Martin's Press, 1967); Thomas Green, *The Descent from Heaven: A Study in Epic Continuity* (New Haven: Yale University Press, 1963); Isabel G. MacCaffrey, *Paradise Lost as "Myth,"* (Cambridge, Mass.: Harvard University Press, 1967); William G. Madsen, *From Shadowy Types to Truth: Studies in Milton's Symbolism* (New Haven: Yale University Press, 1968); C. A. Patrides, ed., *Approaches to "Paradise Lost"* (London: Edward Arnold, 1968); Irene Samuel, *Dante and Milton: The "Commedia" and "Paradise Lost"* (Ithaca: Cornell University Press, 1966); Howard Schultz, *Milton and Forbidden Knowledge* (New York: Modern Language Association, 1955); John M. Steadman, *Milton and the Renaissance Hero* (Oxford: Clarendon Press, 1967); Joseph H. Summers, *The Muse's Method: An Introduction to Paradise Lost* (Cambridge, Mass.: Harvard University Press, 1962).

2. The phrase is of course Stanley Fish's.

3. See Fata, "Landino on Dante," pp. 15–17 and *passim*.

4. For more extensive treatment of these ideas, see my *Epic to Novel* and Peter Hägin, *The Epic Hero and the Decline of Heroic Poetry* (Bern: A. Francke AG Verlag, The Cooper Monographs 8, 1964).

5. One of the basic defining characteristics of the mock epic hero is his endeavoring to remake the world in his own image; see *Epic to Novel*, pp. 176–77 and passim.

6. Here as in many other places in this essay I have availed myself of the excellent notes in Merritt Y. Hughes's edition of *Paradise Lost*: compare the passage with *Aeneid* 2.275–76.

7. The following discussion of the structure of *Paradise Lost* utilizes, in a slightly altered form, some materials from *Epic to Novel*, pp. 97–103.

8. The phrase is taken from Spenser's *Letter to Raleigh* and of course is used therein to describe *The Faerie Queene*.

9. See Cirillo, "Noon-Midnight and the Temporal Structure of *Paradise Lost*."

10. See Wind, *Pagan Mysteries in the Renaissance*.

11. It does not seem to me farfetched to hear, in Adam's and Eve's descent "To the subjected plain," an echo of the geographical beginning of Red Crosse Knight's adventures "on the plaine."

12. Landino is quite explicit about this from the point of view of Dante's understanding of Virgil and their similarity of poetic practice: "Dante imagines that Vergil is his guide on that journey in which he traverses the entire universe from the depth of Tartarus to the heights of heaven; searching for the *summum bonum* of man, he selects—with remarkable genius—the *Aeneid* as his sole model. And although he seems to excerpt very few things from it [*Aeneid*], we see nevertheless, if we look rather more carefully, that he never departs from it. Are not those things which he wrote from the very beginning (concerning the midpoint of life, the forest, the three beasts, the mountain-top already lighted by the son's rays) derived hence? I pass over other things which are so concealed in Dante's poem that they cannot be discovered except by a few very learned men. The fact is, then, that Dante chooses Vergil as his leader in a matter which looks to the *summum bonum* and not to anything physical" (Stahel, "Cristoforo Landino's Allegorization of the *Aeneid*," pp. 162–63). See also pp. 184–85, 255ff.

13. Landino understands Plato's poetic *furor* in a remarkably similar manner: "For in the *Ion* Plato says that poetry is not given through human art; rather, it insinuates itself into our minds by a divine madness. ... While they were in the celestial realms, our souls were participators in that harmony which resides in the eternal mind of God and which brings about the heavens' motions. Afterwards, indeed, weighed down by the desire for mortal things and therefore already fallen to the inferior, our souls were consigned to bodies. Impeded now by earthly limbs and moribund members, our souls are scarcely able to perceive by ear those harmonies made by human artifice. Even if these human harmonies are a far cry from the celestial harmony, nevertheless (because they are, as it were, likenesses and images of it), they lead us to a certain ineffable recollection of heavenly things and inflame us with the most ardent desire of flying back to our former fatherland so that we might truly know that

very music of which this is an adumbration. In the meantime it is permitted to us—insofar as we can with this most irksome prison of the body—to strive to imitate that divine music with this music of ours" (Stahel, *ibid.*, pp. 41–42).

CHAPTER 3

1. The text of Chaucer's poems quoted here and throughout this essay is *The Works of Geoffrey Chaucer*, ed. F. N. Robinson, 2nd ed., (Boston: Houghton Mifflin, 1957). The critical works that I have found most useful to my discussion of *Troilus and Criseyde* are the following: Ida L. Gordon, *The Double Sorrow of Troilus: A Study of Ambiguities in "Troilus and Criseyde"* (Oxford: Clarendon Press, 1970); Donald R. Howard, *The Three Temptations: Medieval Man in Search of the World* (Princeton: Princeton University Press, 1966); Robert M. Jordan, *Chaucer and the Shape of Creation: The Aesthetic Possibilities of Inorganic Structure* (Cambridge, Mass.: Harvard University Press, 1967); Sanford B. Meech, *Design in Chaucer's Troilus* (New York: Greenwood Press, 1969; reprinted from Syracuse University Press, 1959); Charles Muscatine, *Chaucer and the French Tradition: A Study in Style and Meaning* (Berkeley: University of California Press, 1969); D. W. Robertson, *A Preface to Chaucer: Studies in Medieval Perspectives* (Princeton: Princeton University Press, 1962); John M. Steadman, *Disembodied Laughter: Troilus and the Apotheosis Tradition* (Berkeley: University of California Press, 1972). I have also consulted the textual readings and annotation of R. K. Root's edition of *"The Book of Troilus and Criseyde" by Geoffrey Chaucer* (Princeton: Princeton University Press, 1926). I owe a special debt, in this study as in the others in this book, to E. R. Curtius's *European Literature and the Latin Middle Ages*, trans. Willard R. Trask (New York: Pantheon Books, Bollingen Series, 1953), a work indispensable to any serious study of literary continuities.

2. All quotations from the works of Fulgentius are taken from the translation of Leslie George Whitbread, *Fulgentius the Mythographer*.

3. On this point, see Stahel, "Landino's Allegorization of the *Aeneid*," pp. 162–63, 184–85, and Fata, "Landino on Dante," pp. 13–17.

4. See Dante, Epistle 10.7, *Dantis Alagherii Epistolae*, ed. and trans. Paget Toynbee, 2nd. ed., (Oxford: Clarendon Press, 1966), p. 199.

5. Throughout this study I quote from *Joseph of Exeter: The Iliad of Dares Phrygius*, trans. Gildas Roberts (Cape Town: A. A. Balkema, 1970). See pp. 4 and 86–87.

6. See for instance the allegorization of this tale provided in the *Metamorphosis Ovidiana* attributed to Thomas Walleys and printed by

Badius Ascensius in 1509 (folio 80 M recto; the work is actually by Pierre Bersuire).

7. Page references are to *The Commentary on the First Six Books of the Aeneid Commonly Attributed to Bernardus Silvestris*, ed. Julian Ward Jones and Elizabeth Frances Jones. All quotations from Bernardus are taken from the translation by Earl G. Schreiber and myself, and are based on the Joneses' text.

8. See for instance Bishop Haymo's *De Varietate Librorum* 3.26, *Patrologia Latina* vol. 118, col. 946.

9. While I have no wish to denigrate the sound scholarship of Robinson's edition of Chaucer, I think it is important to point out that his notes on the sources of the conception of the sorrowing Furies are misleading: neither the locus he cites in Dante (*Inferno* 9.37–51) nor the one from Claudian (*De Raptu Proserpinae* 1.225) actually depicts the Furies as sorrowing. The single point of origin for the sorrowing Furies lies in the Orpheus myth, in Ovid, Boethius, and perhaps in others treating the same tale.

10. I quote from the Loeb Library edition of *Ovid's Metamorphoses*, ed. and trans. Frank Justus Miller (London: William Heinemann, 1956). Statius too mentions the Furies weeping at Orpheus's song: *Thebaid* 8.58–59.

11. See *Epic to Novel*, pp. 95–96.

12. Contrary to D. W. Robertson's view of the matter, I take this bell to parodically correspond to the first bell of the mass, the offertory as opposed to the consecration: that will follow in the very literal going-to-flesh of Troilus's and Criseyde's sexual union, the climax of the poem as the consecration and communion are the climax of the mass.

EPILOGUE

1. See *Epic to Novel*, pp. 71–72, 176–77.

2. I am not speaking here of a growth in mass or popular consciousness, but rather of an advance in the way in which the thinking members of a culture—a cultural elite, if you will—apprehend their world. Epic cannot and does not reflect popular consciousness because epic is not myth but a controlled continuation, a deliberate and profound extension, of myth: a partially rationalized extrapolation from it, but never identical with it.

INDEX

In the following index, all literary works are listed under the author's name. Individual characters from literary works are listed separately.

217

D. W. Rowe, *O Love, O Charite!: Contraries*
Harmonized in Ch's Tr (1976)

[Muriale. McAlpine, *The Genre of Troilus & Cr* (1978)